A Longman

M000045110

Body and Culture

GREG LYONS
Central Oregon Community College

PEARSON
Longman

New York San Francisco Boston
London Toronto Sydney Tokyo Singapore Madrid
Mexico City Munich Paris Cape Town Hong Kong Montreal

Publisher: Joseph Opiela
Senior Supplements Editor: Donna Campion
Media Supplements Editor: Jenna Egan
Senior Marketing Manager: Alexandra Rivas-Smith
Production Manager: Eric Jorgensen
Project Coordination, Text Design, and Electronic Page Makeup:
    GGS Book Services
Cover Design Manager: Wendy Ann Fredericks
Cover Photo: Copyright © Corbis Royalty-Free
Senior Manufacturing Buyer: Dennis J. Para
Printer and Binder: RR Donnelley & Sons Company
Cover Printer: The Lehigh Press

For permission to use copyrighted material, grateful acknowledgment is made to the copyright holders on page 248, which is hereby made part of this copyright page.

Library of Congress Cataloging-in-Publication Data

Body and culture / [edited by] Greg Lyons.
        p. cm.—(A Longman topics reader)
      ISBN 0-321-31742-4
    1. Body, Human—Social aspects. I. Lyons, Greg, 1950–
II. Longman topics.

GN298.B615 2006
306.4—dc22

2005050973

Visit us at http://www.ablongman.com

ISBN 0-321-31742-4

1 2 3 4 5 6 7 8 9 10—DOH—08 07 06 05

In this reader, *Body and Culture*, the second term of the title is purposely broad and necessarily vague. Culture is not merely the subjects of study in higher education: music, philosophy, art, languages, literature, sciences, and history. Likewise, it includes not only the "mediated" objects of entertainment and fandom—*The Matrix*, Madonna, reports of alien spaceships, super-hero comics, and ballroom dancing—but also the Barnum and Bailey Circus, 4-H swine competitions, designer jeans, fast-food fries, Bikram yoga, diamond nose studs, wet poodles in microwave ovens, the GI Joe action figure doll (with bazooka), and even Viagra. Indeed, what is *not* culture in contemporary American life?

The readings represent a few of the various intersections between body and culture—specifically how the human body is imagined, perceived, or interpreted through social, communicative, and symbolic practices that characterize our contemporary American way of life. The six chapters also represent a cross-disciplinary sampling, including the perspectives of religious studies, psychology, sociology, history, medicine, health and human performance, economics, anthropology, and philosophy. The body as a physical entity is virtually ignored. The body as a cultural matrix of meaning is the topic for exploration.

Just to begin the process of thinking about what the body means in our culture, consider these reflections from Wendell Berry's *The Art of the Commonplace* (2002):

> The so-called identity crisis . . . is a disease that seems to have become prevalent after the disconnection of body and soul. . . . "Finding yourself," the pseudo-ritual by which the identity crisis is supposed to be resolved . . . can be an excuse for irresponsibility or a fashionable mode of self-dramatization. . . . The fashionable cure for this condition . . . is "autonomy," another illusory condition, suggesting that the self can be self-determining and independent. . . . This seems little more than a jargon term for indifference to the opinions and feelings of other people. . . .

Here, in an essay titled "The Body and the Earth," Berry typically identifies personal responsibility with a commitment to both the on the contemporary psychosis of body–soul alienation by reflecting on the social origins of individual "identity crisis":

> One of the commonplaces of modern existence is dissatisfaction with the body. . . . The appropriate standard for the body—that is, health—has been replaced, not even by another standard, but by very exclusive physical *models*. . . . Girls are taught to want to be leggy, slender, large-breasted, curly-haired, unimposingly beautiful. Boys are instructed to be "athletic" in build, tall but not too tall, broad-shouldered, deep-chested, narrow-hipped, square-jawed, straight-nosed, not bald, unimposingly handsome. . . .
>
> Though many people, in health, are beautiful, very few resemble these models. The result is widespread suffering that does immeasurable damage both to individual persons and to the society as a whole. . . . Like the crisis of identity, this crisis of the body brings a helpless dependence on cures. One spends one's life dressing and "making up" to compensate for one's supposed deficiencies. Again, the cure preserves the disease. And the putative healer is the guru of style and beauty aid. The sufferer is by definition a customer. . . .

Thus, Wendell Berry strives to identify the connection between a psychological disaffection and an unhealthy society. He is forever trying to enlighten individual problems through resolving a "cultural crisis" by promoting authentic social relationships. In this way, Berry can help readers to contextualize social meanings of the body—connected as they are to self-esteem, personal identity, and a sense of individual striving toward improvement: "Be all you can be." Likewise, he suggests the fundamental economic basis of the "models" in consumer society, where personal "needs" are mediated by advertising and satisfied by products.

So far, the students working with these readings have realized the relevance of social trends to personal experiences. They have been able to reach broader conclusions in their own essays by incorporating the readings' cultural perspectives on the body. Excerpts from student writing are suggestive:

> In the article "Never Just Pictures," Susan Bordo states, "Children in this culture grow up knowing that you can never be thin enough and that being fat is one of the worst things one can be." At the time my bulimia was at its peak, I couldn't have agreed more with this quote. Being thin meant that I would

fit in and that people would like me. It meant that I could have a boyfriend. . . . Being thin meant that I would be normal. . . .

For about the first three months of my eating disorder I lost quite a bit of weight. People were telling me how wonderful I looked and this positive attention only fed my bulimia even more. Everyone around me simply thought I was "dieting" and had no idea I was vomiting everything I ate. I didn't tell a single person about my eating disorder because it gave me a sense of power and control to have my own little secret. . . .

The majority of *Seventeen* subscribers are teenaged girls . . . who are looking for self-confidence through lots of frivolous material possessions. These young ladies are mainly interested in getting attention from boys [and] want to look eternally flawless like the airbrushed models of the magazine. . . . By gaining acceptance about the way that they look, these girls feel they will somehow give meaning to their superficial lives. . . .

While flipping through the magazine, some girls get discouraged because their bodies are not as close to ideal, like the models and celebrities. . . . The idea explored by Susan Bordo in her article "Never Just Pictures," is that "these ads are not telling us that beauty is trivial," but that it must be obtained. . . .

A few years ago I saw a documentary on the Inuit people of Alaska, and they interviewed a teenage girl who had a labret piercing. She talked about wanting to keep the traditions of her people alive. Young people in her culture get this piercing as part of a coming of age ritual, a kind of rite of passage. At that point in my life I was at a low point (I hated my job, my longtime girlfriend dumped me, I wasn't in college, etc.) and I thought that borrowing another culture's traditions to help me feel better wasn't a bad idea. It worked. Modifying my body in a way that some people might find offensive has helped my self-image. I no longer see myself as the compliant, "good kid" that I was growing up. . . . In my mind the whole "nice guy" image has a more offensive stigma attached to it than any other. . . .

Shenk's article compares the world of prescription drugs with that of illegal drugs and very effectively shows how this country's perception of both is very warped. . . .

Pharmaceutical companies are big business. They want us to buy their products. If we have a weight problem, they do not want us to rely on changing our diet or exercising more. They want us to take their pills. If we want to quit smoking they do not want us to have the will and determination to quit on our own. They want us to buy their nicotine pills, or gum, or patch. . . . This attitude of Americans to just pop a pill to ease all of our ills is also encouraging these drug companies to make more drugs. . . .

In these passages, the students seem to be exploring a variety of social responsibilities, as well as new-found insights on the relationships between culture and some of the practices by which the body can express desires and aspects of identity. They grapple with understanding their own lives and with the social and psychological meanings of the physical being.

New students engaging the readings in *Body and Culture* will be able to draw on their own interests in popular culture, such as sports, music, movies, television, magazines, fashion, and dance. While some of the readings are merely descriptive of cultural phenomena, most are analytical—providing various theories for how and why social behaviors arise. Likewise, like Wendell Berry, many of the authors in the text explicitly consider the ethics of these behaviors. Throughout the collection, an effort has been made to select readings that illuminate social issues and that open a dialog about the consequences of choices that people must make about their own bodies and even others' bodies.

Teachers will find the text useful in both introductory composition and argumentative writing. Faculty can also expect to engage their own knowledge of cultural criticism, media studies, gender studies, and the metaphors of postmodernism. Those familiar with composition research may trace—in the discussion questions and writing topics—the influences of David Bartholomae, James Berlin, Linda Brodkey, Alan France, Henry Giroux, and John Trimbur. Teachers can also use the readings and the writing assignments to encourage visual literacy and critical reading of cultural "texts." In most cases, the readings are accessible and compelling for first-year college students.

In bringing this text to print, I wish to express my appreciation to publisher's representative Ciadelle Harguess for encouraging me to submit the original proposal, to publisher Joe Opiela for supporting the project, to reviewer Robert Schwegler for guiding me to focus the readings and to develop the pedagogical framework, and to Elaine Bridwell for manuscript assistance.

GREG LYONS

Writing in Country

One problem of analyzing our *own* culture is that we are often too close to the subject matter to see it objectively. Thus, it is easier to write about what we learn of American society when we travel to Mexico, for instance, and make comparisons with that foreign culture. In effect, the readings in *Body and Culture* ask you to do just this—to stand outside American culture momentarily and to critically evaluate customary practices or behaviors in which we are usually immersed.

Since the analytical tools suggested by the readings are those of the academic disciplines common to higher education, the text necessarily introduces writing students to the modes of thinking and means of argument that characterize research and writing done by professionals in the fields of humanities, science, and social science. Because the topics in *Body and Culture* emphasize social phenomena, the writings and analytical methods of the social sciences predominate among the articles here. Of the twenty-five selections, about half are written from the perspectives of psychology, anthropology, sociology, or history, while only two (those by Henig and Wilmut in Chapter 5) are scientific reports, six are humanistic studies (mostly in Chapters 1 and 6), and five are journalistic reports (two of which cite research in medicine and social science). In any case, all the selections present a variety of solutions to the problems of what counts as data, how we go about interpreting these data, and how we demonstrate reasonable conclusions about the cultural practices studied.

Since the social science model of research is the most common in the text, it may be useful to review its typical structure for presenting an argument or interpretation: (1) review of literature, (2) methodology, (3) discussion of findings or discoveries, and (4) conclusion. (This structure is most closely followed by

Becky Beal in Chapter 2.) The review of literature explains the context of previous research and its relevance to the present study. The methodology section explains how a researcher gathers "data"—selecting "informants" or people expected to have some specialized knowledge on a topic and recording words or observations through surveys, interviews, audiotapes, or videotapes. The discussion section—the bulk of a social science research report—presents interpretations of the data, which may be supported by previous research or may advance new understandings that previous research did not consider. Finally, the conclusion section emphasizes the importance of the discoveries and proposes questions for further research.

As an extended example, we might adopt the social science research model informally in writing about the popularity of brightly unnatural hair color among American youth. For example, in a brief review of the literature, we might cite statistics from a magazine article about the rise in hair-coloring appointments at salons or the increased sales of home do-it-yourself hair-dying kits among adolescents. In the methodology section, we might explain that we interviewed fifteen teenagers displaying bright hair color, along with members of their families and two of their teachers. In the discussion section, we might explain the various motivations that teenagers expressed for changing their hair color, as well as biographical background that helped us to understand and explain these motivations. This section might also refer to a concept we learned from another source (a college class, television program, or news article) that explained a broader view of teenage behavior, such as the importance of self-expression. The conclusion section might emphasize that hair coloring allows an immediate, positive exploration of identity. In this example, writing in response to reading should involve a personal exploration of cultural behavior through evaluating accessible data, relating to previous commentary, and arguing for compelling interpretations.

ORGANIZATION OF THE TEXT

All six chapters share a similar structure: a chapter introduction highlighting the modes of research, means of argument, and writing strategies of each article; a biographical note before each reading, including prereading hints; discussion questions for each selection, including critical reading, content and rhetorical analysis, personal response, and comparisons to other readings; and finally topics for exploration and writing at the chapter's end. The readings in each chapter portray a particular set of bodily practices in our culture, along with various ways of interpreting them.

Chapter 1, "Mind, Body, Spirit," tries to break down preconceptions and sets out some of the problems of understanding the meanings of the body in contemporary America. Through a personal narrative, and then the perspectives of psychology and medicine, and meditation, these articles question the notion of the body as a physical entity separate from the mind, soul, or the culture in which a body lives. In other words, this chapter presents our culture's ideas about the body as a "problem" to be investigated, but more questions are raised here than answered. What are the influences of mind over body? What is the relationship between our health and our mental state? How can this relationship be tracked or measured? How do physical and emotional pains in our lives relate to spiritual yearnings toward belonging and interconnectedness with the "web of life"? All these questions explore possibilities of what "the body" means in a variety of cultural contexts.

Chapter 2, "Sports and Difference," focuses on a particular social context to explore how gender, sexuality, class, and race are expressed and perceived through athletic activities. These articles express the idea that exercise and sports are much more than physical activities; individuals' attitudes about these activities express the social values of competition and individuality, as well as sexist and racist stereotypes about masculinity, femininity, and black athleticism. Again, the writers try to raise cultural awareness by attempting to answer several related questions. What social goals are achieved through pumping iron or working out? Do men and women have different reasons for seeking physical fitness? How do our goals in bodybuilding symbolize our ambitions for ego satisfaction or social success? How do heterosexual males and gay males define their masculinity through athletic performance? Are their standards of "play" similar or different? How are "alternative" athletic activities, such as skateboarding, different from and similar to organized sports, such as football? How does the participation of men and women differ in this alternative sport, and how do skateboarders perceive gender as a meaningful difference in their evaluations of performance? How does athletic performance impact the notions of black social success and identity? How is black athletic performance perceived by a white majority? All these questions complicate the expectation that sports are mostly about individual bodily health, training and excellence. The articles in Chapter 2, then, explore how culture invests social meanings in various practices of the physical body.

Chapter 3, "Body Modification," explores the varieties of physical decoration or "enhancements" that individuals choose to permanently alter their bodies, including tattoos, piercings, and breast implants. The chapter begins with a historical, anthropological perspective to tattooing among "primitive" peoples. Subsequent articles explore the contemporary popularity of body modification in the United States and other "advanced" or industrialized Western countries, as well as Japan, along with comparisons to "tribal" customs in Asia, the Pacific Islands, and Africa. The readings raise a variety of questions to consider about the phenomena of "body art." What were the motivations for tattooing and body piercing among Western cultures in the previous two centuries? Have those motivations changed in the last forty years? How can we account for the enormous mainstream appeal of body modification today? To what extent is this practice still considered "outlaw" behavior that is socially stigmatized? To what extent is tattooing an "art" form or a cosmetic accessory? How do tattooing and piercing relate to breast enhancements? Are the motivations similar? Why are substantial breast implants more popular than smaller ones? Why do some people push the limits of body modification with horn implants, scarring, skin braiding, and branding? How can permanent body modifications seem beautiful to some people and grotesque to others? The readings explore these questions, but generally force readers to reach their own conclusions about the aesthetics, the ethics, and the social significance of these behaviors that treat the body as a living canvas, rather than a holy temple.

Chapter 4, "Body, Image, Media," explores the ways in which American commercial culture—especially through advertising—creates images of certain physical types to symbolize bodily ideals that supposedly can be attained only through buying specific products. Beginning with a personal narrative defining a Latina's experience of her body in Puerto Rico and then in the United States, the readings consider the anorexic fashion model and other popularized body fantasies of both women and men, including the Maidenform bra ad campaigns of the 1960s and 1980s and the changes in male advertising images from powerful to self-indulgent. These articles analyze the ways in which male and female body ideals respond to changes in American society—such as feminism—and appeal to consumers' personal insecurities and ambitions. The readings, then, explore questions of male and female desires couched in the images of idealized bodies. What are the impacts of such cultural ideals on individual behavior? How do the popular images of waiflike, undernourished models provoke anorexia and bulimia among American teenage girls? Moreover, what is the root cause of their insecurities that convince young women that skinny is pretty, or that being pretty is the most important social attainment they can strive for? How does advertising manipulate consumers into having emotional responses to supposedly sexy images of women and men? How do such responses translate to product popularity and sales—in merchandise as varied as underwear, cars, shampoo, watches, and cologne? Where do the ideals for male and female bodily appearance originate? What flaws in American society and our notions of gender roles allow advertising to manipulate our yearnings and even our sense of self? Again, a variety of theories are proposed to answer these questions, but ultimately readers must grapple with these topics and their own conceptions of sexuality, gender, and body image in order to reach some resolutions for themselves.

Chapter 5, "Medicine and Technology," explores various definitions of the body as proposed by medical science. The readings consider the problem of how traditional limits of bodily identity and function are challenged by the now routine practice of making test-tube babies, by the frontiers of cloning research, by the widespread selling of human organs, and by the popularity of both legal and illegal drugs to "cure" what are considered "pathological" conditions of both body and mind. In effect, these readings challenge the boundaries that have traditionally separated two bodies, as well as body from mind. Several articles ask what does it mean to mothers, fathers, babies, relationships, religions, and all of society when organs or genetic tissues are technologically transferred across biological boundaries from one organism to another? And what does it mean to pay for such a medical service? How are the costs for such an operation distributed throughout society? Who can *never* buy one? And why not? How are we to comprehend the new technologies of conception, prenatal genetic testing, and fetal tissue therapies? Is it ethical to "harvest" and incubate unborn, undifferentiated cells in order to improve or save the lives of ailing siblings or even strangers? Who "owns" human tissues once they are removed from an individual body—the mother or donor, the nonviable fetus, or the recipient? Likewise, how are we to understand, monitor, control, or condone the massive public reliance on chemistry to alter the biology of human organisms for years and years on end in the lives of individuals and huge subsets of society, such as crackheads, high-blood-pressure sufferers, or rowdy ADD children? Why, in America, is the "quick fix" perceived as the only fix or, at least, as the most practical fix to our problems? How do our values determine our pathologies, our health practices, our medicines, and our addictions? These questions all concern how the human body, ensconced in culture, is shaped by the social forces of economy, the national faith in technology, and a widespread divorce from nature. The readings, then, investigate both scientific frontiers and ethical borders, exploring to what extent our beliefs about our bodies shape the patterns of our humanity.

Chapter 6, "Dance," explores definitions of the body as an artistic medium; as a fountain of creativity, rapturous worship, and intoxicating prayer; and as a primal, nonverbal expression of the self. On the one hand, these articles also consider to what extent the forms of dance as performance or experience have been determined by social trends, which can prohibit sensual movement in one era or locale, but celebrate the body as an "instrument of pleasure" and erotic courtship in another time or place. Thus, the "unleashed sexuality" of 1970s disco dancing is juxtaposed to the therapeutic value of "structured movement" in evoking "inner perceptions"—a practice among psychotherapists in the 1990s. The readings in this chapter also serve to cycle back to some of the mind–body concerns of Chapter 1 and to some of the health-and-wellness concerns of Chapters 2 and 5. These articles explore a set of questions that oppose the physicality to the spirituality of the body in order to reveal its multiple nature. How can dance express both the tribal history of the human race and a transitory jimmy-and-jive fad—the alligator, the twelve-step, the Macarena, or the salsa? Why is socially organized movement so popular that the steps come and go, but the dance lives on? To what extent does the dancer express not only a joyful celebration of the body's possibilities, but also the sacredness of life and a striving toward transcendence? How can dance both create an unhealthy ideal of emaciated girlhood in the ballerina and offer a penetrating, fundamental "way of knowing" the world? Again, these questions move beyond the borders of the corporeal frame to include psycho-social, moral, and spiritual concerns. These concerns suggest that to study the body in any depth is, indeed, to study our culture, our human nature, and the relations between the two.

Mind, Body, Spirit

This chapter introduces the concerns of *Body and Culture* by focusing on natural healing, which presupposes a metaphor of disease as disharmony and health as equilibrium. This model recalls the ancient Greek theory of the humors advanced by Hippocrates. In his view, the balance of four fluids (blood, phlegm, choler or yellow bile, and melancholy or black bile) within the body ensures good health and a steady disposition, but an excess of any humor results in pain and disease. Hippocrates also proposed that this balance is influenced by outside forces, but that the humors themselves are secretions from bodily glands. In the second century (A.D.), the Greek physician Galen extended this theory to propose that an imbalance in the humors also explains four psychological temperaments: an excess of blood in the system causes cheerfulness; an excess of phlegm causes apathy or sluggishness; an excess of yellow bile causes anger; and an excess of black bile causes depression. In any case, this early model of the body—popular through the medieval age and the Renaissance—relied on a holistic view of the human system, much the way ancient Chinese medicine or acupuncture operates today.

According to Michel Foucault, modern medicine began in the late eighteenth century only when European doctors developed a technological language and an observing gaze that could interpret signs and locate an invading disease within the three-dimensional space of the body. In *The Birth of the Clinic: An Archeology of Medical Perception* (Vintage, 1975), he explains that once the clinical examination could track the sequence of causes, effects, and life cycle of an alien organism, the physical conditions of the disease became paramount while the person became a mere "object of positive knowledge" (197). As Foucault suggests, the doctor–patient dialog shifted from the interpersonal question "What is the matter with you?" to the more objectifying question "Where does it hurt?" (xviii). According to the modern medical model, treatment then tracks the disease "on the paths followed by nature" (9) so that even if its strength is reduced by medication, the pathology is allowed to run its course in the body.

The following readings reject this model, which assumes an alienation between body and disease. Instead, dis-ease is considered a dis-equilibrium of energies that have a bodily manifestation, as well as a mental component and even a transpersonal dimension. The first article provides a personal experience that calls medical science and hospital routines into question, but Norman Cousins relies not only on his own illness and recovery as an example. He also cites research studies that lend support to his intuitions about his own health.

The second article, "Psychoneuroimmunology," is a bit more scientific treatment of Cousins's realizations through experience. As psychologists trained in medical science, Joan and Miroslav Borysenko gather not only human examples to demonstrate the mind–body connection, but also cite well-established research and offer technical explanations about physiological changes caused by specific hormones and proteins in the immune system. Their approach is rational and historical, although they also provide a practical exercise so that readers can learn from a brief experience exactly how the mind–body connection feels.

The third article, on forms of healing through meditation, takes a decidedly nonmedical approach in applying Buddhist principles to health practices. Jack Kornfield argues for the interrelatedness of body, mind, heart, and soul in the human system so that health is a pathway on a continual journey of life, rather than a steady state defined by the absence of disease. Here, the "data" of his argument are a set of ethical principles that he asks the reader to share, as well as examples from people's stories of healing that he learned in his practice as a psychotherapist and meditation teacher.

Together, these three readings raise fundamental questions about how we can understand our bodies in nonphysiological ways that challenge the accepted culture of medicine, hospitals, and the expert–client relationship. Moreover, the readings ask you to probe your own experience of the body through reflection on how American society shapes your understanding of health and disease.

Anatomy of an Illness as Perceived by the Patient
NORMAN COUSINS

An editor and writer at Saturday Review *for nearly forty years, Norman Cousins was the author of a dozen books and hundreds of essays. The magazine itself, now defunct, was dedicated to literature and the arts, and to ethical questions about science, religion, and politics in America. In the 1950s Cousins began acting as a citizen diplomat, promoting world peace and an international government that would supercede the authority of individual nations. In the early 1960s he facilitated communication among the Vatican, the Kremlin, and the White House, which helped the United States and the former Soviet Union reach the first nuclear test ban treaty. In the late 1960s and early 1970s he was a vocal opponent of the Vietnam War. In the 1960s he also suffered the illness that brought about his own profound realization of holistic healing, the basis of his best-selling book* Anatomy of an Illness as Perceived by the Patient: Reflections on Healing and Regeneration *(1979). In 1980 he experienced a heart attack and a second recovery that he later reported in* The Healing Heart: Antidotes to Panic and Helplessness *(1983). By 1978 he had retired from publishing and become Professor of Medical Humanities at the UCLA School of Medicine, teaching ethics and continuing his research on the relationship between mental attitude and bodily health. At UCLA, he also founded the Norman Cousins Center for Psychoneuroimmunology, where research continues into the holistic practice of medicine that integrates the interactions between mind and body. In 1990 he died of cardiac arrest at age 75—having outlived his doctors' predictions by years. The first chapter of his 1979 book, reprinted below, records his initial experience with disease and healing that challenged the conventions of medical science.*

─────────── ✦ ───────────

This book is about a serious illness that occurred in 1964. I was reluctant to write about it for many years because I was fearful of creating false hopes in others who were similarly afflicted. Moreover, I knew that a single case has small standing in the annals of medical research, having little more than "anecdotal" or "testimonial" value. However, references to the illness surfaced from time to time in the general and medical press. People wrote to ask whether it was true that I "laughed" my way out of a crippling disease that doctors believed to be irreversible. In view of those questions, I thought it useful to provide a fuller account than appeared in those early reports.

In August 1964, I flew home from a trip abroad with a slight fever. The malaise, which took the form of a general feeling of achiness, rapidly deepened. Within a week it became difficult to move my neck, arms, hands, fingers, and legs. My sedimentation rate was over 80. Of all the diagnostic tests, the "sed" rate is one of the most useful to the physician. The way it works is beautifully simple. The speed with which red blood cells settle in a test tube—measured in millimeters per hour—is generally proportionate to the severity of an inflammation or infection. A normal illness, such as grippe, might produce a sedimentation reading of, say, 30 or even 40. When the rate goes well beyond 60 or 70, however, the physician knows that he is dealing with more than a casual health problem. I was hospitalized when the sed rate hit 88. Within a week it was up to 115, generally considered to be a sign of a critical condition.

There were other tests, some of which seemed to me to be more an assertion of the clinical capability of the hospital than of concern for the well-being of the patient. I was astounded when four technicians from four different departments took four separate and substantial blood samples on the same day. That the hospital didn't take the trouble to coordinate the tests, using one blood specimen, seemed to me inexplicable and irresponsible. Taking four large slugs of blood the same day even from a healthy person is hardly to be recommended. When the technicians came the second day to fill their containers with blood for processing in separate laboratories, I turned them away and had a sign posted on my door saying that I would give just one specimen every three days and that I expected the different departments to draw from one vial for their individual needs.

I had a fast-growing conviction that a hospital is no place for a person who is seriously ill. The surprising lack of respect for basic sanitation; the rapidity with which staphylococci and other pathogenic organisms can run through an entire hospital; the extensive and sometimes promiscuous use of X-ray equipment; the seemingly indiscriminate administration of tranquilizers and powerful painkillers, sometimes more for the convenience of hospital staff in managing patients than for therapeutic needs; and the regularity with which hospital routine takes precedence over the rest requirements of the patient (slumber, when it comes for an ill person, is an uncommon blessing and is not to be wantonly interrupted)—all these and other practices seemed to me to be critical shortcomings of the modern hospital.

• • •

My doctor did not quarrel with my reservations about hospital procedures. I was fortunate to have as a physician a man who was able to put himself in the position of the patient. Dr. William Hitzig supported me in the measures I took to fend off the random sanguinary assaults of the hospital laboratory attendants.

We had been close friends for more than twenty years, and he knew of my own deep interest in medical matters. We had often discussed articles in the medical press, including the *New England Journal of Medicine (NEJM)*, and *Lancet*. He was candid with me about my case. He reviewed the reports of the various specialists he had called in as consultants. He said there was no agreement on a precise diagnosis. There was, however, a consensus that I was suffering from a serious collagen illness—a disease of the connective tissue. All arthritic and rheumatic diseases are in this category. Collagen is the fibrous substance that binds the cells together. In a sense, then, I was coming unstuck. I had considerable difficulty in moving my limbs and even in turning over in bed. Nodules appeared on my body, gravel-like substances under the skin, indicating the systemic nature of the disease. At the low point of my illness, my jaws were almost locked.

Dr. Hitzig called in experts from Dr. Howard Rusk's rehabilitation clinic in New York. They confirmed the general opinion, adding the more particularized diagnosis of ankylosing spondylitis, which would mean that the connective tissue in the spine was disintegrating.

I asked Dr. Hitzig about my chances for full recovery. He leveled with me, admitting that one of the specialists had told him I had one chance in five hundred. The specialist had also stated that he had not personally witnessed a recovery from this comprehensive condition.

All this gave me a great deal to think about. Up to that time, I had been more or less disposed to let the doctors worry about my condition. But now I felt a compulsion to get into the act. It seemed clear to me that if I was to be that one in five hundred I had better be something more than a passive observer.

• • •

10   I knew that the full functioning of my endocrine system—in particular the adrenal glands—was essential for combating severe arthritis or, for that matter, any other illness. A study I had read in the medical press reported that pregnant women frequently have remissions of arthritic or other rheumatic symptoms. The reason is that the endocrine system is fully activated during pregnancy.

How was I to get my adrenal glands and my endocrine system, in general, working well again?

I remembered having read, ten years or so earlier, Hans Selye's classic book, *The Stress of Life*. With great clarity, Selye showed that adrenal exhaustion could be caused by emotional tension, such as frustration or suppressed rage. He detailed the negative effects of the negative emotions on body chemistry.

The inevitable question arose in my mind: what about the positive emotions? If negative emotions produce negative chemical changes in the body, wouldn't the positive emotions produce positive chemical changes? Is it possible that love, hope, faith, laughter, confidence, and the will to live have therapeutic value? Do chemical changes occur only on the downside?

Obviously, putting the positive emotions to work was nothing so simple as turning on a garden hose. But even a reasonable degree of control over my emotions might have a salutary physiologic effect. Just replacing anxiety with a fair degree of confidence might be helpful.

15   A plan began to form in my mind for systematic pursuit of the salutary emotions, and I knew that I would want to discuss it with my doctor. Two preconditions, however, seemed obvious for the experiment. The first concerned my medication. If that medication were toxic to any degree, it was doubtful whether the plan would work. The second precondition concerned the hospital. I knew I would have to find a place somewhat more conducive to a positive outlook on life.

Let's consider these preconditions separately.

First, the medication. The emphasis had been on pain-killing drugs—aspirin, phenylbutazone (butazolidine), codeine, colchicine, sleeping pills. The aspirin and phenylbutazone were anti-inflammatory and thus were therapeutically justifiable. But I wasn't sure they weren't also toxic. It developed that I was hypersensitive to virtually all the medication I was receiving. The hospital had been giving me maximum dosages: twenty-six aspirin tablets and twelve phenylbutazone tablets a day. No wonder I had hives all over my body and felt as though my skin were being chewed up by millions of red ants.

It was unreasonable to expect positive chemical changes to take place so long as my body was being saturated with, and toxified by, pain-killing medications. I had one of my research assistants at the *Saturday Review* look up the pertinent references in the medical journals and found that drugs like phenylbutazone and even aspirin levy a heavy tax on the adrenal glands. I also learned that phenylbutazone is one of the most powerful drugs being manufactured. It can produce bloody stools, the result of its antagonism to fibrinogen. It can cause intolerable itching and sleeplessness. It can depress bone marrow.

Aspirin, of course, enjoys a more auspicious reputation, at least with the general public. The prevailing impression of aspirin is that it is not only the most harmless drug available but also one of the most effective. When I looked into research in the medical journals, however, I found that aspirin is quite powerful in its own right and warrants considerable care in its use. The fact that it can be bought in unlimited quantities without prescription or doctor's guidance seemed indefensible. Even in small amounts, it can cause internal bleeding. Articles in the medical press reported that the chemical composition of aspirin, like that of phenylbutazone, impairs the clotting function of platelets, disc-shaped substances in the blood.

It was a mind-boggling train of thought. Could it be, I asked   20
myself, that aspirin, so universally accepted for so many years, was actually harmful in the treatment of collagen illnesses such as arthritis?

• • •

Suppose I stopped taking aspirin and phenylbutazone? What about the pain? The bones in my spine and practically every joint in my body felt as though I had been run over by a truck.

I knew that pain could be affected by attitudes. Most people become panicky about almost any pain. On all sides they have been so bombarded by advertisements about pain that they take this or that analgesic at the slightest sign of an ache. We are largely illiterate about pain and so are seldom able to deal with it rationally. Pain is part of the body's magic. It is the way the body transmits a sign to the brain that something is wrong. Leprous patients pray for the sensation of pain. What makes leprosy such a terrible disease is that the victim usually feels no pain when his extremities are being injured. He loses his fingers or toes because he receives no warning signal.

I could stand pain so long as I knew that progress was being made in meeting the basic need. That need, I felt, was to restore the body's capacity to halt the continuing breakdown of connective tissue.

There was also the problem of the severe inflammation. If we dispensed with the aspirin, how would we combat the inflammation? I recalled having read in the medical journals about the usefulness of ascorbic acid in combating a wide number of illnesses—all the way from bronchitis to some types of heart disease. Could it also combat inflammation? Did vitamin C act directly, or did it serve as a starter for the body's endocrine system—in particular, the adrenal glands? Was it possible, I asked myself, that ascorbic acid had a vital role to play in "feeding" the adrenal glands?

• • •

25   Even before we had completed arrangements for moving out of the hospital we began the part of the program calling for the full exercise of the affirmative emotions as a factor in enhancing body chemistry. It was easy enough to hope and love and have faith, but what about laughter? Nothing is less funny than being flat on your back with all the bones in your spine and joints hurting. A systematic program was indicated. A good place to begin, I thought, was with amusing movies. Allen Funt, producer of the spoofing television program "Candid Camera," sent films of some of his CC classics, along with a motion-picture projector. The nurse was instructed in its use. We were even able to get our hands on some old Marx Brothers films. We pulled down the blinds and turned on the machine.

It worked. I made the joyous discovery that ten minutes of genuine belly laughter had an anesthetic effect and would give me at least two hours of pain-free sleep. When the pain-killing effect of the laughter wore off, we would switch on the motion-picture projector again, and, not infrequently, it would lead to another pain-free sleep interval. Sometimes, the nurse read to me out of a trove of humor books. Especially useful were E. B. and Katharine White's *Subtreasury of American Humor* and Max Eastman's *The Enjoyment of Laughter*.

How scientific was it to believe that laughter—as well as the positive emotions in general—was affecting my body chemistry for the better? If laughter did in fact have a salutary effect on the body's chemistry, it seemed at least theoretically likely that it would enhance the system's ability to fight the inflammation. So we took sedimentation rate readings just before as well as several hours after the laughter episodes. Each time, there was a drop of at least five points. The drop by itself was not substantial, but it held and was cumulative. I was greatly elated by the discovery that there is a physiologic basis for the ancient theory that laughter is good medicine.

There was, however, one negative side-effect of the laughter from the standpoint of the hospital. I was disturbing other patients. But that objection didn't last very long, for the arrangements were now complete for me to move my act to a hotel room.

One of the incidental advantages of the hotel room, I was delighted to find, was that it cost only about one-third as much as the hospital. The other benefits were incalculable. I would not be awakened for a bed bath or for meals or for medication or for a change of bed sheets or for tests or for examinations by hospital interns. The sense of serenity was delicious and would, I felt certain, contribute to a general improvement.

What about ascorbic acid and its place in the general pro-   30
gram for recovery? In discussing my speculations about vitamin C with Dr. Hitzig, I found him completely open-minded on the subject, although he told me of serious questions that had been raised by scientific studies. He also cautioned me that heavy doses of ascorbic acid carried some risk of renal damage. The main problem right then, however, was not my kidneys; it seemed to me that, on balance, the risk was worth taking. I asked Dr. Hitzig about previous recorded experience with massive doses of vitamin C. He ascertained that at the hospital there had been cases in which patients had received up to 3 grams by intramuscular injection.

As I thought about the injection procedure, some questions came to mind. Introducing the ascorbic acid directly into the bloodstream might make more effective use of the vitamin, but I wondered about the body's ability to utilize a sudden, massive infusion. I knew that one of the great advantages of vitamin C is that the body takes only the amount necessary for its purposes and excretes the rest. Again, there came to mind [Walter] Cannon's phrase—the wisdom of the body.

Was there a coefficient of time in the utilization of ascorbic acid? The more I thought about it, the more likely it seemed to me that the body would excrete a large quantity of the vitamin because it couldn't metabolize it fast enough. I wondered whether a better procedure than injection would be to administer the ascorbic acid through slow intravenous drip over a period of three or four hours. In this way we could go far beyond 3 grams. My hope was to start at 10 grams and then increase the dose daily until we reached 25 grams.

Dr. Hitzig's eyes widened when I mentioned 25 grams. This amount was far beyond any recorded dose. He said he had to caution me about the possible effect not just on the kidneys but on the veins in the arms. Moreover, he said he knew of no data to support the assumption that the body could handle 25 grams over a four-hour period, other than by excreting it rapidly through the urine.

As before, however, it seemed to me we were playing for bigger stakes: losing some veins was not of major importance alongside the need to combat whatever was eating at my connective tissue.

35 To know whether we were on the right track we took a sedimentation test before the first intravenous administration of 10 grams of ascorbic acid. Four hours later, we took another sedimentation test. There was a drop of nine full points.

Seldom had I known such elation. The ascorbic acid was working. So was laughter. The combination was cutting heavily into whatever poison was attacking the connective tissue. The fever was receding, and the pulse was no longer racing.

We stepped up the dosage. On the second day we went to 12.5 grams of ascorbic acid, on the third day 15 grams, and so on until the end of the week, when we reached 25 grams. Meanwhile, the laughter routine was in full force. I was completely off drugs and sleeping pills. Sleep—blessed, natural sleep without pain—was becoming increasingly prolonged.

At the end of the eighth day I was able to move my thumbs without pain. By this time, the sedimentation rate was somewhere in the 80s and dropping fast. I couldn't be sure, but it seemed to me that the gravel-like nodules on my neck and the backs of my hands were beginning to shrink. There was no doubt in my mind that I was going to make it back all the way. I could function, and the feeling was indescribably beautiful.

I must not make it appear that all my infirmities disappeared overnight. For many months I couldn't get my arms up far enough to reach for a book on a high shelf. My fingers weren't agile enough to do what I wanted them to do on the organ keyboard. My neck had a limited turning radius. My knees were somewhat wobbly, and off and on, I have had to wear a metal brace.

40 Even so, I was sufficiently recovered to go back to my job at the *Saturday Review* full time again, and this was miracle enough for me.

• • •

It was seven years after the onset of the illness before I had scientific confirmation about the dangers of using aspirin in the treatment of collagen diseases. In its May 8, 1971 issue, *Lancet* published a study by Drs. M. A. Sahud and R. J. Cohen showing that aspirin can be antagonistic to the retention of vitamin C in the body. The authors said that patients with rheumatoid arthritis should take vitamin C supplements, since it has often been noted that they have low levels of the vitamin in their blood. It was no surprise, then, that I had been able to absorb such massive amounts of ascorbic acid without kidney or other complications.

What conclusions do I draw from the entire experience?

The first is that the will to live is not a theoretical abstraction, but a physiologic reality with therapeutic characteristics. The second is that I was incredibly fortunate to have as my doctor a man who knew that his biggest job was to encourage to the fullest the patient's will to live and to mobilize all the natural resources of body and mind to combat disease. Dr. Hitzig was willing to set aside the large and often hazardous armamentarium of powerful drugs available to the modern physician when he became convinced that his patient might have something better to offer. He was also wise enough to know that the art of healing is still a frontier profession. And, though I can't be sure of this point, I have a hunch he believed that my own total involvement was a major factor in my recovery.

• • •

Until comparatively recently, medical literature on the phenomenon of the placebo has been rather sparse. But the past two decades have seen a pronounced interest in the subject. Indeed, three medical researchers at the University of California, Los Angeles, have compiled an entire volume on a bibliography of the placebo. (J. Turner, R. Gallimore, C. Fox, *Placebo: An Annotated Bibliography*. The Neuropsychiatric Institute, University of California, Los Angeles, 1974.) Among the medical researchers who have been prominently engaged in such studies are Arthur K. Shapiro, Stewart Wolf, Henry K. Beecher, and Louis Lasagna. In connection with my own experience, I was fascinated by a report citing a study by Dr. Thomas C. Chalmers, of the Mount Sinai Medical Center in New York, which compared two groups that were being used to test the theory that ascorbic acid is a cold preventative. "The group on placebo who thought they were on ascorbic acid," says Dr. Chalmers, "had fewer colds than the group on ascorbic acid who thought they were on placebo."

45   I was absolutely convinced, at the time I was deep in my illness, that intravenous doses of ascorbic acid could be beneficial—and they were. It is quite possible that this treatment—like everything else I did—was a demonstration of the placebo effect.

At this point, of course, we are opening a very wide door, perhaps even a Pandora's box. The vaunted "miracle cures" that abound in the literature of all the great religions all say something about the ability of the patient, properly motivated or stimulated, to participate actively in extraordinary reversals of disease and disability. It is all too easy, of course, to raise these possibilities and speculations to a monopoly status—in which case the entire edifice of modern medicine would be reduced to little more than the hut of an African witch doctor. But we can at least reflect on William Halse Rivers's statement, as quoted by Shapiro, that "the salient feature of the medicine of today is that these psychical factors are no longer allowed to play their part unwittingly, but are themselves becoming the subject of study, so that the present age is serving the growth of a rational system of psychotherapeutics."

What we are talking about essentially, I suppose, is the chemistry of the will to live. In Bucharest in 1972, I visited the clinic of Ana Aslan, described to me as one of Romania's leading endocrinologists. She spoke of her belief that there is a direct connection between a robust will to live and the chemical balances in the brain. She is convinced that creativity—one aspect of the will to live—produces the vital brain impulses that stimulate the pituitary gland, triggering effects on the pineal gland and the whole of the endocrine system. Is it possible that placebos have a key role in this process? Shouldn't this entire area be worth serious and sustained attention?

If I had to guess, I would say that the principal contribution made by my doctor to the taming, and possibly the conquest, of my illness was that he encouraged me to believe I was a respected partner with him in the total undertaking. He fully engaged my subjective energies. He may not have been able to define or diagnose the process through which self-confidence (wild hunches securely believed) was somehow picked up by the body's immunologic mechanisms and translated into antimorbid effects, but he was acting, I believe, in the best tradition of medicine in recognizing that he had to reach out in my case beyond the usual verifiable modalities. In so doing, he was faithful to the first dictum in his medical education: above all, do not harm.

Something else I have learned. I have learned never to underestimate the capacity of the human mind and body to regenerate—even when the prospects seem most wretched. The life-force may be the least understood force on earth. William James said that human beings tend to live too far within self-imposed limits. It is possible that these limits will recede when we respect more fully the natural drive of the human mind and body toward perfectibility and regeneration. Protecting and cherishing that natural drive may well represent the finest exercise of human freedom.

Discussion Questions

1. Cousins resents the hospital's demands for blood samples and complains of its unhealthy environment where, he says, decisions are sometimes made "for the convenience of hospital staff" (paragraphs 3–5). In these responses, do you consider him a cranky or uncooperative patient or a responsible health services consumer? Why?

2. Based on your experience and observations, to what extent do you believe that medical personnel and/or hospitals have improved, since 1964, in their healthful treatment of patients? Explain with examples.

3. Describe your personal viewpoint about relying on drugs, such as aspirin or even vitamin C, for recurring problems with your body.

4. In the concluding paragraphs of Cousins's essay, he reports some of the medical research on vitamin C and on "the placebo effect." In your opinion, do these citations add to the validity of Cousins's personal experience, detract from the value of his treatment, or not affect your conviction either way? Explain.

Psychoneuroimmunology: Where Mind and Body Meet

JOAN AND MIROSLAV BORYSENKO

Joan Borysenko completed her Ph.D. in medical sciences at Harvard Medical School, where she continued post-doctoral studies in experimental pathology, behavioral medicine, and psychoneuroimmunology. She is also a licensed psychologist and cofounder of the Mind–Body clinical programs at Boston's Beth Israel/Deaconess Medical Center. These programs became the basis for her bestselling 1987 book Minding the Body, Mending the Mind. *As an inspirational workshop leader and author of eleven books, she integrates scientific training and spirituality to promote healing. The following selection is from* The Power of the Mind to Heal *(1994), coauthored with her husband Miroslav.*

As you read, consider to what extent the argument depends on (1) technical explanations about medical science, (2) citations to previous research, and (3) nontechnical examples addressed to the general (nonspecialist) reader. Among the three kinds of evidence, consider which you find to be the most important evidence offered and why you think so.

———————— ✦ ————————

In 1978, Miron took a year's sabbatical as a visiting professor at Harvard Medical School to begin doing research in a fledgling field called psychoneuroimmunology. Partway through the year, he returned to Tufts Medical School to attend a staff meeting for faculty who were planning the following year's immunology course. When he explained that the study of psychoneuroimmunology sought to establish a link between our thoughts and the function of our immune cells, he was met by a stunned silence. On the way out the door, one of his colleagues stopped him, literally pointing the finger of disbelief. "Do you really mean that you actually believe that what we think can affect the activity of lymphocytes?" he challenged.

Miron held his ground. He did believe exactly that, and research has backed him up. There is an old metaphysical principle stating that "thoughts are things." Now, that might be a workable concept for metaphysicians, but many conventional physicians still blanch at the concept. As Miron tells the story, within a few weeks of his announcing his new research interest, there was a joke afoot in the corridors that he had become a psychotic, neurotic immunologist!

Only a few years later, the fact that conditions such as stress have a serious impact on immunity is no longer in question. Temporary stress, like studying for an exam, can completely wipe out the body's interferon levels, literally reducing them to zero. Interferon is necessary for certain cells of the immune system to do their jobs. For example, one kind of immune cell is a lymphocyte known as the natural killer cell. Natural killer cells have two functions. First, they patrol the body and seek out virus-infected cells for elimination. Second, they seek out and destroy cancer cells. Unfortunately, current medical science has not yet found a cure for viruses, and cancer treatment is still in a very rudimentary stage. How incredible that our bodies have lymphocytes that can perform these important functions.

In students, the stress of exam week often results in colds, cold sores, or other "minor" illnesses—perhaps as a result of the poor natural killer cell activity brought about by low interferon levels. Have you ever gone through a particularly stressful period and then, right after it was over, contracted a cold or the flu? Probably so, but fortunately, the body recovers very quickly from acute stress and the immune dysfunction that accompanies it. In terms of our long-term health, chronic stress is much more important than short-term stress.

Harvard physiologist Walter Cannon first described the body's response to acute stress, which he called the "fight-or-flight response," in 1929. From time to time you may have opened your morning paper and found a photograph that defies belief—for example, a 110-pound mother lifting a two-ton truck off her injured child. These seemingly miraculous feats are due to a physiological symphony that plays flawlessly when we are faced with an emergency. Adrenaline pours out of the adrenal glands, causing blood pressure to rise and the heart to beat more forcefully. At the same time, sugar is liberated from storage in the liver and pours into the bloodstream. This rapidly burning fuel is quickly delivered to our muscles, giving us uncommon strength. Adrenaline simultaneously improves visual acuity, short-term memory, and mental sharpness. We can make decisions fast and then act on them. We can survive.

The fight-or-flight response is mediated by the sympathetic, or activating branch, of the autonomic nervous system. These neural pathways respond to fear by triggering an outpouring of adrenaline that is then broken down very quickly by the body. If you have a scare in traffic, for example, your body responds instantly. A minute later, calm prevails again unless you decide to wallow in anger or frustration. And often, that's exactly what we do. For example, sometimes the stress of marriage is so taxing that we finally get a divorce, but by hanging on to ancient anger for years, we turn an old situation into a current stressor. Stress then becomes chronic.

In 1936, physician and physiologist Dr. Hans Selye described the physiology of chronic stress, which he called the *general adaptation syndrome*. When rats were chronically stressed, he noticed that their adrenal glands got very big and that their thymus glands—the source of T-lymphocytes—became very small. Although little was known about the immune system in the 1930s, it was obvious that chronic stress led to increased illness. What Selye was observing had a great deal to do with a hormone called corticosterone. In humans the analogous hormone is called cortisol. When we are chronically stressed, the hypothalamus of our brain secretes a hormone called ACTH, or adrenocorticotropin. This hormone then binds to cells in the outer cortex of the adrenal gland and causes them to manufacture and secrete cortisol. Over time, the gland gets bigger and bigger if it is constantly challenged with the need to make more cortisol. In the short run, cortisol is a repair hormone. But in the long run, it is an immunosuppressant. Cortisol not only prevents the formation of new immune cells, it also inhibits the activities of the ones already in our system.

Hans Selye himself had a spontaneous remission from an often rapidly lethal type of cancer called mesothelioma. When his physician informed him that he might have only a few months left to live, Selye decided to write his memoirs. As he was poring through old journals, his memory was jarred by several painful situations that had occurred in his past. One of them was the theft of his research findings by supposed mentors when he was still in medical school. He reasoned that he could either release the old hurt or belabor it. He decided to let it go and leave it out of his memoirs. He continued the retrospective of his life in that manner—that is, letting go of old hurts. When he returned for a check-up about a year later, his physician found that the cancer had disappeared! Was his remission related to his practice of forgiveness and the relief of chronic stress? We have no way of knowing the answer to that question definitively, but it's certainly a reasonable hypothesis.

Chronic stress not only takes the form of long-held regrets and resentments, it also shows up as feelings of hopelessness and helplessness when we feel that we have neither the skills nor the strength to cope with the challenges of life. The best definition of stress that Miron and I have found is "the perception of physical or emotional threat coupled with the perception that our responses are inadequate to cope." The key words here are *perception* and *coping*.

10   Miron often jokes that two people confronted with a large black dog may perceive the animal very differently. On the basis of past experience, one person may love dogs and be attracted to the animal; the other may fear dogs and be repelled. But if the dog were growling and foaming at the mouth, both people would be afraid. Then, coping skills would become important. A poor coper might freeze at the sight of the dog, and a good coper might hide behind the person who had frozen!

Whenever Miron tells that story, I am reminded of the two hikers who are set upon by a lion. One drops to the ground and puts on his sneakers, while the other berates him for thinking that he can outrun such a beast. The one donning his sneakers replies, "I don't have to outrun the lion; I just have to outrun you!"

People who are good copers are often referred to as *stress-hardy*. Psychologist Suzanne Kobasa has identified three attitudes that sustain such individuals during demanding times. These attitudes are called the three C's: challenge, commitment, and control. A stress-hardy person sees change and crisis as a challenge rather than a threat. Even when they cannot control the outer situation, they realize that they always have control over their response to the things that are happening. There is a wise, old saying that relates to this phenomenon: Suffering is inevitable, but misery is optional.

Stress-hardy people who can endure the inevitable sufferings of life without becoming mired in misery are often able to thrive in hard times because they are committed to a set of values that puts crisis and difficulty into a positive frame of reference. For example, people who have to work very hard, but who are committed to their jobs because they believe that they are helping people, are less stressed than those who do not feel this type of commitment. The *meaning* that we ascribe to any stressful situation—be it a job, an illness, or the death of a loved one—makes a tremendous difference in our ability to cope. At times it can mean the difference between life and death.

Viktor Frankl, the renowned psychiatrist who wrote the beautiful and inspiring book, *Man's Search for Meaning*, is a survivor of the Nazi holocaust who was finally liberated from Auschwitz at the end of World War II. He observed that people who could find some meaning in their suffering often managed to hang on to the will to live, and if the Nazis didn't kill them first, they often survived until liberation. These were the good copers. He also wrote about how people who lost the will to live often died within hours from heart attacks, or simply succumbed to infection. Frankl was one of the first people to write about psychoneuroimmunology: "Those who know how close the connection is between the mind of a man—and his courage and hope or lack of them—and the state of immunity of his body will understand that the sudden loss of hope and courage can have a deadly effect."

The molecular mechanisms through which attitudes such as helplessness, hopelessness, and despair can impact the immune system have to do both with the autonomic nervous system and some tiny proteins called *neuropeptides*. Our brains are like pharmacies, compounding a wide range of drugs that affect both our moods and all of our biological systems, including the immune system. For example, when threatened with death—that is, if a saber-toothed tiger had you in its jaws—thanks to neuropeptides called *endorphins* and *encephalins,* you would feel somewhat peaceful, sleepy, and numb as you took your place in the food chain. Our brains also secrete valium and other natural tranquilizers, as well as dozens of other peptides related to the control and expression of emotion.

When you react to the very thought of your boss as if he were a saber-toothed tiger, your body secretes chemicals that prepare you to die, rather than helping you to live. The amazing thing is that these drugs are pumped out of the brain into the bloodstream and eventually bind to the surface of all the cells in your body, the way that a lock fits into a key. They then affect the function of all your cells. The area of the brain in which thought is transformed into emotional response is called the *limbic system*. Cells of the limbic system are particularly active in the manufacture and secretion of neuropeptides—a direct line of communication between emotions and the body.

For example, let's say that you've just had a joyful thought. Better still, bring a joyful thought to mind right now. Take a few letting-go breaths, close your eyes, and either recall something that made you happy, such as a baby's first smile or a delightful joke, or imagine something that might make you joyful in the future. Allow yourself to imagine—that is, to enter into—the scene with all your senses. What do you see or sense around you? Above and below you? Are there any sounds? Any special fragrances? Are you moving, touching, sitting, standing? What is the emotional or deep-felt sense of the memory in your body? Now, if you've recalled joy, pause for another minute or two and really notice how your body responded to joy. Feel it in your cells.

Perhaps you feel somewhat different now than you did a few minutes ago. Your brief meditation on joy caused cells in your limbic system to release neuropeptides that crossed the blood/brain barrier and entered your bloodstream. In a matter of seconds, these clever little chemicals fit into receptor sites all over your body. When the key slid into the lock, various genes in your cells were turned on or off, starting or stopping the synthesis of proteins. Depending on what proteins were activated or deactivated, the function of all your systems was potentially altered. This is one of the many pathways through which thoughts become things.

So, if you feel joy, every cell in your body responds to that emotion. And if you are depressed, that image, too, is broadcast throughout the entire body/mind by the neuropeptide system. Furthermore, the brain is not the only organ that makes neuropeptides. The cells that line your gut are also neuropeptide factories, as are some lymphocytes. So what goes on in the digestive tract or the immune system in turn affects brain function and mood. Dr. Candace Pert, a neuroscientist who was one of the co-discoverers of the endorphins, has quipped that neuropeptides released by the gut may be the physiological basis of gut feelings!

Some of us are very aware of the way that our moods affect   20
our bodies—how anxiety tenses the muscles, how depression leads to fatigue, how joy creates energy, and how gratitude and love open the heart. Dr. Pert and her colleague, neuroscientist Michael Ruff, believe that the mind and body cannot be separated—that each cell is imbued with mind. Our very cells are conscious, aware beings that communicate with each other, affecting our emotions and choices. When people speak of the body/mind connection, they are often referring to only one side of the equation—the effect of mind on body. But body also affects mind. What we eat, whether we are touched, how and whether we exercise, how we breathe—all these seemingly physical acts have a profound effect on our moods and on our ability to be clear-headed, loving, and creative.

Discussion Questions

1. State the thesis of the Borysenkos's article. Then, in a well-developed paragraph, write a personal example that demonstrates your agreement or disagreement with that thesis.

2. Among the three kinds of evidence (examples, reference to previous research, and technical explanations), consider which you find to be the most convincing evidence offered and why you think so.

3. Describe your response to the scientific details about the immune system. Do these details help convince you of the Borysenkos's thesis? Explain.

4. Why do the authors include the example of Victor Frankl and the Nazi Holocaust? How does this example relate to Cousins's report in "Anatomy of an Illness"?

Necessary Healing
JACK KORNFIELD

After training as a Buddhist monk in Thailand, Burma, and India for five years, Jack Kornfield has taught meditation around the world since 1974. However, with a Ph.D. in clinical psychology, he combines the teachings of East and West as a practicing therapist, believing that psychotherapy can unblock personal fears and delusions. He is also a cofounder of the Insight Meditation Society in Barre, Massachusetts, and of the Spirit Rock Meditation Center in Woodacre, California, near his home. His books include Teachings of the Buddha *(1993) and* After the Ecstasy, the Laundry *(2001). One key to his teachings is that "to undertake a genuine spiritual path is not to avoid difficulties but to learn the art of making mistakes wakefully, to bring them to the transformative power of our heart." The following essay is from his 1993 best-seller,* A Path with Heart: A Guide through the Perils and Promises of Spiritual Life.

Consider the title, "Necessary Healing," in the context of Kornfield's entire book. Describe your expectations for how "healing" might be a "necessary" step to prepare us for something else. Also, as you read, notice where Kornfield relies on the modern beliefs of psychotherapy, which he integrates with ancient religious teachings.

──────────── ✦ ────────────

True maturation on the spiritual path requires that we discover the depth of our wounds. As Achaan Chah put it, "If you haven't cried a number of times, your meditation hasn't really begun."

Almost everyone who undertakes a true spiritual path will discover that a profound personal healing is a necessary part of his or her spiritual process. When this need is acknowledged, spiritual practice can be directed to bring such healing to body, heart, and mind. This is not a new notion. Since ancient times, spiritual practice has been described as a process of healing. The Buddha and Jesus were both known as healers of the body, as well as great physicians of the spirit.

I encountered a powerful image of the connection of these two teachers in Vietnam, during the war years. In spite of active fighting in the area, I was drawn to visit a temple built by a famous master known as the Coconut Monk on an island in the Mekong Delta. When our boat arrived, the monks greeted us and showed us around. They explained to us their teachings of peace and nonviolence. Then they took us to one end of the island where on top of a hill was an enormous sixty-foot-tall statue of a standing Buddha. Just next to Buddha stood an equally tall statue of Jesus. They had their arms around each other's shoulders, smiling. While helicopter gunships flew by and war raged around them, Buddha and Jesus stood there like brothers expressing compassion and healing for all who would follow their way.

Wise spiritual practice requires that we actively address the pain and conflict of our life in order to come to inner integration and harmony. Through the guidance of a skillful teacher, meditation can help bring this healing. Without including the essential step of healing, students will find that they are blocked from deeper levels of meditation or are unable to integrate them into their lives.

• • •

One man I knew practiced as a yogi in India for ten years. He had come to India after a divorce, and when he left his home in England, he was depressed and unhappy in his work as well. As a yogi he did years of deep and strict breath practices that led to long periods of peace and light in his mind. These were healing in a certain way. But, later, his loneliness returned, and he found himself drawn back home, only to discover that the unfinished issues that had ended his marriage, made him unhappy in his work, and, worst of all, contributed to his depression, all arose again as strong as before he had left. After some time, he saw that a deep healing of his heart was necessary. He realized he could not run from himself and began to seek a healing in the midst of his life. So he found a teacher who wisely guided him to include his depression and loneliness in his meditation. He sought a reconciliation (though not remarriage) with his former wife. He joined support groups that could help him to understand his childhood; he found communal work with people he liked. Each of these became part of the long process of healing his heart that had only begun in India.

• • •

This healing is necessary if we are to embody spiritual life 5 lovingly and wisely. Unhealed pain and rage, unhealed traumas from childhood abuse or abandonment, become powerful unconscious forces in our lives. Until we are able to bring awareness and understanding to our old wounds, we will find ourselves repeating their patterns of unfulfilled desire, anger, and confusion over and over again. While many kinds of healing can come through spiritual life in the form of grace, charismatic revivals, prayer, or ritual, two of the most significant kinds develop naturally through a systematic spiritual practice.

The first area of healing comes when we develop a relationship of trust with a teacher.... A healthy relationship with a teacher serves as a model for trust in others, in ourselves, in our bodies, in our intuitions, our own direct experience. It gives us a trust in life itself. Teachings and teacher become a sacred container to support our awakening....

Another kind of healing takes place when we begin to bring the power of awareness and loving attention to each area of our life with the systematic practice of mindfulness. The Buddha spoke of cultivating awareness in four fundamental aspects of life that he called the Four Foundations of Mindfulness. These areas of mindfulness are: awareness of the body and senses, awareness of the heart and feelings, awareness of the mind and thoughts, and awareness of the principles that govern life. (In Sanskrit these principles are called *the dharma*, or the *universal laws*.)

• • •

HEALING THE BODY

Meditation practice often begins with techniques for bringing us to an awareness of our bodies. This is especially important in a culture such as ours, which has neglected physical and instinctual life. James Joyce wrote of one character, "Mr. Duffy lived a short distance from his body." So many of us do. In meditation, we can slow down and sit quietly, truly staying with whatever arises. With awareness, we can cultivate a willingness to open to physical experiences without struggling against them, to actually live in our bodies. As we do so, we feel more clearly its pleasures and its pains. Because our acculturation teaches us to avoid or run from pain, we do not know much about it. To heal the body we must study pain. When we bring close attention to our physical pains, we will notice several kinds. We see that sometimes pain arises as we adjust to an unaccustomed sitting posture. Other times, pains arise as signals that we're sick or have a genuine physical problem. These pains call for a direct response and healing action from us.

However, most often the kinds of pains we encounter in meditative attention are not indications of physical problems. They are the painful, physical manifestations of our emotional, psychological, and spiritual holdings and contractions. Reich called these pains our muscular armor, the areas of our body that we have tightened over and over in painful situations as a way to protect ourselves from life's inevitable difficulties. Even a healthy person who sits somewhat comfortably to meditate will probably become aware of pains in his or her body. As we sit still, our shoulders, our backs, our jaws, or our necks may hurt. Accumulated knots in the fabric of our body, previously undetected, begin to reveal themselves as we open. As we become conscious of the pain they have held, we may also notice feelings, memories, or images connected specifically to each area of tension.

As we gradually include in our awareness all that we have previously shut out, and neglected, our body heals. Learning to work with this opening is part of the art of meditation. We can bring an open and respectful attention to the sensations that make up our bodily experience. In this process, we must work to develop a feeling awareness of what is actually going on in the body. We can direct our attention to notice the patterns of our breathing, our posture, the way we hold our back, our chest, our belly, our pelvis. In all these areas we can carefully sense the free movement of energy or the contraction and holding that prevents it.

When you meditate, try to allow whatever arises to move through you as it will. Let your attention be very kind. Layers of tension will gradually release, and energy will begin to move. Places in your body where you have held the patterns of old illness and trauma will open. Then a deeper physical purification and opening of the energy channels will occur as the knots release and dissolve. Sometimes with this opening we will experience a powerful movement of the breath, sometimes a spontaneous vibration and other physical sensations.

Let your attention drop beneath the superficial level that just notices "pleasure," "tension," or "pain." Examine the pain and unpleasant sensations you usually block out. With careful mindfulness, you will allow "pain" to show itself to have many layers. As a first step, we can learn to be aware of pain without creating further tension, to experience and observe pain physically as pressure, tightness, pinpricks, needles, throbbing, or burning. Then we can notice all the layers around the "pain." Inside are the strong elements of fire, vibration, and pressure. Outside is often a layer of physical tightness and contraction. Beyond this may be an emotional layer of aversion, anger, or fear and a layer of thoughts and attitudes such as, "I hope this will go away soon," or "If I feel pain, I must be doing something wrong," or "Life is always painful." To heal, we must become aware of all these layers.

Everyone works with physical pain at some time in their spiritual practice. For some people it is a perennial theme. In my own practice, I have had periods of deep physical release that have been organic and very peaceful, and other times have felt like painful and powerful purifications, where my body would shake, my breathing was labored, sensations of heat and fire would move through my body, and strong feelings and images would arise. I would feel as if I were being wrung out. Staying with this process inevitably led to a great opening in my body, often accompanied by tremendous feelings of rapture and well-being. Such physical openings, both gentle and intense, are a common part of prolonged meditation. As you deepen your practice of the body, honor what arises, stay present with an open and loving awareness so that the body itself can unfold in its own way.

Other attitudes toward the body can be found in meditation: ascetic practices, warrior training, and inner yogas to conquer the body. Sometimes healers will recommend consciously aggressive meditation for healing certain illnesses. For instance, in one such practice cancer patients picture their white blood cells as little white knights who spear and destroy the cancer. For certain people this has been helpful, but for myself and others such as Stephen Levine, who has worked so extensively with healing meditation, we have found that a deeper kind of healing takes place when instead of sending aversion and aggression to wounds and illness, we bring loving-kindness. Too often we have met our pain and disease, whether a simple backache or a grave illness, by hating it, hating the whole afflicted area of our body. In mindful healing we direct a compassionate and loving attention to touch the innermost part of our wounds, and healing occurs. As Oscar Wilde put it, "It's not the perfect but the imperfect that is in need of our love."

15   One woman student came to her first meditation retreat with cancer throughout her body. Although she had been told she would die within weeks, she was determined to heal herself using meditation as a tool. She undertook a regimen of excellent Chinese medicine, acupuncture, and daily healing meditations. Though her belly was hot and distended with the cancer the whole time, she so bolstered her immune system that she lived well for ten more years. She credited her healing attention as a key to keeping her cancer in check.

Bringing systematic attention to our body can change our whole relationship to our physical life. We can notice more clearly the rhythms and needs of our bodies. Without mindfully attending to our bodies, we may become so busy in our daily lives that we lose touch with a sense of appropriate diet, movement, and physical enjoyment. Meditation can help us find out in what ways we are neglecting the physical aspects of our lives and what our body asks of us.

A mistaken disregard for the body is illustrated in a story of Mullah Nasrudin, the Sufi wise and holy fool. Nasrudin had bought a donkey, but it was costing him a lot to keep it fed, so he hatched a plan. As the weeks went on, he gradually fed the donkey less and less. Finally, he was only feeding it one small cupful of grain throughout the day. The plan seemed to be succeeding, and Nasrudin was saving a lot of money. Then, unfortunately, the donkey died. Nasrudin went to see his friends in the tea shop and told them about his experiment. "It's such a shame. If that donkey had been around a little longer, maybe I could have gotten him used to eating nothing!"

To ignore or abuse the body is mistaken spirituality. When we honor the body with our attention, we begin to reclaim our feelings, our instincts, our life. Out of this developing attention we can then experience a healing of the senses. The eyes, the tongue, the ears, and the sense of touch are rejuvenated. Many people experience this after some period of meditation. Colors are pure, flavors fresh, we can feel our feet on the earth as if we were children again. This cleansing of the senses allows us to experience the joy of being alive and a growing intimacy with life here and now.

HEALING THE HEART

Just as we open and heal the body by sensing its rhythms and touching it with a deep and kind attention, so we can open and heal other dimensions of our being. The heart and the feelings go through a similar process of healing through the offering of our attention to their rhythms, nature, and needs. Most often, opening the heart begins by opening to a lifetime's accumulation of unacknowledged sorrow, both our personal sorrows and the universal sorrows of warfare, hunger, old age, illness, and death. At times we may experience this sorrow physically, as contractions and barriers around our heart, but more often we feel the depth of our wounds, our abandonment, our pain, as unshed tears. The Buddhists describe this as an ocean of human tears larger than the four great oceans.

As we take the one seat and develop a meditative attention, the heart presents itself naturally for healing. The grief we have carried for so long, from pains and dashed expectations and hopes, arises. We grieve for our past traumas and present fears, for all of the feelings we never dared experience consciously.

Whatever shame or unworthiness we have within us arises—much of our early childhood and family pain, the mother and father wounds we hold, the isolation, any past abuse, physical or sexual, are all stored in the heart. Jack Engler, a Buddhist teacher and psychologist at Harvard University, has described meditation practice as primarily a practice of grieving and of letting go. At most of the spiritual retreats I have been a part of, nearly half of the students are working with some level of grief: denial, anger, loss, or sorrow. Out of this grief work comes a deep renewal.

Many of us are taught that we shouldn't be affected by grief and loss, but no one is exempt. One of the most experienced hospice directors in the country was surprised when he came to a retreat and grieved for his mother who had died the year before. "This grief," he said, "is different from all the others I work with. It's *my* mother."

Oscar Wilde wrote, "Hearts are meant to be broken." As we heal through meditation, our hearts break open to feel fully. Powerful feelings, deep unspoken parts of ourselves arise, and our task in meditation is first to let them move through us, then to recognize them and allow them to sing their songs. A poem by Wendell Berry illustrates this beautifully.

> *I go among trees and sit still.*
> *All my stirring becomes quiet*
> *around me like circles on water.*
> *My tasks lie in their places*
> *Where I left them, asleep like cattle . . .*
>
> *Then what I am afraid of comes.*
> *I live for a while in its sight.*
> *What I fear in it leaves it,*
> *And the fear of it leaves me.*
> *It sings, and I hear its song.*

What we find as we listen to the songs of our rage or fear, loneliness or longing, is that they do not stay forever. Rage turns into sorrow; sorrow turns into tears; tears may fall for a long time, but then the sun comes out. A memory of old loss sings to us; our body shakes and relives the moment of loss; then the armoring around that loss gradually softens; and in the midst of the song of tremendous grieving, the pain of that loss finally finds release.

● ● ●

Naomi Remen, a physician who uses art, meditation, and other spiritual practices in the healing of cancer patients, told me a moving story that illustrates the process of healing the heart, which accompanies a healing of the body. She described a young man who was twenty-four years old when he came to her after one of his legs had been amputated at the hip in order to save his life from bone cancer. When she began her work with him, he had a great sense of injustice and a hatred for all "healthy" people. It seemed bitterly unfair to him that he had suffered this terrible loss so early in his life. His grief and rage were so great that it took several years of continuous work for him to begin to come out of himself and to heal. He had to heal not simply his body, but also his broken heart and wounded spirit.

He worked hard and deeply, telling his story, painting it, meditating, bringing his entire life into awareness. As he slowly healed, he developed a profound compassion for others in similar situations. He began to visit people in the hospital who had also suffered severe physical losses. On one occasion, he told his physician, he visited a young singer who was so depressed about the loss of her breasts that she would not even look at him. The nurses had the radio playing, probably hoping to cheer her up. It was a hot day, and the young man had come in running shorts. Finally, desperate to get her attention, he unstrapped his artificial leg and began dancing around the room on his one leg, snapping his fingers to the music. She looked at him in amazement, and then she burst out laughing and said, "Man, if you can dance, I can sing."

When this young man first began working with drawing, he made a crayon sketch of his own body in the form of a vase with a deep black crack running through it. He redrew the crack over and over and over, grinding his teeth with rage. Several years later, to encourage him to complete his process, my friend showed him his early pictures again. He saw the vase and said, "Oh, this one isn't finished." When she suggested that he finish it then, he did. He ran his finger along the crack, saying, "You see here, this is where the light comes through." With a yellow crayon, he drew light streaming through the crack into the body of the vase and said, "Our hearts can grow strong at the broken places."

This young man's story profoundly illustrates the way in which sorrow or a wound can heal, allowing us to grow into our fullest, most compassionate identity, our greatness of heart. When we truly come to terms with sorrow, a great and unshakable joy is born in our heart.

HEALING THE MIND

Just as we heal the body and the heart through awareness, so can we heal the mind. Just as we learn about the nature and rhythm of sensations and feelings, so can we learn about the nature of thoughts. As we notice our thoughts in meditation, we discover that they are not in our control—we swim in an uninvited constant stream of memories, plans, expectations, judgments, regrets. The mind begins to show how it contains all possibilities, often in conflict with one another—the beautiful qualities of a saint and the dark forces of a dictator and murderer. Out of these, the mind plans and imagines, creating endless struggles and scenarios for changing the world.

Yet the very root of these movements of mind is dissatisfaction. We seem to want both endless excitement and perfect peace. Instead of being served by our thinking, we are driven by it in many unconscious and unexamined ways. While thoughts can be enormously useful and creative, most often they dominate our experience with ideas of like versus dislikes, higher versus lower, self versus other. They tell stories about our successes and failures, plan our security, habitually remind us of who and what we think we are.

This dualistic nature of thought is a root of our suffering. Whenever we think of ourselves as separate, fear and attachment arise and we grow constricted, defensive, ambitious, and territorial. To protect the separate self, we push certain things away, while to bolster it we hold on to other things and identify with them.

A psychiatrist from the Stanford University School of Medicine discovered these truths when he attended his first ten-day intensive retreat. While he had studied psychoanalysis and been in therapy, he had never actually encountered his own mind in the nonstop fashion of fifteen hours a day of sitting and walking meditation. He later wrote an article on this experience in which he described how a professor of psychiatry felt sitting and watching himself go crazy. The nonstop flood of thought astounded him, as did the wild variety of stories it told. Especially repetitious were thoughts of self-aggrandizement, of becoming a great teacher or famous writer or even world savior. He knew enough to look at the source of these thoughts, and he discovered they were all rooted in fear: during the retreat he was feeling insecure about himself and what he knew. These grand thoughts were the mind's compensation so he would not have to feel the fear of not knowing. Over the many years since, this professor has become a very skillful meditator, but he first had to make peace with the busy and fearful patterns of an untrained mind. He has also learned, since that time, not to take his own thoughts too seriously.

Healing the mind takes place in two ways: In the first, we bring attention to the content of our thoughts and learn to redirect them more skillfully through practices of wise reflection. Through mindfulness, we can come to know and reduce the patterns of unhelpful worry and obsession, we can clarify our confusion and release destructive views and opinions. We can use conscious thought to reflect more deeply on what we value. Asking the question, Do I love well? is an example of this, and we can also direct our thought into the skillful avenues of loving-kindness, respect, and ease of mind. Many Buddhist practices use the repetition of certain phrases in order to break through old, destructively repetitious patterns of thought to effect change.

However, even though we work to reeducate the mind, we can never be completely successful. The mind seems to have a will of its own no matter how much we wish to direct it. So, for a deeper healing of the conflicts of the mind, we need to let go of our identification with them. To heal, we must learn to step back from all the stories of the mind, for the conflicts and opinions of our thoughts never end. As the Buddha said, "People with opinions just go around bothering one another." When we see that the mind's very nature is to think, to divide, to plan, we can release ourselves from its iron grip of separatism and come to rest in the body and heart. In this way, we step out of our identification, out of our expectations, opinions, and judgments and the conflicts to which they give rise. The mind thinks of the self as separate, the heart knows better. As one great Indian master, Sri Nisargadatta, put it, "The mind creates the abyss, and the heart crosses it."

• • •

HEALING THROUGH EMPTINESS

The last aspect of mindful healing is awareness of the universal laws that govern life. Central to it is an understanding of emptiness. This is most difficult to describe in words. In fact, while I can try to describe it here, the understanding of openness and emptiness will need to come directly through the experience of your own spiritual practice.

In Buddhist teaching, "emptiness" refers to a basic openness and nonseparation that we experience when all small and fixed notions of our self are seen through or dissolved. We experience it when we see that our existence is transitory, that our body, heart, and mind arise out of the changing web of life, where nothing is disconnected or separate. The deepest experiences in meditation lead us to an intimate awareness of life's essential openness and emptiness, of its ever-changing and unpossessable nature, of its nature as an unstoppable process.

35 The Buddha described human life as comprising a series of ever-changing processes: a physical process, a feeling process, a memory and recognition process, a thought and reaction process, and a consciousness process. These processes are dynamic and continuous, without a single element we can call our unchanging self. We ourselves are a process, woven together with life, without separateness. We arise like a wave out of the ocean of life, our tentative forms still one with the ocean. Some traditions call this ocean the Tao, the divine, the fertile void, the unborn. Out of it, our lives appear as reflections of the divine, as a movement or dance of consciousness. The most profound healing comes when we sense this process, this life-giving emptiness.

• • •

One hospice director experienced this interconnectedness as he sat with the children of a dying sixty-five-year-old man outside his room. They had just received news that their father's younger brother had been killed in a car accident and were struggling with whether or not to tell him. Their father was close to death and, fearing it would upset him, they decided not to speak of it. As they entered the room he looked up and said, "Don't you have something to tell me?" They wondered what he could mean. "Why didn't you tell me that my brother died?" Astonished, they asked how he had found out. "I've been talking with him for the past half hour," said their father, who then called them to his bedside. He spoke some last words to each child and in ten minutes rested his head back and died.

The Tibetan teacher Kalu Rinpoche puts it this way:

> You live in illusion and the appearance of things. There is a reality, but you do not know this. When you understand this, you will see that you are nothing, and being nothing you are everything. That is all.

Healing comes in touching this realm of nonseparation. We discover that our fears and desires, our attempts to enhance and defend ourselves, are based on delusion, on a sense of separateness that is fundamentally untrue.

In discovering the healing power of emptiness, we sense that everything is intertwined in a continuous movement, arising in certain forms that we call bodies or thoughts or feelings, and then dissolving or changing into new forms. With this wisdom we can open to one moment after another and live in the ever-changing Tao. We discover we can let go and trust, we can let the breath breathe itself and the natural movement of life carry us with ease.

Each dimension of our being, the body, the heart, and the mind, is healed through the same loving attention and care. Our attention can honor the body and discover the blessings of the physical life that has been given us. Attention can bring us fully into the heart to honor the whole range of our human feelings. It can heal the mind and help us to honor thought without being trapped by it. And it can open us to the great mystery of life, to the discovery of the emptiness and wholeness that we are and our fundamental unity with all things.

Discussion Questions

1. Kornfield claims that our culture "has neglected physical and instinctual life" (paragraph 8). If you agree, provide your own example that suggests this assumption is true. If you disagree, provide your own example that suggests this assumption is false.

2. Through the article, Kornfield develops the concept of "mindfulness" (first mentioned in paragraph 7). In your own words, define this concept.

3. Describe some consequences of giving due attention to the physical body in the section "Healing the Body." Explain the role of compassion in "Healing the Heart." Explain why "Healing the Mind" is a necessary process in meditation. Explain the essential goal of "Healing through Emptiness."

4. Kornfield offers several examples of people whom he has observed in order to illustrate his explanations about healing through meditation. Do you find these examples *essential* to his argument, somewhat distracting or unimportant, or even unconvincing? Explain.

5. Kornfield uses *classification* as a means of organizing this essay from his book. One feature of *classification* is to consider all possible types of a particular subject. For example, if you were writing an essay on popular music, you would include as many types as you could think of: rock, country, jazz, folk, etc. Reflecting on Kornfield's essay, do you think that his four types of

healing comprise all the possibilities? If so, explain. If not, describe the type or types he does *not* consider.

6. Reflecting on the three essays of this chapter, discuss one or two common themes or ideas that each author explores.

Topics for Exploration and Writing

You have been reading about and discussing mind–body connections and beliefs about ways of healing. To explore these topics, focus on one activity or sequence of events, drawing on examples from your observation and experience. Instead, you may write about someone close to you, but ask your informant for details about his or her experience and perceptions of the activity. While most of your content should be original, brief comparisons to the articles may explain your viewpoint (refer to authors by last name and to article titles). Your job as a writer is to inform readers by presenting specific examples that you can explain in detail and then generalize about these examples by presenting a significant understanding. If race, ethnicity, gender, sexual preference, age, body size or image, or disability relates to your analysis, include these dimensions in your essay.

1. Analyze a physical activity, such as playing a sport, biking, dancing, or working out at the gym. Explain the mind–body connection you feel when participating in this activity. Include not only descriptions of physical sensations, but also analysis of the activity's effect on attitude, mood, or changes in behavior. Try to assess the effect of this activity on your own self-image, especially as that has changed over the period of time you have been engaged in the activity.

2. Analyze a bodily practice, such as dieting or fasting, meditation, yoga, or massage. Include not only descriptions of physical sensations, but also analysis of the mental, emotional, and/or spiritual dimensions of this practice. How does it affect your attitude or mood, or bring about changes in behavior? Try to assess the effect of this practice on your own self-image since you have been engaged in the practice.

3. Analyze your recent experience with a particular illness, or your regular use of natural medicine to alleviate particular symptoms or conditions. If examining an illness, describe not only the physical sensations of the sickness and the treatment, but also the psychological manifestations of your dis-ease. Explain how the illness affected your own sense of self. If examining your use of herbal or natural remedies, describe the symptoms and the effects of such remedies. Analyze the mental and emotional consequences of your holistic health practices and assess the effect of these practices on your own self-image.

CHAPTER 2

Sports and Difference

Athletic activities and working out in the gym have long been associated with "manly" bodies. However, since the women's liberation movement began in the 1960s, pumping iron, aerobic exercise, and sports have become womanly pursuits as well. In *A Primer for Daily Life* (Routledge, 1991), Susan Willis analyzes this rather recent cultural phenomenon, noting that Jane Fonda's 1981 *Workout* book represents a consciousness-raising experiment in "defining women-centered notions about the female body" (67). The book also was another of many successful attempts to capitalize on and privatize culture, turning exercise into commodities for consumption at expensive members-only spas. Willis observes that a strong difference between men and women exercising is that women are encouraged by advertising and their peers to buy and display the workout look: the hot leotards, the bright leg-warmers, the stylish headbands—the accessories that acknowledge and reproduce "male domination through the gendered look of exercise" (72).

The articles in this chapter examine the "gendering" of sports, but also consider differences of sexual identity, class, and race in the realm of athletic performance and body image. Willis's insights suggest how social movements can change some behaviors of (mostly) middle-class white Americans without altering basic social structures. However, the women's movement did result in the 1972 Title IX legislation that revolutionized the funding and access to team sports for girls and women in every public high school and college in the United States. Although this book does not address the debates about Title IX's merits, the articles in this chapter reflect an awareness of dramatic changes in the "gendering" of sports and also reveal a political consciousness of the compatibility between work and leisure, or economics and culturally motivated athletic activities.

The first article, "Hard Bodies," equates the self-absorption of money-driven careerism with the narcissism of bodybuilding in the 1980s. Moreover, author Stuart Ewen comments on the role of commercial advertising in reinforcing muscle definition as an ideal for both men and women. Oddly enough, Ewen suggests that advertisers treat women as equal to men in pursuing "a conception of *self* as an object of competitive display." Ewen's method in developing his article is to begin with a grounding in sociology, then to analyze a human example drawn from interview and observation, and finally to draw comparable examples from a series of print ads. Basically, he writes as a social psychologist while incorporating illustrations from popular media.

The second article, "Sport and Gender Relations," also takes a sociological approach to defining mainstream masculinity in American culture as a continual demonstration of male–female differences. In describing a study of the "social definition of gender," author Michael A. Messner notes that "homophobia and misogyny were the key bonding agents among male athletes." Therefore, his central task is explaining the social and psychological formation of masculine identities through athletes' experiencing their own bodies "as instruments of power and domination." In opposition to this mainstream, socially reinforced model of masculinity, Messner cites numerous sources and uses data from interviews to describe two male groups who strive to advance their own models: lower-class black athletes and gay athletes. Finally, Messner shows how these groups express themselves through sport, but often redefine athletic success and undermine cultural stereotypes.

The third article, "Alternative Masculinity," actually relies on Messner's research, and then applies it to the non-mainstream sport of skateboarding. Again, as a sports sociologist, author Becky Beal emphasizes "the social construction of gender," citing previous research to lay the groundwork for her argument that the subculture of skateboarding reveals an alternative masculinity while sharing the sexism of the mainstream model. Unlike the previous two selections that formed chapters in books, this reading was first published as a research study in the *Journal of Sports Behavior*, so it is a self-contained argument. Therefore, Beal describes her "methodology"—how she gathered her data, who her "subjects" or participants were, and how she refined her interpretations. To analyze her data, she also makes use of the sophisticated concept of "hegemonic masculinity," which refers to the unquestioned and socially reinforced ideal of manliness that most males conform to in America. Thus, in her interpretation of the skateboarders' own self-affirmations, they act as rebels against the formal structures and masculine roles typical in organized team sports. However, she notes that the male skateboarders in her study do accept mainstream notions of "femininity," relegating the few female skateboarders to the limited and inferior role of "skate Betties." It seems that even young men who seek to define an alternative masculinity for themselves still define the male body as tolerant of pain and consider bodily injury a badge of courage or a medal of athletic performance.

The fourth article, "The Sports Taboo," returns to the concerns of mainstream sports, but with a focus on the physiology, psychology, and social identity of the black athlete. Here, author Malcolm Gladwell explores an idea, perhaps wishing to change the reader's viewpoint on that idea, but the structure and "data" of his writing are not driven by the models of academic sociology. Thus, it has the classic essay style of trying out different explanations, drawing from different disciplines of research, illuminating the "problem" of black athleticism in our culture from various perspectives in order to quash stereotypical representations and understandings. Certainly, Gladwell is concerned with black athletic masculinity as an "alternative" to the mainstream white model. However, he seems more concerned with changing a society that cannot accept the notion of black superiority in any field, even in running or basketball, where the population of high achievers is racially skewed. Finally, Gladwell's goal is persuasion, but through the course of his essay he offers facts that previous writers and researchers have confirmed.

Collectively, the readings in Chapter 2 approach the body as a social invention determined by our cultural definitions of manliness, womanliness, blackness, and gayness. The corporeal guts and bones, though of biological interest in several readings, disappear behind the fabric of social ideals for body image and athletic performance.

Hard Bodies

STUART EWEN

Professor of media studies at Hunter College, Stuart Ewen incorporates history, psychology, architecture, advertising, and the interpretation of images in research on the public impact of the media. His early book Captains of Consciousness: Advertising and the Social Roots of Consumer Culture *(1976) tells the story of how corporate advertising shapes society by creating "new conceptions of individual attainment and community desire" that institute a mass consumer market. A second popular work by Ewen, in collaboration with his wife Elizabeth, is* Channels of Desire: Mass Images and the Shaping of American Consciousness *(1982), which became the basis for* The Public Mind, *Bill Moyers's PBS series on the politics of the image in a visual culture. The selection below is from his 1988 book,* All Consuming Images: The Politics of Style in Contemporary Culture.

As you read, consider in what ways the "world of work" is hard. Likewise, consider what kinds of "hardness" are achieved through weight lifting.

———————— ✦ ————————

Writing in 1934, the sociologists George A. Lundberg, Mirra Komarovsky, and Mary Alice McInerny addressed the question of "leisure" in the context of an emerging consumer society. Understanding the symbiotic relationship between mass-production industries and a consumerized definition of leisure, they wrote of the need for society to achieve a compatibility between the worlds of work and daily life. "The ideal to be sought," they proposed, "is undoubtedly the gradual obliteration of the psychological barrier which today distinguishes work from leisure."[1]

That ideal has been realized in the daily routine of Raymond H-------, a thirty-four-year-old middle-management employee of a large New York City investment firm. He is a living cog in what Felix Rohatyn has termed the new "money culture," one in which making things no longer counts; making money, as an end in itself, is the driving force.[2] His days are spent at a computer terminal, monitoring an endless flow of numerical data.

When his workday is done, he heads toward a local health club for the relaxation of a "workout." Three times a week this means a visit to the Nautilus room, with its high, mirrored walls, and its imposing assembly line of large, specialized "machines." The workout consists of exercises for his lower body and for his upper body, twelve "stations" in all. As he moves from Nautilus machine to Nautilus machine, he works on his hips, buttocks, thighs, calves, back, shoulders, chest, upper arms, forearms, abdomen, and neck, body part by body part.

At the first station, Raymond lies on the "hip and back machine," making sure to align his hip joints with the large, polished, kidney-shaped cams which offer resistance as he extends each leg downward over the padded roller under each knee. Twelve repetitions of this, and he moves on to the "hip abduction machine," where he spreads his legs outward against the padded restraints that hold them closed. Then leg extensions on the "compound leg machine" are followed by leg cuffs on the "leg cuff machine." From here, Raymond H-------- proceeds to the "pullover/torso arm machine," where he begins to address each piece of his upper body. After a precise series of repetitions on the "double chest machine," he completes his workout on the "four-way neck machine."

While he alternates between different sequential workouts, and different machines, each session is pursued with deliberate precision, following exact instructions.

Raymond H-------- has been working on his body for the past three years, ever since he got his last promotion. He is hoping to achieve the body he always wanted. Perhaps it is fitting that this quintessential, single, young, urban professional—whose life has become a circle of work, money culture, and the cultivation of an image—has turned himself, literally, into a piece of work. If the body ideal he seeks is *lean*, devoid of fatty tissue, it is also *hard*. "Soft flesh," once a standard phrase in the American erotic lexicon, is now—within the competitive, upscale world he inhabits—a sign of failure and sloth. The hard shell is now a sign of achievement, visible proof of success in the "rat race." The goal he seeks is more about *looking* than *touching*.

To achieve his goal, he approaches his body piece by piece; with each machine he performs a discrete task. Along the way he also assumes the job of inspector, surveying the results of each task in the mirrors that surround him. The division of labor, the fragmentation of the work process, and the regulating function of continual measurement and observation—all fundamental to the principles of "scientific management"—are intrinsic to this form of recreation. Like any assembly line worker, H-------- needs no overall knowledge of the process he is engaged in, only the specific tasks that comprise that process. "You don't have to understand *why* Nautilus equipment works," writes bodybuilder Mike Mentzer in the foreword to one of the most widely read Nautilus manuals. "With a tape measure in hand," he promises, "you will see what happens."[3]

The body ideal Raymond H-------- covets is, itself, an aestheticized tribute to the broken-down work processes of the assembly line. "I'm trying to get better definition," H-------- says. "I'm into Nautilus because it lets me do the necessary touchup work. Free weights [barbells] are good for building up mass, but Nautilus is great for definition."[4] By "definition," H-------- is employing the lingo of the gym, a reference to a body surface upon which each muscle, each muscle group, appears segmented and distinct. The perfect body is one that ratifies the fragmentary process of its construction, one that mimics—in flesh—the illustrative qualities of a schematic drawing, or an anatomy chart.

Surveying his work in the mirror, H-------- admires the job he has done on his broad, high pectorals, but is quick to note that his quadriceps "could use some work." This ambivalence, this mix of emotions, pursues him each time he comes for a workout, and the times in between. He is never quite satisfied with the results. The excesses of the weekend-past invariably leave their blemish. An incorrectly struck pose reveals an over-measure of loose skin, a sign of weakness in the shell. Despite all efforts, photogenic majesty is elusive.

10   The power of the photographic idiom, in his mind's eye, is reinforced, again and again, by the advertisements and other media of style visible everywhere. The ideal of the perfectly posed machine—the cold, hard body in response—is paraded, perpetually, before his eyes and ours. We see him, or her, at every glance.

An advertisement for home gym equipment promises a "Body By Soloflex." Above is the silent, chiaroscuro portrait of a muscular youth, his torso bare, his elbows reaching high, pulling a thin-ribbed undershirt up over his head, which is faceless, covered by shadow. His identity is situated below the neck, an instrumentally achieved study in brawn. The powerful expanse of his chest and back is illuminated from the right side. A carefully cast shadow accentuates the paired muscle formations of his abdominal wall. The airbrush has done its work as well, effecting a smooth, standardized, molded quality, what John Berger has termed "the skin without a biography." A silent, brooding hulk of a man, he is the unified product of pure engineering. His image is a product of expensive photographic technology, and expensive technical expertise. His body—so we are informed—is also a technical achievement. He has reached this captured moment of perpetual perfection on a "machine that fits in the corner" of his home. The machine, itself, resembles a stamping machine, one used to shape standardized, industrial products. Upon this machine, he has routinely followed instructions for "twenty-four traditional iron pumping exercises, each correct in form and balance." The privileged guidance of industrial engineering, and the mindless obedience of work discipline, have become legible upon his body; yet as it is displayed, it is nothing less than a thing of beauty, a transcendent aspiration.

This machine-man is one of a generation of desolate, finely tuned loners who have cropped up as icons of American style. Their bodies, often lightly oiled to accentuate definition, reveal their inner mechanisms like costly, open-faced watches, where one can see the wheels and gears moving inside, revealing—as it were—the magic of time itself. If this is eroticism, it is one tuned more to the mysteries of technology than to those of the flesh.

In another magazine advertisement, for Evian spring water from France, six similarly anatomized figures stand across a black and white two-page spread. From the look of things, each figure (three men and three women) has just completed a grueling workout, and four of them are partaking of Evian water as part of their recovery. The six are displayed in a lineup, each one displaying a particularly well-developed anatomical region. These are the new icons of beauty, precisely defined, powerful machines. Below, on the left, is the simple caption: "Revival of the Fittest." Though part of a group, each figure is conspicuously alone.

Once again, the modern contours of power, and the structures of work discipline, are imprinted upon the body. In a world of rampant careerism, self-absorption is a rule of thumb. If the division of labor sets each worker in competition with every other, here that fragmentation is aestheticized into the narcissism of mind and body.

Within this depiction, sexual equality is presented as the meeting point between the anorectic and the "nautilized." True to gender distinctions between evanescent value and industrial work discipline, the three women are defined primarily by contour, by the thin lines that their willowy bodies etch upon the page. Although their muscles are toned, they strike poses that suggest pure, disembodied form. Each of the men, situated alternately between the women, gives testimony on behalf of a particular fraction of segmented flesh: abdomen, shoulders and upper arms, upper back. In keeping with the assembly line approach to muscle building, each man's body symbolizes a particular station within the labor process. 15

Another ad, for a health and fitness magazine, contains an alarmingly discordant statement: "Today's women workers are back in the sweat shop." There is a basis to this claim. In today's world, powerful, transnational corporations search the globe looking for the cheapest labor they can find. Within this global economy, more and more women—from Chinatown to Taiwan—are employed at tedious, low-paying jobs, producing everything from designer jeans to computer parts.

Yet this is not the kind of sweatshop the ad has in mind. The photographic illustration makes this clear. Above the text, across the two-page color spread, is the glistening, heavily muscled back of a woman hoisting a chrome barbell. Her sweat is self-induced, part of a "new woman" lifestyle being promoted in *Sport* magazine, "the magazine of the new vitality." Although this woman bears the feminine trademark of blonde, braided hair, her body is decidedly masculine, a new body aesthetic in the making. Her muscles are not the cramped, biographically induced muscles of menial labor. Hers is the brawn of the purely symbolic, the guise of the middle-class "working woman."

While the text of the advertisement seems to allude to the real conditions of female labor, the image transforms that truth into beauty, rendering it meaningless. Real conditions are copywritten into catchy and humorous phrases. The harsh physical demands of women's work are reinterpreted as regimented, leisure-time workouts at a "health club." Real sweat is reborn as photogenic body oil.

The migration of women into the social structures of industrial discipline is similarly aestheticized in an ad for Jack LaLanne Fitness Centers. A black and white close-up of a young woman wrestling with a fitness "machine" is complemented by the eroticized grimace on her face. Once again, the chiaroscuro technique accentuates the straining muscles of her arms. The high-contrast, black and white motif may also suggest the "night and day" metamorphosis that will occur when one commits to this particular brand of physical discipline.

20 In large white letters, superimposed across the shadowy bottom of the photograph, are the words: "Be taut by experts." With a clever play on words the goal of education moves from the mind to the body. Muscle power is offered as an equivalent substitute for brain power. No problem. In the search for the perfectly regulated self, it is implicit that others will do the thinking. This woman, like the Soloflex man, is the product of pure engineering, of technical expertise:

> We were building bodies back when you were building blocks. . .
> We know how to perfectly balance your workout between swimming, jogging, aerobics and weight training on hundreds of the most advanced machines available. . . Sure it may hurt a little. But remember. *You only hurt the one you love.* [Emphasis added.]

These advertisements, like Raymond H-------'s regular visits to the Nautilus room, are part of the middle-class bodily rhetoric of the 1980s. Together they mark a culture in which self-absorbed careerism, conspicuous consumption, and a conception of *self* as an object of competitive display have fused to become the preponderant symbols of achievement. The regulated body is the nexus where a cynical ethos of social Darwinism, and the eroticism of raw power, meet.

Endnotes

1. George A. Lundberg et al., *Leisure: A Suburban Study* (1934), p. 3.
2. *New York Times*, 3 June 1987, p. A27.
3. Ellington Darden, *The Nautilus Bodybuilding Book* (1986), pp. viii–ix.
4. Style Project, interview I–13.

Discussion Questions

1. Explain the similarities that Ewen finds between contemporary work and the activity of bodybuilding.
2. The first part of the essay describes the meaning of "hard bodies" by interpreting a particular example, Raymond H--------. The second part develops this meaning by interpreting various advertisements depicting athletic bodies. To what extent do the two parts work together? Which part do you think is more effective in demonstrating Ewen's thesis? Explain how the "data" or evidence in the two parts is similar and how it is different.
3. To what extent do you believe that most men are concerned about their own image as well-muscled and powerful? Do you agree with Ewen's criticism of the "machine man" who seeks such muscular "definition"? Explain.
4. To what extent do you believe that many women are seeking a similar muscular image through bodybuilding or gym workouts?
5. Do you think that desirable body images for men and women in America have changed since the 1980s, when this selection was first published? If so, how?

Sport and Gender Relations: Continuity, Contradiction, and Change

MICHAEL A. MESSNER

A professor of sociology and gender studies at the University of Southern California, Michael A. Messner earned his Ph.D. at the University of California, Berkeley, and teaches such courses as Men and Masculinity; Social Issues in Gender, Sexuality, and Society; and Gender and Sport. His research studies the visual images of advertising and televised athletic competitions in order to reveal relationships among beer and liquor companies, organized sports, and mass media. He is especially interested in contemporary changes in the images of men, women, gender, and sexuality in sports. His most recent books include Politics of Masculinities: Men in Movements *(1997) and* Taking the Field: Women, Men, and Sports *(2002). The following selection is from* Power at Play: Sports and the Problem of Masculinity *(1992).*

Before you read, consider the activities and games "typical" of boys and those "typical" of girls. Did you ever participate in the activities "typical" of the other gender? If so, write down some examples, recording how other people responded to your interest in the games of the "other."

———————— ✦ ————————

In 1973, conservative writer George Gilder, later to become a central theorist of the antifeminist family policies of the Reagan administration, was among the first to sound the alarm that the contemporary explosion of female athletic participation might threaten the very fabric of civilization. "Sports," Gilder wrote, "are possibly the single most important male rite in modern society." The woman athlete "reduces the game from a religious male rite to a mere physical exercise, with some treacherous danger of psychic effect." Athletic performance, for males, embodies "an ideal of beauty and truth," while women's participation represents a "disgusting perversion" of this truth.[1] In 1986, over a decade later, a similar view was expressed by John Carroll in a respected academic journal. Carroll lauded the masculine "virtue and grace" of sport, and defended it against its critics, especially feminists. He concluded that in order to preserve sport's "naturally conserving and creating" tendencies, especially in the realms of "the moral and the religious . . . , women should once again be prohibited from sport: They are the true defenders of the humanist values that emanate from the household, the values of tenderness, nurture and compassion, and this most important role must not be confused by the military and political values inherent in sport. Likewise, sport should not be muzzled by humanist values: it is the living arena for the great virtue of manliness."[2]

The key to Gilder's and Carroll's chest-beating about the importance of maintaining sport as a "male rite" is their neo-Victorian belief that male-female biological differences predispose men to aggressively dominate public life, while females are naturally suited to serve as the nurturant guardians of home and hearth. As Gilder put it, "The tendency to bond with other males in intensely purposeful and dangerous activity is said to come from the collective demands of pursuing large animals. The female body, on the other hand, more closely resembles the body of nonhunting primates. A woman throws, for example, very like a male chimpanzee."[3] This perspective ignores a wealth of historical, anthropological, and biological data that suggest that the equation of males with domination of public life and females with the care of the domestic sphere is a cultural and historical construction.[4] In fact, Gilder's and Carroll's belief that sport, *a socially constructed* institution, is needed to sustain male-female difference contradicts their assumption that these differences are "natural." As R. W. Connell has argued, social practices that exaggerate male-female difference (such as dress, adornment, and sport) "are part of a continuing effort to sustain a social definition of gender, an effort that is necessary precisely *because the biological logic . . . cannot sustain the gender categories.*[5]

Indeed, I must argue against the view that sees sport as a natural realm within which some essence of masculinity unfolds. Rather, sport is a social institution that, in its dominant forms, was created by and for men. It should not be surprising, then, that my research with male athletes reveals an affinity between the institution of sport and men's developing identities. As the young males in my study became committed to athletic careers, the gendered values of the institution of sport made it extremely unlikely that they would construct anything but the kinds of personalities and relationships that were consistent with the dominant values and power relations of the larger gender order. The competitive hierarchy of athletic careers encouraged the development of masculine identities based on very narrow definitions of public success. Homophobia and misogyny were the key bonding agents among male athletes, serving to construct a masculine personality that disparaged anything considered "feminine" in women, in other men, or in oneself. The fact that winning was premised on physical power, strength, discipline, and willingness to take, ignore, or deaden pain inclined men to experience their own bodies as machines, as instruments of power and domination—and to see other peoples bodies as objects of their power and domination. . . .

THE COSTS OF ATHLETIC MASCULINITY

As boys, the men in my study were initially attracted to playing sport because it was a primary means to connect with other people—especially fathers, brothers, and male peers. But as these young males became committed to athletic careers, their identities became directly tied to continued public success. Increasingly, it was not just "being there with the guys" but beating the other guys that mattered most. As their need for connection with others became defined more abstractly, through their relationships with "the crowd," their actual relationships with other people tended to become distorted. Other individuals were increasingly likely to be viewed as (male) objects to be defeated or (female) objects to be manipulated and sexually conquered. As a result, the socially learned means through which they constructed their identities (public achievement within competitive hierarchies) did not deliver what was most craved and needed: intimate connection and unity with other people. More often than not, athletic careers have exacerbated existing insecurities and ambivalences in young men's developing identities, thus further diminishing their capacity for intimate relationships with others.

5   In addition to relational costs, many athletes—especially those in "combat sports" such as football—paid a heavy price in terms of health. While the successful operation of the male body-as-weapon may have led, for a time, to victories on the athletic field, it also led to injuries and other health problems that lasted far beyond the end of the athletic career.

It is extremely unlikely that a public illumination of the relational and health costs paid by male athletes will lead to a widespread rejection of sport by young males. There are three reasons for this. First, the continued affinity between sport and developing masculine identities suggests that many boys will continue to be attracted to athletic careers for the same reasons they have in the past. Second, since the successful athlete often basks in the limelight of public adoration, the relational costs of athletic masculinity are often not apparent until after the athletic career ends, and he suddenly loses his connection to the crowd. Third, though athletes may recognize the present and future health costs of their athletic careers, they are likely to view them as dues willingly paid. In short, there is a neat enough fit between the psychological and emotional tendencies of young males and the institution of sport that these costs—if they are recognized at all—will be considered "necessary evils," the price men pay for the promise of "being on top."[6]

COMPETING MASCULINITIES

Boys' emerging identities may influence them to be attracted to sport, but they nevertheless tend to experience athletic careers differently, based upon variations in class, race, and sexual orientation. Despite their similarities, boys and young men bring different problems, anxieties, hopes, and dreams to their athletic experiences, and thus tend to draw different meanings from, and make different choices about, their athletic careers.

Race, Class, and the Construction of Athletic Masculinity

My interviews reveal that within a social context stratified by class and by race, the choice to pursue—or not to pursue—an athletic career is determined by the individual's rational assessment of the available means to construct a respected masculine identity. White middle-class men were likely to reject athletic careers and shift their masculine strivings to education and nonsport careers. Conversely, men from poor and blue-collar backgrounds, especially blacks, often perceived athletic careers to be their best chance for success in the public sphere. For nearly all of the men from lower-class backgrounds, the status and respect that they received through sport was temporary—it did not translate into upward mobility.

One might conclude from this that the United States should adopt a public policy of encouraging young lower-class black males to "just say no" to sport. This strategy would be doomed to failure, because poor young black men's decisions to pursue athletic careers can be viewed as rational, given the constraints that they continue to face. Despite the increased number of black role models in nonsport professions, employment opportunities for young black males actually deteriorated in the 1980s, and nonathletic opportunities in higher education also declined. By 1985, blacks constituted 14 percent of the college-aged (18–24 years) U.S. population, but as a proportion of students in four-year colleges and universities, they had dropped to 8 percent. By contrast, black men constituted 49 percent of male college basketball players, and 61 percent of male basketball players in institutions that grant athletic scholarships.[7] For young black men, then, organized sport appears to be more likely to get them to college than their own efforts in nonathletic activities.

In addition to viewing athletic careers as an arena for career success, there is considerable evidence that black male athletes have used sport as a cultural space within which to forge a uniquely expressive style of masculinity, a "cool pose." As Majors puts it,

> Due to structural limitations, a black man may be impotent in the intellectual, political, and corporate world, but he can nevertheless display a potent personal style from the pulpit, in entertainment, and in athletic competition, with a verve that borders on the spectacular. Through the virtuosity of a performance, he tips the socially imbalanced scales in his favor and sends the subliminal message: "See me, touch me, hear me, but, white man, you can't copy me!"[8]

In particular, black men have put their "stamp" on the game of basketball. There is considerable pride in U.S. black communities in the fact that black men have come to dominate the higher levels of basketball—and in the expressive style with which they have come to do so. The often aggressive "cool pose" of black male athletes can thus be interpreted as a form of masculinity that symbolically challenges the class constraints and the institutionalized racism that so many young black males face.

Sexual Orientation and the Construction of Athletic Masculinity

Until very recently, it was widely believed that gay men did not play organized sports. Nongay people tended to stereotype gay men as "too effeminate" to be athletic. This belief revealed a confusion between sexual orientation and gender. We now know that there is no neat fit between how "masculine" or "feminine" a man is, and whether or not he is sexually attracted to women, to men, to both, or to neither.[9] Interestingly, some gay writers also believed that gay men were not active in sport. For instance, Dennis Altman wrote in 1982 that most gay men were not interested in sport, since they tended to reject the sexual repression, homophobia, and misogyny that are built into the sportsworld.[10]

The belief that gay men are not interested or involved in sport has proven to be wrong. People who made this assumption were observing the overtly masculine and heterosexual culture of sport and then falsely concluding that all of the people within that culture must be heterosexual. My interview with Mike T. and biographies of gay athletes such as David Kopay suggest that young gay males are often attracted to sport because they are just as concerned as heterosexual boys and young men with constructing masculine identities.[11] Indeed, a young closeted gay male like Mike T. may view the projection of an unambiguous masculinity as even more critical than his nongay counterparts do. As Mike told me, "There are a *lot* of gay men in sports," but they are almost all closeted and thus not visible to public view.

As Mike's story illustrates, gay male athletes often share similar motivations and experiences with nongay athletes. This suggests that as long as gay athletes stay closeted, they are contributing to the construction of culturally dominant conceptions of masculinity. However, Brian Pronger's recent research suggests that many gay male athletes experience organized sport in unique ways. In particular, Pronger's interviews with gay male athletes indicate that they have a "paradoxical" relationship to the male athletic culture. Though the institution itself is built largely on the denial (or sublimation) of any erotic bond between men, Pronger argues, many (but not all) gay athletes experience life in the locker room, as well as the excitement of athletic competition, as highly erotic. Since their secret desires (and, at times, secret actions) run counter to the heterosexist culture of the male locker room, closeted gay male athletes develop ironic sensibilities about themselves, their bodies, and the sporting activity itself.[12] Gay men are sexually oppressed through sport, Pronger argues, but the ironic ways they often redefine the athletic context can be interpreted as a form of resistance with the potential to undermine and transform the heterosexist culture of sport.

The Limits of Masculine Resistances

• • •

My research also suggests how homophobia within athletic masculine cultures tends to lock men—whether gay or not—into narrowly defined heterosexual identities and relationships. Within the athletic context, homophobia is closely linked with misogyny in ways that ultimately serve to bond men together as superior to women. Given the extremely oppressive levels of homophobia within organized sport, it is understandable why the vast majority of gay male athletes would decide to remain closeted. But the public construction of a heterosexual/masculine status requires that a closeted gay athlete actively participate in (or at the very least, tolerate) the ongoing group expressions of homophobia and

15

misogyny—what Mike T. called "locker room garbage." Thus, though he may feel a sense of irony, and may even confidentially express that sense of irony to gay male friends or to researchers, the public face that the closeted gay male athlete presents to the world is really no different from that of his nongay teammates. As long as he is successful in this public presentation-of-self as heterosexual/masculine, he will continue to contribute to (and benefit from) men's power over women.

Sport in Gay Communities

The fissuring of the category "men," then, as it is played out within the dominant institution of sport, does little to threaten—indeed, may be a central mechanism in—the reconstruction of existing class, racial, sexual, and gender inequalities.[13] Nevertheless, since the outset of the gay liberation movement in the early 1970s, organized sport has become an integral part of developing gay and lesbian communities. The ways that "gay" sports have been defined and organized are sometimes different—even radically different—than the dominant institution of sport in society.

The most public sign of the growing interest in athletics in gay communities was the rapid growth and popularity of bodybuilding among many young, urban gay men in the 1970s and early 1980s. The meanings of gay male bodybuilding are multiple and contradictory.[14] On the one hand, gay male bodybuilding overtly eroticizes the muscular male body, thus potentially disrupting the tendency of sport to eroticize male bodies under the guise of aggression and competition. On the other hand, the building of muscular bodies is often motivated by a conscious need by gay men to prove to the world that they are "real men." Gay bodybuilding thus undermines cultural stereotypes of homosexual men as "nelly," effeminate, and womanlike. But it also tends to adopt and promote a very conventional equation of masculinity with physical strength and muscularity.[15] In effect, then, as gay bodybuilders attempt to sever the cultural link between masculinity and heterosexuality, they uncritically affirm a conventional dichotomization of masculinity/male vs. femininity/female.

By contrast, some gay athletes have initiated alternative athletic institutions that aim to challenge conventional views of sexuality and gender. Originally Mike T. had gone into sport to prove that he was "male," and cover up the fact that he was gay. When his career as an Olympic athlete finally ended, he came out publicly, and soon was a very active member of the San Francisco

Bay area gay community. He rekindled his interest in the arts and dance. He also remained very active in athletics, and he increasingly imagined how wonderful it would be to blend the beauty and exhilaration of sport, as he had experienced it, with the emergent, liberating values of the feminist, gay, and lesbian communities of which he was a part. In 1982, his dream became a reality, as 1,300 athletes from twelve different nations gathered in San Francisco to participate in the first ever Gay Games.[16]

Though many of the events in the Gay Games are "conventional" sports (track and field, swimming, etc.), and a number of "serious athletes" compete in the events, overall the Games reflect a value system and a vision based on feminist and gay liberationist ideals of equality and universal participation. As Mike T. said,

> You don't win by beating someone else. We defined winning as doing your very best. That way, everyone is a winner. And we have age-group competition, so all ages are involved. We have parity: If there's a men's sport, there's a women's sport to complement it. And we go out and recruit in Third World and minority areas. All of these people are gonna get together for a week, they're gonna march in together, they're gonna hold hands, and they'll say, "Jesus Christ! This is wonderful!" There's this *discovery:* "I had no *idea* women were such fun!" and, "God! Blacks are okay—I didn't do anything to offend him, and we became *friends!*" and, "God, that guy over there is in his sixties, and I had no idea they were so sexually *active!*"—[laughs].

This emphasis on bridging differences, overcoming prejudices, and building relationships definitely enhanced the athletic experience for one participant I interviewed. This man said that he loved to swim, and even loved to compete, because it "pushed" him to swim "a whole lot better." Yet in past competitions, he had always come in last place. As he put it, "The Gay Games were just wonderful in many respects. One of them was that people who came in second, or third, and last got standing ovations from the crowd—the crowd genuinely recognized the thrill of giving a damn good shot, regardless of where you came in, and gave support to that. Among the competitors, there was a whole lot of joking and supportiveness."

In 1986, 3,482 athletes participated in Gay Games II in San Francisco. In 1990, at Gay Games III in Vancouver, 7,200 athletes continued the vision of building, partly through sport, an

20

"exemplary community" that eliminates sexism, homophobia, and racism. Mike T. described what the Gay Games mean to him:

> To me, it's one of those steps in a thousand-mile journey to try and raise consciousness and enlighten people—not just people outside the gay community, but within the gay community as well, [because] we're just as racist, ageist, nationalistic, and chauvinistic as anybody else. Maybe it's simplistic to some people, you know, but why does it have to be complicated? Put people in a position where they can experience this process of discovery, and here it is! I just hope that this is something that'll take hold and a lot of people will get the idea.

The Gay Games represent a radical break from past and current conceptions of the role of sport in society. But they do not represent a major challenge to sport as an institution. Alternative athletic venues like the Gay Games, since they exist outside of the dominant sports institution, do not directly confront or change the dominant structure. On the other hand, these experiments are valuable in terms of demonstrating the fact that alternative value systems and structures are possible.[17]

Endnotes

1. G. Gilder, *Sexual Suicide* (New York: Bantam Books, 1973), pp. 216, 218.
2. J. Carroll, "Sport: Virtue and Grace," *Theory, Culture and Society* 3 (1986), pp. 91–98. Jennifer Hargreaves delivers a brilliant feminist rebuttal to Carroll's masculinist defense of sport in the same issue of the journal. See J. Hargreaves, "Where's the Virtue? Where's the Grace? A Discussion of the Social Production of Gender through Sport," pp. 109–121.
3. G. Gilder, p. 221.
4. For a critical overview of the biological research on male-female difference, see A. Fausto-Sterling, *Myths of Gender: Biological Theories about Men and Women* (New York: Basic Books, 1985). For an overview of the historical basis of male domination, see R. Lee and R. Daly, "Man's Domination and Woman's Oppression: The Question of Origins," in M. Kaufman, ed., *Beyond Patriarchy: Essays by Men on Pleasure, Power, and Change* (Toronto: Oxford University Press, 1987), pp. 30–44.

5. R. W. Connell, *Gender and Power* (Stanford: Stanford University Press, 1987), p. 81 (emphasis in original text).

6. Indeed, "men's liberationists" of the 1970s were overly optimistic in believing that a public illumination of the "costs of masculinity" would induce men to "reject the male role." See, for instance, W. Farrell, *The Liberated Man* (New York: Bantam Books, 1975); J. Nichols, *Men's Liberation: A New Definition of Masculinity* (New York: Penguin Books, 1975). These men's liberationists underestimated the extent to which the costs of masculinity are linked to the promise of power and privilege. One commentator went so far as to argue that the privileges of masculinity were a "myth" perpetrated by women to keep men in destructive success-object roles. See H. Goldberg, *The Hazards of Being Male: Surviving the Myth of Masculine Privilege* (New York: Signet, 1976). For more recent discussions of the need to analyze both the "costs" and the "privileges" of dominant conceptions of masculinity, see M. E. Kann, "The Costs of Being on Top," *Journal of the National Association for Women Deans, Administrators, and Counselors* 49 (1986): 29–37; and M. A. Messner, "Men Studying Masculinity: Some Epistemological Questions in Sport Sociology," *Sociology of Sport Journal* 7 (1990): 136–153.

7. W. J. Wilson and K. M. Neckerman, "Poverty and Family Structure: The Widening Gap between Evidence and Public Policy Issues," in S. H. Danzinger and D. H. Weinberg, eds., *Fighting Poverty* (Cambridge: Harvard University Press, 1986), pp. 232–259; F. J. Berghorn et al., "Racial Participation in Men's and Women's Intercollegiate Basketball: Continuity and Change, 1958–1985." *Sociology of Sport Journal* 5 (1988), 107–124.

8. R. Majors, "'Cool Pose': Black Masculinity and Sports," in M. A. Messner and D. F. Sabo, *Sport, Men, and the Gender Order: Critical Feminist Perspectives* (Champaign, Ill.: Human Kinetics Publishers, 1990), p. 111.

9. See S. Kleinberg, "The New Masculinity of Gay Men, and Beyond," in Kaufman, *Beyond Patriarchy*, pp. 120–138.

10. D. Altman, *The Homosexualization of America* (Boston: Beacon Press, 1982).

11. See D. Kopay and P. D. Young, *The Dave Kopay Story* (New York: Arbor House, 1977).

12. B. Pronger, "Gay Jocks: A Phenomenology of Gay Men in Athletics," in Messner and Sabo, *Sport, Men, and the Gender Order*, pp. 141–152; and *The Arena of Masculinity: Sports, Homosexuality, and the Meaning of Sex* (New York: St. Martin's Press, 1990).

13. One potentially important, but largely unexplored, fissure among men is that between athletes and nonathletes. There are tens of

millions of boys who do not pursue athletic careers. Many boys dislike sport. Others may yearn to be athletes, but may not have the body size, strength, physical capabilities, coordination, emotional predisposition, or health that is necessary to successfully compete in sports. What happens to these boys and young men? What kinds of adult masculine identities and relationships do they eventually develop? Does the fact of not having been an athlete play any significant role in their masculine identities, goals, self-images, and relationships? The answers to these questions, of course, lie outside the purview of my study. But they are key to understanding the contemporary role that sport plays in constructions of gender.

14. For interesting discussions of bodybuilding, gender, and sexuality, see B. Glassner, *Bodies: Why We Look the Way We Do (and How We Feel about It)* (New York: G. P. Putnam's Sons, 1988); A. M. Klein, "Little Big Man: Hustling, Gender Narcissism, and Homophobia in Bodybuilding," in Messner and Sabo, *Sport, Men, and the Gender Order*, pp. 127–140.

15. Alan Klein's research revealed that nongay male bodybuilders are also commonly motivated by a need to make a public statement with their muscular bodies that they are indeed "masculine." To the nongay bodybuilder, muscles are the ultimate sign of heterosexual masculinity. But, ironically, as one nongay male bodybuilder put it, "We're everything the U.S. is supposed to stand for: strength, determination, everything to be admired. But it's not the girls that like us, it's the fags!" Interestingly, Klein found that many male bodybuilders who defined themselves as "straight" (including the one quoted above) made a living by prostituting themselves to gay men. See Klein, "Little Big Man," p. 135.

   For a thought-provoking feminist analysis of the contradictory relationship between gay male sexuality and masculinity, see T. Edwards, "Beyond Sex and Gender: Masculinity, Homosexuality and Social Theory," in J. Hearn and D. Morgan, eds., *Men, Masculinities, and Social Theory* (London: Unwin Hyman, 1990), pp. 110–123.

16. The Gay Games were originally called the "Gay Olympics," but the U.S. Olympic Committee went to court to see that the word "Olympics" was not used to denote this event. Despite the existence of "Police Olympics," "Special Olympics," "Senior Olympics," "Xerox Olympics," "Armenian Olympics," even "Crab Cooking Olympics," the U.S.O.C. chose to enforce their control legally over the term "Olympics" when it came to the "Gay Olympics." For further discussion of the politics of the Gay Games, see M. A. Messner, "Gay Athletes and the Gay Games: An Interview with Tom Waddell," *M: Gentle Men for Gender Justice* 13 (1984): 13–14.

17. During the 1982 Gay Games in San Francisco, the major local newspapers tended to cover the Games mostly in the "lifestyle" sections of the paper, not in the sports pages. Alternative sports demonstrate the difficulties of attempting to change sport in the absence of larger institutional transformations. For instance, the European sport of korfball was developed explicitly as a sex egalitarian sport. The rules of korfball aim to neutralize male-female biological differences that may translate into different levels of ability. But recent research shows that old patterns show up, even among the relatively "enlightened" korfball players. Korfball league officials are more likely to be male than female. More important, the more "key" roles within the game appear to be dominated by men, while women are partially marginalized. See D. Summerfield and A. White, "Korfball: A Model of Egalitarianism?" *Sociology of Sport Journal* 6 (1989): 144–151.

Discussion Questions

1. Messner suggests that "public success" in sports serves to prevent the development of "intimate connections and unity with other people" (paragraph 4). In your experience, have you found this pattern to be true in school, in work, or in another social setting? Explain, using a particular example.
2. To what extent do you believe that there are essential differences between men and women in the *meaning* of their athletic performance? Explain.
3. In your own experience of participating in or watching athletic competitions, describe some differences you have felt or noticed in male and female behavior.
4. Describe any examples of homophobia and/or sexism you have experienced or witnessed among athletes or spectators at sporting events.
5. According to Messner, in what ways do gay male perceptions of athletic participation differ from the "dominant sports institution" among heterosexual male athletes? To what extent do you agree with his analysis?
6. Messner notes that the Gay Games promote the values of "equality," "bridging differences," and "building relationships" (paragraph 19). Examine another social setting—such as coed soccer, campfire girls, boy scouts, boys and girls club, T-ball, a service club, volunteer work, team bowling, hunting, fishing, city league softball, or a church organization—explaining to what extent these values are also encouraged. If these values are negligible in the activity you analyze, explain to what extent it promotes the typical organized sport values of competition, personal power, and domination.
7. Compare the analysis of gender in Messner's and Ewen's articles.

Alternative Masculinity and Its Effects on Gender Relations in the Subculture of Skateboarding

BECKY BEAL

A former college runner herself, Becky Beal now teaches sport sociology and philosophy in the Department of Sport Science at the University of the Pacific. She continues to participate as an athlete, having taken first place in her age division at the Avenue of the Giants Marathon in 2004. Her research concerns gender issues in sports subcultures, including the influences of peer and university culture on female student athletes. With Belinda Wheaton, at the University of Surrey, England, she has also studied the issues of identity and authenticity, as affected by the commercialization of such "extreme and lifestyle sports" as skateboarding and windsurfing. Finding that corporations have capitalized on such activities by producing and marketing an assortment of equipment and clothing, Beal and Wheaton have analyzed participant responses to images in specialized advertising. The athletes report that action photos best express authenticity and commitment, although racial minorities and women are often excluded from these role models.

Before you read, write a brief definition of "subculture" and explain a particular example. As you read, consider how well your definition applies to the "subculture of skateboarders" that Beal describes.

✦

With the recent movement in men's studies there has been a growing popularity of investigating different forms of masculinity and their consequences for men, their relationships with each other, and their relationships with women. According to Clatterbaugh (1990) there have been several avenues of the men's movement including a conservative, profeminist, socialist, and gay and black perspective. Each avenue carries with it different social agendas with priorities for addressing social problems. For example, a conservative approach can be correlated with a pro-family values orientation which asserts traditional gender norms and family relations as a way of reestablishing social order. On the other hand, a profeminist approach sees traditional masculinity as the root of women's oppression, and therefore seeks to change traditional gender roles as a way of promoting a more democratic society. The black and gay perspectives have demonstrated that there is not just one form of masculinity from which all men equally benefit. Gay men must deal with homophobia and blacks must deal with racism, and—to more of an extent than whites—poverty. Both these circumstances show that minority men have a different experience of masculinity.

Carrigan, Connell, and Lee (1987) effectively summarized the history of research on masculinity as moving from a "sex roles" (or an assumption of "natural" differences determining social behavior) approach to an emphasis on the social construction of gender. The latter approach has emphasized power relations associated with different genders. Carrigan et al. (1987) clarified that power relations are not only between masculinity and femininity, but among different forms of masculinity as well (e.g., gay and black perspective). The most powerful form of masculinity is called hegemonic masculinity. They stated "what emerges from this line of argument is the very important concept of hegemonic masculinity, not as 'the male role,' but as a particular variety of masculinity to which others—among them young and effeminate as well as homosexual men—are subordinated" (p. 174).

This paper will combine a profeminist and critical perspective to describe how one group of young males created a non-hegemonic or alternative form of masculinity. The subculture of skateboarders I investigated chose not to live completely by the traditional and hegemonic forms of masculinity. In doing so, they created an alternative masculinity, one which explicitly critiqued the more traditional form. This paper will not only describe how they distinguished their subculture from traditional sport and hegemonic masculinity, but also investigate the resulting gender relations within the subculture, particularly how the males maintained the privilege of masculinity by differentiating and elevating themselves from females and femininity.

• • •

HEGEMONIC MASCULINITY IN SPORT

Sport is one of the most significant institutions of male bonding and male initiation rites. Sabo and Panepinto (1990) described football as a male initiation ritual which promotes hegemonic masculinity. In their analysis they described five characteristics of male initiation rituals in patriarchal societies. The first is man-boy relationships in which the older men direct the participants through the rituals. The second characteristic is the use of a variety of means to ensure conformity to the rules of the rituals. Through this process arises the third characteristic, which is learning to defer to male authority. Sabo and Panepinto stated "the initiation rites process at once introduces boys to the wider male status hierarchy and acclimates them to male authority" (p. 117). Pain is also another characteristic of these rituals, for it is the tolerance of pain that often "proves" one's manhood. In addition, these rituals take place in a segregated environment. Family members and females are not present during these rituals. These attributes illustrate many male sporting environments.

5 As noted by several sport sociologists (e.g., Curry, 1991; Kidd, 1987; Messner, 1992a; Sabo, 1989), the paradigm of hegemonic masculinity which abounds in mainstream sport includes physical domination, aggression, competition, sexism, and homophobia. These are often seen as the ideal of manliness, which affects male athletes' views about themselves, their relationships with other men, and their attitudes about women.

• • •

METHODOLOGY

I used qualitative methods of observation, participant-observation and semistructured in-depth interviews to investigate the subculture of skateboarding in northeastern Colorado. My research began in June 1989, when I started observing skateboarders in Jamestown and Welton, Colorado, at local hangouts, skateboard shops, and even a locally sponsored skateboard exhibition.

Most of my participants I met by stopping them while they were skateboarding on the streets, and asking if I could talk with them. (They call themselves "skaters," and the act of skateboarding they call "skating.") I met other skaters through interactions I had with their parents. In addition, I met one female skater (a rarity) through mutual membership in a local feminist group. These initial contacts snowballed to many others. Over a two year period (1990–1992) I talked with 41 skaters, skateboard shop owners, and several parents and siblings.

Thirty-seven of the 41 participants were male and 4 were female. In addition, all were anglo except two, who were Hispanic males. The average age of those participating was 16, but ranged from 10 to 25 years. The participants had skateboarded for an average of four years, but the range of their participation was from one to 15 years. Of the 41 skateboarders, 24 I interviewed more than once—6 of whom I had on-going communication with, which gave me a vital source of feedback and helped to refine my conclusions and questions. In addition, I spent over 100 hours observing skateboarders many of whom I had not interviewed (they were observed in public spaces).

After I finished gathering data, the information and analysis of their subculture was presented to approximately one third of the participants. Their comments served to confirm and fine tune my conclusions. They especially wanted me to note that although they shared many norms and values, they did not share all values and, therefore, just because they were all skateboarders did not mean that they were all good friends. This was evident in the variety of friendship groups within skateboarding, such as "hippies," "punks," "Skinheads," and "old-timers."

• • •

CONFORMITY AND SELF-EXPRESSION

The popular practice of skateboarding lacked a strict formal structure. In fact, the appeal for many skaters was precisely to use skateboarding as a means of self-expression and of challenging their own physical limits. Generally, a skating "session" (the time spent skateboarding) involves creating and practicing certain techniques, finding fun places to skate, and trying new tricks on the obstacles found. For example, a favorite spot of skaters in Welton was a loading dock located on the backside of a grocery store. The space used for the trucks to dock was lower than the parking area which created a U-shaped ramp where the skaters did a variety of tricks. The flexibility of skateboarding was one of the main attractions. Many skaters commented on their attraction to a sport in which there are no rules, referees, set plays, nor coaches. For example, Paul claimed that to skateboard "[you] don't need uniforms, no coach to tell you what to do and how to do it." Philip added, "I quit football because I didn't like taking orders." Skaters' general disregard for conforming to an authority carried over into a criticism of those who did. Many of the skaters distinguished themselves by considering themselves more reflective than their average peers. Philip and Jeff discussed the issue: "We might look at everything twice whereas everybody else will just go 'oh ya. . . .'. We're not saying skating doesn't have any conformity, but it's more by your own choice." Jeff:

> It's not conformist conformity. . . . I think skaters are more aware of conformity than jocks, I think jocks just seem to deal with it and say "OK, well that's just the way it is," but skaters go "geez, why do I have to do that, man. I don't want to buy these shoes, I don't want to have to buy 100 dollar shoes just to fit in," you know, that kind of thing.

The flexibility within skating was a key component, for example, Mark claimed that there are different styles of skating and all of them are accepted, unlike football, in which he felt that a participant would be kicked off the team for having a different style of play. In a separate interview, Jeff stated a similar concern, "Skating is a lot less confined [than organized sport], people are open to new things when you skate." The lack of a formal structure allowed and encouraged the participants to control their sport; they were the ones to determine what tricks they practiced and for how long, as well as creating their own individualized standards of excellence. This environment often led to the feelings that skateboarding allowed for more freedom of expression than other sports. Doug, a 25-year-old skateboarder and public school teacher, commented:

> A lot of them [skaters] are really involved with artistic endeavors, are very artistic. You can see the parallel; it's a kind of freedom of expression that skating is. How do you express yourself playing football, playing basketball? When you're skating it's, basically skating reflects your mood at the time and how you're skating, what you are doing, you know, it's definitely, you know, a way to express yourself.

Many athletes as well as sport sociologists would claim that one can express themselves through organized sport, but the point is that these skateboarders felt that they had more freedom to be creative in skateboarding than in traditional organized sport. The lack of a formal structure controlled by adult males is an essential element in this subculture, which is reflected in the lack of standardized criteria to judge performance. As Craig commented, "There is no such thing as a perfect '10' for a trick." What particularly stood out was the skaters' preference not to be judged by adult authority figures. For example, Grace discussed her anxiety over skateboarding becoming a sport, "For who's to say what trick is better? I like to do stuff that feels cool, that gives me butterflies in my stomach." The use of the skaters' own standards for personal worth was common as Eric's following comment reflects, "Skating is more challenging than organized sports! You see yourself improve, you amaze yourself." Alan, a fifth grade student and a skateboarder, wrote an essay for his school about why he liked to skateboard:

> The reason I love to skate is because it's a challenging sport. It's the way I express myself. It's something I can do by myself and nobody's there to judge me.

This subculture resisted many of the tenets of organized sport and of hegemonic masculinity with particular regard to the deference to adult male authority in formal structures. Another alternative behavior encouraged in the subculture is the emphasis on participation and cooperation as opposed to elite competition found in traditional sport: "You never lose when you skate."

COMPETITION AND PARTICIPATION

The subculture that I investigated represents those who prefer not to compete on an elite level. There are people who skateboard who are involved in a highly structured and competitive circuit. This bureaucratized version of skateboarding is coordinated through the National Skateboard Association. Although skateboarding can be practiced as a highly competitive sport, the vast majority of skaters I interviewed described their sport as different from competition. Jeff stated: "I don't know if I would classify it (skating) as a sport. I suppose I just find sport as competition; unless you are on the pro or amateur circuit you're not really competing against anybody." Pamela, an 18-year-old skater made this comparison:

> Soccer is a lot of pressure. . . . You have to be good if not better than everybody else, you have to be otherwise you don't play at all. Skating you can't do that, you just push yourself harder and harder. . . . Swimming is just sort of there, you get timed, now for

me you go against the clock. Now when you skate you don't go against anything, you just skate. That's what it is.

15   While [I was] discussing the issue of competition with Doug, he suggested:

> Most skaters don't, you know, I don't hear, I don't hear skaters whining about, you know, other people being better than them or striving to be, or bumming out about because they're not mastering something, whereas in other athletics they do. . . . There's a pressure to succeed where there isn't in skateboarding because there's not huge goals to attain. How do you measure success in skateboarding if you're not skating in contests, which most people don't. . . . Skaters, even in contests, it's more an attitude of having your best run, making all your tricks, as opposed to beating somebody. . . . It's not "I got to beat this guy, this is the guy I'm going to beat."

• • •

CONTRADICTIONS IN THE ALTERNATIVE SUBCULTURE

The subculture of skateboarding is not solely or purely an alternative form of masculinity. It differs from traditional sport in that it demotes competition and rule-bound behavior while it promotes self-expression. Yet (to my initial surprise), it also serves as an alternative conduit for promoting an ideology of male superiority and of patriarchal relations within the subculture. This contradiction resulted because the subculture of skateboarding provided an informal structure for its participants to create their own rules, yet it simultaneously provided an avenue for the participants to create gender stratification.

As stated previously, organized sport has historically been a realm in which males have bonded and created and reinforced a hegemonic masculinity which has demoted femininity, females, and homosexuals. The subculture of skateboarding I investigated had similar elements. It was male dominated (90% of the participants were male) and promoted a separation and stratification of males and females and of masculinity and femininity.

One of my formal questions addressed female participation. The responses generally reflected the dominant ideology that males and females "naturally" have different social roles, and that sport, and by extension skateboarding, is a male role.

SEX-SEGREGATION

While talking with the skateboarders, I commented on the lack of female participation and asked their opinion about why it occurred. Most males were taken aback and they spent time reflecting on it (as if they had not given it much thought before), and their explanations ranged from describing "natural" differences to social preferences of males and females. All the females discussed the issue directly and with depth, and it is my interpretation that they thought about this often. For both males and females the sex-segregation of skateboarding was typically justified as a reflection of feminine and masculine behaviors. In their explanations they did not distinguish between sex (as biological behaviors) and gender (as socially expected behaviors). It appeared that the dominant ideology of "natural" differences between males and females was a fundamental assumption of these skaters.

None of the skaters I met would consciously or deliberately exclude women from skating, as reflected by Philip's statement: 20

> Well, the first time you set up boundaries it's like the first nail in the coffin, when you say well no more skating in the street or no more skating for women, that's just saying, well we can't go any further with skating, it stops as far as, you know, "only guys can skate and that's it." I really don't think anybody wants to limit it, especially skaters.

Even though these skaters' sexism was not intentional, it is my contention that their assumptions of "natural" differences specifically affected how this predominately male subculture related with females, and therefore, affected female participation. These males did not relate to females as equals; they commonly viewed females as significantly different and especially as an object to view and as a sexual partner. The following categories reflect the varying assumptions of male and female behavior as a means to explain the lack of female participation.

FEMALE APPEARANCE

One common explanation for the low number of female participants was that skateboarding does not promote the traditional feminine appearance of the immaculately groomed, petite female. The skaters' assumption is that women want to appear traditionally feminine in all realms of their lives. Part of a feminine appearance is frailness and purity. Most males could not reconcile the physical risk-taking nature of skateboarding with female behavior. For example, Craig stated that skating "is a rough sport where people get scarred, and girls don't want to have scars on their shins, it wouldn't look good." He also added that girls would get tired of wearing tennis shoes all the time. In a separate interview another skater, Stuart, a 21-year-old male stated, "Girls probably don't skate because they don't look good with bruises." Along the same line, Francis commented that in skateboarding one has to get totally hurt before one can learn, and girls don't want to get bruised to learn. This type of response was very common. An 11-year-old male skater asserted, "They [girls] don't want to fall and get their butts dirty." All these comments reflect the assumption that females do not want to do anything that may disrupt appearing traditionally feminine, such as taking physical risks which may lead to bruises or to getting dirty. One female skater, Shelley, made a similar remark, "Girls don't want to do anything harsh or bruise their legs."

The bruising of one's body demonstrates a traditional masculine characteristic of risking bodily injury. Most males flaunted their bruises, and often proudly told stories of past injuries. Overall, the skaters did not associate courageous injury as a feminine (and, therefore, in their assumptions, a female) attribute. It appeared that these males thought that bruises did not look good or "appropriate" on females which reflected their expectations of females as much (if not more) as females' expectations of themselves.

• • •

FEMALE SOCIAL ROLES

Most of the skaters presumed that males and females have different social roles.

25   Doug replied to my question of what is a cool skater by stating, "Someone who is not ashamed of it. They don't hide it in the closet around their girlfriends." The statement reflects the assumption of different social realms for males and females; skaters are male (assuming heterosexuality), and females are not typically exposed to skating. I then asked directly about female participation, and Doug responded, "there's not nearly as many, it's too bad." He seemed sincere, so I commented on the idea that it appeared to be an open sport, and he replied: "Ya, but it's also pretty aggressive, kinda, I mean, there's that end of it, it kind of looks aggressive

maybe, and women don't get into it." This switch in mid-sentence from a natural difference ("but, it's also pretty aggressive") to a matter of choice ("it kind of looks aggressive, and women don't get into it") was a typical response. I interpreted him as saying: it's not that women can't be aggressive, but it's that they choose not to. Either way, women are relegated to a different social role; they could choose differently but it's not in their "nature" to do so. Males did not expect masculine behavior from women, and therefore did not interact with females in such a way as to encourage it. Tim stated that his sister wants to skate but, "she would rather spend her time doing her hair or talking on the phone." Brian commented on female interests: "No, um, I'm not too sure why girls don't like to skate, maybe because they are so interested in other things like going to the mall and hanging out with friends, their friends don't skate." Jeff, an 18-year-old skater, described the lack of female participation as a social choice of females:

> Not as many women take an interest in it, it's not intended to be a sexist point of view or anything, but I don't know if women take as much interest in it, maybe it's that, or maybe it's that women prefer to pursue other sports. Maybe it's just a male-dominated sport like football is, I don't know, I don't think it is. I don't see any reason why women shouldn't be able to skate.

Many of the skaters saw no physical or tangible barriers to females' involvement, and therefore assumed that females freely choose not to be involved. Other skaters were aware of social forces that may hinder females from skating, such as lack of other female participants and lack of peer support. Rarely did the male skaters ever consider their behavior as a reason why females did not participate more regularly. Through my interviews, I became aware that males thought of the female skater as an exception. More often, they commented about females as playing a marginalized role in the subculture of skateboarding. "Skate Betties" is the name given to most females associated with skating. Skate Betties are female groupies whose intentions (according to males) are instrumental: to meet cute guys and associate with an alternative crowd. Females are not perceived as expressive or fully engaged in the values of the subculture. Doug, a 25-year-old skater, explained skate Betties in this way:

> They do it because they want to meet cute guys, or their boyfriends do it. It's the alternative crowd; it's like the girls that are kind of

into alternative music and that stuff, and kind of skating goes along with it, not as much punk, but not mainstream, and um, they like the clothes; it's a cool look, I think it's a cool look.

Male skaters often labeled females who were attempting to skate as "Betties." James was describing two women he knew that skated: "They were like skating Betties, you know, you always saw them downtown trying to skate around." The last phrase "trying to skate around" is a derogatory statement with the assumption that these females could never fully be skaters. Brian, a 13-year-old, illustrates the marginalization that many females who try to skate face. I had asked him if "girls get into skating." He replied, "Oh, sometimes, there are girls that like skaters, like they hang out, but they don't really, they aren't like, they just try to balance on the board." Female efforts were often belittled. Philip stated, "there were some girls at my school that used to skate but they weren't, I don't know, I guess they just didn't quite have the dedication for it." These comments illustrate the assumption that females are not capable or dedicated enough to be true skaters. Male skaters tend to lump all females into the marginalized role of a "skate Betty": an instrumental role, and a role that looks to the male for identity. A skate Betty's only identity is her association with, not participation in, the subculture. In addition, skate Betties are frequently seen as a reserve stock of girlfriends, similar to the cheerleader role women play in mainstream sport. As Mark stated: "some skaters think women are only there when you get done with skating." It is my contention that males act on the assumptions stated above: that males are potential skaters and females are only affiliated with male skaters. The actions derived from those assumptions affect female participation. Females do not feel as welcomed to the subculture. Some of the following comments from the female skaters illustrate this differential treatment.

DIFFERENTIAL TREATMENT OF FEMALES

Pamela, an 18-year-old skater, described her barriers with male skaters. She felt that she had to be a better skater than males in order to be accepted by them.

> With my friends they look at me as just one of the guys, that was fine, now when you go skating and meet new people you pretty

much have to prove yourself and they say, "Oh, a girl skater, she probably can't do anything," so you, you got to pull off a bunch of tricks and then they say, "Oh, oh, she's pretty cool." That pretty much breaks the ice if you show your skill. . . . If you don't prove yourself you get hassled.

She followed that statement by saying guys don't have to prove themselves like girls do in order to be accepted. Once she proved herself, she did feel accepted. Acceptance based on being "one of the guys" reinforces that females and femininity are not accepted; it is only when females prove their masculinity ([being] one of the guys) that they are accepted within the subculture of skateboarding.

For Shelley, this meant that she actually had to split her personality in two parts: masculine and feminine. When she skates she "stops thinking like a girl" and then she can do better. While she skates she wants to be treated like "one of the guys"; she doesn't want to "be scammed on." Then she stated, after she skates she can get "dressed up." While she skates she thinks in a masculine manner, and after she skates she can be feminine. Her statement also implies that part of being feminine is to be open to being scammed on, to being viewed as a sexual object—to "dress up."

The perceived masculine role of skateboarding was reflected in the perceived masculinization of females through participation in skating: females become "one of the guys." Francis, an 18-year-old male skater, portrayed another facet of this masculinization: "You don't want your girlfriend to skate, but it's cool for others [females]." He could not explain why he felt this way, but it is my contention that these males could not conceive of being intimate with someone else they perceived to be masculine. Part of being treated as one of the guys means that female masculinity is accepted (as a rare exception to the rule), but this often meant that males would not consider being physically intimate with a masculine female. This may partially explain why Shelley divided her personality into a skater who would not be "scammed on," and someone who could "dress up" after she skates.

Grace, a 21-year-old skater, also stated that her acceptance was based on being masculine because "skating is perceived as unfeminine." Therefore, when she skates she is "one of the guys." She stated that males "feel threatened by her," and thus treat her differently. For example, they are more concerned when she falls, and more enthusiastic when she learns tricks which do not warrant the enthusiasm. Her male friends tend to be overprotective, which annoyed her.

The bonding that does occur in the subculture of skateboarding happens more immediately for males than females. As described above, males unconsciously create barriers through this assumption. These assumptions of sex difference created barriers to female participation, which effectively promoted the reification of sex difference through the maintenance of social boundaries. Females are accepted once they prove themselves by overcoming these barriers. As noted previously, females enjoy skating for the same reasons that males do. Yet, two of the females described feelings of isolation. Grace specifically stated that she gets lonely as a female skater. Shelley indirectly addressed this when she said that she got support from males, but she really got psyched when she saw a video with a "girl" skater in it. These feelings of isolation reflect a lack of complete acceptance into the subculture.

SUMMARY AND CONCLUDING REMARKS

• • •

35   This study of skateboarding is also an example of how masculinity is not naturally predetermined or universal, but instead a creation of the participants which varies according to the social context. The emphasis on participant control, self-expression, and open participation differs greatly from the hegemonic values of adult authority, conformity, and elite competition.

An interesting contradiction arises within this subculture. Even though the participants' challenged mainstream masculinity, they defined skateboarding as primarily a male activity. This subculture of skateboarding illustrates some of the incongruities that arise when people negotiate new social relations. For on one level skateboarding displayed resistance by redefining masculine behavior, yet on another level it reproduced patriarchal relations similar to Young's findings within the rugby subculture. What is essential for the maintenance of patriarchy is creating different social roles for males and females, and marginalizing the female role. Skaters did this by redefining masculinity, which preserved skateboarding as a male realm.

Because many of these male skateboarders did not participate in mainstream athletics (either by choice or size/ability), it is my contention that they created an alternative sport which met some of their specific needs, such as participant control and a deemphasis on elite competition. And skateboarding also served to meet social needs that traditional athletics have met for other males—a place where boys create friendships and differentiate themselves from girls and that which is labeled feminine. Although the weight of this paper is on the males' attitudes and behaviors, it is evident that both the males and the females have internalized the dominant ideology of sport as a male social role. This affects how females negotiate their position within the subculture. Some of the responses are typical of females in male-dominated settings, such as feeling a need to constantly demonstrate one's ability as well as fitting into the dominant culture by being "one of the boys" (Theberge, 1993). And as Theberge (1993) noted, as long as females are judged by a standard of masculinity in a patriarchal society, they will always be marginalized.

References

Carrigan, T., Connell, B., & Lee, J. (1987). "Hard and heavy: Toward a new theory of masculinity." In M. Kaufman (Ed.), *Beyond patriarchy: Essays by men on pleasure, power, and change*. New York: Oxford University.

Clatterbaugh, K. (1990). *Contemporary perspectives on masculinity: Men, women, and politics in modern society*. Boulder, CO: Westview.

Curry, T. J. (1991). "Fraternal bonding in the locker room: A profeminist analysis of talk about competition and women." *Sociology of Sport Journal, 8,* 119–135.

Kidd, B. (1987). "Sports and masculinity." In M. Kaufman (Ed.), *Beyond patriarchy: Essays by men on pleasure, power, and change*. New York: Oxford University.

Messner, M. (1992a). *Power at play: Sports and the problem of masculinity*. Boston: Beacon.

Messner, M. (1992b). "Like family: Power, intimacy, and sexuality in male athletes' friendships." In P. Nardi (Ed.), *Men's friendships*. Newbury Park: Sage.

Sabo, D. (1989). "Pigskin, patriarchy, and pain." In Kimmel & Messner (Eds.), *Men's lives*. New York: Macmillan.

Sabo, D., & Panepinto, J. (1990). "Football ritual and the social reproduction of masculinity." In M. Messner & D. Sabo (Eds.), *Sport, men and the gender order: Critical feminist perspectives*. Champaign, IL: Human Kinetic Books.

Theberge, N. (1993). "The construction of gender in sport: Women coaching, and the naturalization of difference." *Social Problems, 40,* 301–313.

Young, R. (1983). "The subculture of rugby players: A form of resistance and incorporation." Unpublished master's thesis, McMaster University.

Discussion Questions

1. Which of the "five characteristics of male initiation rituals" (paragraph 4) seem to apply to the skateboarders that Beal describes?
2. To what extent does Beal's analysis of "alternative forms of masculinity" apply to other athletic activities (e.g. snowboarding, rock climbing, mountain biking, water sports, etc.)? Give examples.
3. Explain how "masculinity" is defined first in Messner's article and then in Beal's article. Then, explain how each author describes forms of "alternative masculinity." Account for any contrasts you find in their viewpoints.
4. To what extent do you believe that some women participate in sports in order to challenge "mainstream masculinity"? Give specific examples from your own experience or observation.
5. Consider a social activity in which you have participated with both men and women. Explain to what extent the men treat the women differently within the setting of that activity. Explain to what extent the women treat the men differently? To what extent do you *feel* different from members of the other gender while engaged in the activity?
6. To what extent do you believe that sport is generally *perceived* in America as "a male social role"?

The Sports Taboo
Malcolm Gladwell

Of Jamaican heritage, Malcolm Gladwell was born in Britain and grew up in Canada, earning a history degree from the University of Toronto in 1984. At The Washington Post, *he served from 1987 to 1996 as a business and science writer. Writing for* The New Yorker *since 1996, he has tackled a variety of topics, including "The Coolhunt" (1997)—a portrait of the merchandisers who track new trendsetters in fashion and create products that commercialize the latest "cool" look. In "The Talent Myth" (2002), he made quite a splash in the business world when he exposed the failures of the star system for rewarding young executives at Enron, which at the time was facing bankruptcy. In "Getting Over It" (2004), he describes "a kind of psychological immune system" that overcomes such traumatic*

*events as war and sexual abuse through an "unexpected strength
and resilience of the human spirit." All his articles explore a particular idea, bringing social science research to bear and citing individual human examples along with historical perspectives in order to
change the reader's perception of that idea. His latest books have
made him something of a business guru, speaking to CEOs and executives for up to $40,000 per engagement as many as two dozen
times a year.* The Tipping Point *(2000), on the* New York Times
*best-seller list for six months, explains how ideas, attitudes, behav-
iors, and products spread contagiously through a culture. Here, he
makes his argument by using research from epidemiology, sociology, and psychology, while citing practical examples from fashion,
business, education, and the media.*

*In the following essay (1997), he uses an analogy to describe
the relationship between perceptions of race and sports achievement. Gladwell relies on his own experience to introduce his argument, but also cites evidence from physiologists, statistics of athletic performance, DNA research, and the "social science literature
on male and female math achievement." As you read, consider
which types of evidence you find most convincing.*

✦

The education of any athlete begins, in part, with an education
in the racial taxonomy of his chosen sport—in the subtle, unwritten rules about what whites are supposed to be good at and
what blacks are supposed to be good at. In football, whites play
quarterback and blacks play running back; in baseball whites
pitch and blacks play the outfield. I grew up in Canada, where my
brother Geoffrey and I ran high-school track, and in Canada the
rule of running was that anything under the quarter-mile be-
longed to the West Indians. This didn't mean that white people
didn't run the sprints. But the expectation was that they would
never win, and, sure enough, they rarely did. There was just a
handful of West Indian immigrants in Ontario at that point clus-
tered in and around Toronto—but they owned Canadian sprinting, setting up under the stands at every major championship,
cranking up the reggae on their boom boxes, and then humiliating everyone else on the track. My brother and I weren't from
Toronto, so we weren't part of that scene. But our West Indian
heritage meant that we got to share in the swagger. Geoffrey
was a magnificent runner, with powerful legs and a barrel chest,
and when he was warming up he used to do that exaggerated,

slow-motion jog that the white guys would try to do and never quite pull off. I was a miler, which was a little outside the West Indian range. But, the way I figured it, the rules meant that no one should ever outkick me over the final two hundred metres of any race. And in the golden summer of my fourteenth year, when my running career prematurely peaked, no one ever did.

When I started running, there was a quarter-miler just a few years older than I was by the name of Arnold Stotz. He was a bull-dog of a runner, hugely talented, and each year that he moved through the sprinting ranks he invariably broke the existing four-hundred-metre record in his age class. Stotz was white, though, and every time I saw the results of a big track meet I'd keep an eye out for his name, because I was convinced that he could not keep winning. It was as if I saw his whiteness as a degenerative disease, which would eventually claim and cripple him. I never asked him whether he felt the same anxiety, but I can't imagine that he didn't. There was only so long that anyone could defy the rules. One day, at the provincial championships, I looked up at the results board and Stotz was gone.

Talking openly about the racial dimension of sports in this way, of course, is considered unseemly. It's all right to say that blacks dominate sports because they lack opportunities elsewhere. That's the "Hoop Dreams" line, which says whites are allowed to acknowledge black athletic success as long as they feel guilty about it. What you're not supposed to say is what we were saying in my track days—that we were better because we were black, because of something intrinsic to being black. Nobody said anything like that publicly last month when Tiger Woods won the Masters or when, a week later, African men claimed thirteen out of the top twenty places in the Boston Marathon. Nor is it likely to come up this month, when African-Americans will make up eighty per cent of the players on the floor for the N.B.A. playoffs. When the popular television sports commentator Jimmy (the Greek) Snyder did break this taboo, in 1988—infamously ruminating on the size and significance of black thighs—one prominent N.A.A.C.P. official said that his remarks "could set race relations back a hundred years." The assumption is that the whole project of trying to get us to treat each other the same will be undermined if we don't all agree that under the skin we actually are the same.

The point of this, presumably, is to put our discussion of sports on a par with legal notions of racial equality, which would be a fine idea except that civil-rights law governs matters like housing and employment and the sports taboo covers matters like what can be said about someone's jump shot. In his much heralded new book *Darwin's Athletes,* the University of Texas scholar John Hoberman tries to argue that these two things are the same, that it's impossible to speak of black physical superiority without implying intellectual inferiority. But it isn't long before the argument starts to get ridiculous. "The spectacle of black athleticism," he writes, inevitably turns into "a highly public image of black retardation." Oh, really? What, exactly, about Tiger Woods's victory in the Masters resembled "a highly public image of black retardation"? Today's black athletes are multimillion-dollar corporate pitchmen, with talk shows and sneaker deals and publicity machines and almost daily media opportunities to share their thoughts with the world, and it's very hard to see how all this contrives to make them look stupid. Hoberman spends a lot of time trying to inflate the significance of sports, arguing that how we talk about events on the baseball diamond or the track has grave consequences for how we talk about race in general. Here he is, for example, on Jackie Robinson:

> The sheer volume of sentimental and intellectual energy that has been invested in the mythic saga of Jackie Robinson has discouraged further thinking about what his career did and did not accomplish. . . . Black America has paid a high and largely unacknowledged price for the extraordinary prominence given the black athlete rather than other black men of action (such as military pilots and astronauts), who represent modern aptitudes in ways that athletes cannot.

Please. Black America has paid a high and largely unacknowledged price for a long list of things, and having great athletes is far from the top of the list. Sometimes a baseball player is just a baseball player, and sometimes an observation about racial difference is just an observation about racial difference. Few object when medical scientists talk about the significant epidemiological differences between blacks and whites—the fact that blacks have a higher incidence of hypertension than whites and twice as many black males die of diabetes and prostate cancer as white males, that breast tumors appear to grow faster in black women than in white women, that black girls show signs of puberty sooner than white girls. So why aren't we allowed to say that there might be athletically significant differences between blacks and whites?

According to the medical evidence, African-Americans seem to have, on the average, greater bone mass than do white Americans— a difference that suggests greater muscle mass. Black men have

5

slightly higher circulating levels of testosterone and human-growth hormone than their white counterparts, and blacks overall tend to have proportionally slimmer hips, wider shoulders, and longer legs. In one study, the Swedish physiologist Bengt Saltin compared a group of Kenyan distance runners with a group of Swedish distance runners and found interesting differences in muscle composition: Saltin reported that the Africans appeared to have more blood-carrying capillaries and more mitochondria (the body's cellular power plant) in the fibres of their quadriceps. Another study found that, while black South African distance runners ran at the same speed as white South African runners, they were able to use more oxygen—eighty-nine per cent versus eighty-one per cent—over extended periods: somehow, they were able to exert themselves more. Such evidence suggested that there were physical differences in black athletes which have a bearing on activities like running and jumping, which should hardly come as a surprise to anyone who follows competitive sports.

To use track as an example—since track is probably the purest measure of athletic ability—Africans recorded fifteen out of the twenty fastest times last year in the men's ten-thousand-metre event. In the five thousand metres, eighteen out of the twenty fastest times were recorded by Africans. In the fifteen hundred metres, thirteen out of the twenty fastest times were African, and in the sprints, in the men's hundred metres, you have to go all the way down to the twenty-third place in the world rankings—to Geir Moen, of Norway—before you find a white face. There is a point at which it becomes foolish to deny the fact of black athletic prowess, and even more foolish to banish speculation on the topic. Clearly, something is going on. The question is what. . . .

What are we seeing when we remark on black domination of elite sporting events—an average difference between the races or merely a difference in variability?

This question has been explored by geneticists and physical anthropologists, and some of the most notable work has been conducted over the past few years by Kenneth Kidd, at Yale. Kidd and his colleagues have been taking DNA samples from two African Pygmy tribes in Zaire and the Central African Republic and comparing them with DNA samples taken from populations all over the world. What they have been looking for is variants—subtle differences between the DNA of one person and another—and what they have found is fascinating. "I would say, without a doubt, that in almost any single African population—a tribe or however you want to define it—there is more genetic variation than in all the rest of the world put together," Kidd told me. In a sample of fifty Pygmies, for example, you might find nine variants in one stretch of DNA. In a sample of hundreds of people from around the rest of the world, you might find only a total of six variants in that same stretch of DNA—and probably every one of those six variants would also be found in the Pygmies. If everyone in the world was wiped out except Africans, in other words, almost all the human genetic diversity would be preserved.

The likelihood is that these results reflect Africa's status as   10
the homeland of Homo sapiens: since every human population outside Africa is essentially a subset of the original African population, it makes sense that everyone in such a population would be a genetic subset of Africans, too. So you can expect groups of Africans to be more variable in respect to almost anything that has a genetic component. If, for example, your genes control how you react to aspirin, you'd expect to see more Africans than whites for whom one aspirin stops a bad headache, more for whom no amount of aspirin works, more who are allergic to aspirin, and more who need to take, say, four aspirin at a time to get any benefit—but far fewer Africans for whom the standard two-aspirin dose would work well. And to the extent that running is influenced by genetic factors you would expect to see more really fast blacks—and more really slow blacks—than whites but far fewer Africans of merely average speed. Blacks are like boys. Whites are like girls.

• • •

Elite athletes are elite athletes because, in some sense, they are on the fringes of genetic variability. As it happens, African populations seem to create more of these genetic outliers than white populations do, and this is what underpins the claim that blacks are better athletes than whites. But that's all the claim amounts to. It doesn't say anything at all about the rest of us, of all races, muddling around in the genetic middle. . . .

Or consider, in a completely different realm, the problem of hypertension. Black Americans have a higher incidence of hypertension than white Americans, even after you control for every conceivable variable, including income, diet, and weight, so it's tempting to conclude that there is something about being of African descent that makes blacks prone to hypertension. But it turns out that although some Caribbean countries have a problem with hypertension, others—Jamaica, St. Kitts, and the Bahamas—don't. It also turns out that people in Liberia and Nigeria—two countries where many New World slaves came from—have similar and perhaps even lower blood-pressure rates than white North Americans, while studies of Zulus, Indians, and whites in Durban, South Africa, showed that urban white males had the highest hypertension rates and urban white females had the lowest. So it's likely that the disease has nothing at all to do with Africanness.

The same is true for the distinctive muscle characteristic observed when Kenyans were compared with Swedes. Saltin, the Swedish physiologist, subsequently found many of the same characteristics in Nordic skiers who train at high altitudes and Nordic runners who train in very hilly regions—conditions, in other words, that resemble the mountainous regions of Kenya's Rift Valley, where so many of the country's distance runners come from. The key factor seems to be Kenya, not genes.

Lots of things that seem to be genetic in origin, then, actually aren't. Similarly, lots of things that we wouldn't normally think might affect athletic ability actually do. Once again, the social-science literature on male and female math achievement is instructive. Psychologists argue that when it comes to subjects like math, boys tend to engage in what's known as ability attribution. A boy who is doing well will attribute his success to the fact that he's good at math, and if he's doing badly he'll blame his teacher or his own lack of motivation—anything but his ability. That makes it easy for him to bounce back from failure or disappointment, and gives him a lot of confidence in the face of a tough new challenge. After all, if you think you do well in math because you're good at math, what's stopping you from being good at, say, algebra, or advanced calculus? On the other hand, if you ask a girl why she is doing well in math she will say, more often than not, that she succeeds because she works hard. If she's doing poorly, she'll say she isn't smart enough. This, as should be obvious, is a self-defeating attitude. Psychologists call it "learned helplessness"—the state in which failure is perceived as insurmountable. Girls who engage in effort attribution learn helplessness because in the face of a more difficult task like algebra or advanced calculus they can conceive of no solution. They're convinced that they can't work harder, because they think they're working as hard as they can, and that they can't rely on their intelligence, because they never thought they were that smart to begin with. In fact, one of the fascinating findings of attribution research is that the smarter girls are, the more likely they are to fall into this trap. High achievers are sometimes the most helpless. Here, surely, is part of the explanation for greater math variability among males. The female math whizzes, the ones who should be competing in the top one and two per cent with their male counterparts, are the ones most often paralyzed by a lack of confidence in their own aptitude. They think they belong only in the intellectual middle.

The striking thing about these descriptions of male and female stereotyping in math, though, is how similar they are to black and white stereotyping in athletics—to the unwritten rules holding that blacks achieve through natural ability and whites through effort. Here's how *Sports Illustrated* described, in a recent article, the white basketball player Steve Kerr, who plays alongside Michael Jordan for the Chicago Bulls. According to the magazine, Kerr is a "hard-working overachiever," distinguished by his "work ethic and heady play" and by a shooting style "born of a million practice shots." Bear in mind that Kerr is one of the best shooters in basketball today, and a key player on what is arguably one of the finest basketball teams in history. Bear in mind, too, that there is no evidence that Kerr works any harder than his teammates, least of all Jordan himself, whose work habits are legendary. But you'd never guess that from the article. It concludes, "All over America, whenever quicker, stronger gym rats see Kerr in action, they must wonder, How can that guy be out there instead of me?"

There are real consequences to this stereotyping. As the psychologists Carol Dweck and Barbara Licht write of high-achieving schoolgirls, "[They] may view themselves as so motivated and well disciplined that they cannot entertain the possibility that they did poorly on an academic task because of insufficient effort. Since blaming the teacher would also be out of character, blaming their abilities when they confront difficulty may seem like the most reasonable option." If you substitute the words "white athletes" for "girls" and "coach" for "teacher," I think you have part of the reason that so many white athletes are underrepresented at the highest levels of professional sports. Whites have been saddled with the athletic equivalent of learned helplessness—the idea that it is all but fruitless to try and compete at the highest levels, because they have only effort on their side. The causes of athletic and gender discrimination may be diverse, but its effects are not. Once again, blacks are like boys, and whites are like girls.

15

When I was in college, I once met an old acquaintance from my high-school running days. Both of us had long since quit track, and we talked about a recurrent fantasy we found we'd both had for getting back into shape. It was that we would go away somewhere remote for a year and do nothing but train, so that when the year was up we might finally know how good we were. Neither of us had any intention of doing this, though, which is why it was a fantasy. In adolescence, athletic excess has a certain appeal—during high school, I happily spent Sunday afternoons running up and down snow-covered sandhills—but with most of us that obsessiveness soon begins to fade. Athletic success depends on having the right genes and on a self-reinforcing belief in one's own ability. But it also depends on a rare form of tunnel vision. To be a great athlete, you have to care, and what was obvious to us both was that neither of us cared anymore. This is the last piece of the puzzle about what we mean when we say one group is better at something than another: sometimes different groups care about different things. Of the seven hundred men who play major-league baseball, for example, eighty-six come from either the Dominican Republic or Puerto Rico, even though those two islands have a combined population of only eleven million. But then baseball is something that Dominicans and Puerto Ricans care about—and you can say the same thing about African-Americans and basketball, West Indians and sprinting, Canadians and hockey, and Russians and chess. Desire is the great intangible in performance, and unlike genes or psychological affect we can't measure it and trace its implications. This is the problem, in the end, with the question of whether blacks are better at sports than whites. It's not that it's offensive, or that it leads to discrimination. It's that, in some sense, it's not a terribly interesting question; "better" promises a tidier explanation than can ever be provided. . . .

Discussion Questions

1. Both Beal and Gladwell write about the "rules" of sports, although Gladwell focuses on running. Explain how these "rules" are different. Despite this difference, how are these "rules" similar?

2. Do you believe that other journalists should break the "sports taboo" and write honestly about the racial differences among athletes? Why? What do you think Gladwell's purpose is in doing so?

3. Citing DNA research, Gladwell uses the scientific concept of "genetic variability" to help explain racial differences in sports. Summarize his argument in your own words.

4. Explain the purpose of Gladwell's discussion of boys' and girls' math ability. Do you find this point helpful to his overall argument? In your own experience or observation, to what extent are such gender differences in math ability valid? Explain.

5. Review the different types of evidence Gladwell uses to support his argument (see the introduction to the reading above). Which type do you find most convincing, and which do you find least significant to his argument?

6. Describe your response to Gladwell's assertion in the concluding paragraph that "desire is the great intangible in performance" (paragraph 17).

Topics for Exploration and Writing

You have been reading about and discussing body image and the social meanings of sports. To explore these topics, focus on one activity or sequence of events, drawing on examples from your observation and experience. Instead, you may choose to write about someone close to you, but be sure to ask your informant for details about his or her experience, feelings, and perceptions of the activity. While most of your content should be original, brief comparisons to the articles in this chapter may be helpful to your viewpoint (refer to authors by last name and to article titles). Your job as a writer is to inform your readers by presenting specific examples that you can explain in detail and then generalizing about these examples by presenting a significant understanding. For any of these topics, if race, ethnicity, gender, sexual preference, age, body size or image, or disability relates to your analysis, please include these important dimensions in your essay.

1. Analyze your involvement with a specific athletic activity that you participate in with other people (even if it is not a team sport). Rather than the mind–body connections and individual experience you focused on in the topics of Chapter 1, for this essay analyze the interpersonal dimensions of sport. You may need to explain the activity's effect on individual feelings or psychology, but also explore the group psychology of the sport, including the social motives to participate, the feelings of belonging, interpersonal bonding or "team spirit," and the attitudes of others toward the activity. Consider how the gender of the participants may affect others' responses. Analyze what group satisfactions you gain through the sport. In the course of your essay, try to assess the effects of this activity not merely on your own self-image, but also on group image—thus defining the social consequences or value of the activity.

2. Consider your personal experience or first-hand observation of high school sports or amateur athletics for adults (such as a city league). Analyze the racial dimension of a particular sport. To establish a context for your essay,

first summarize the viewpoint of Messner or Gladwell, or even synthesize their viewpoints about black athletes. Then, describe the participants in your particular sport, analyzing the social dynamics among white players and players from other ethnic groups. To what extent were conventional expectations confirmed or challenged considering leadership roles, athletic ability, and patterns of achievement? In particular, explain the "exceptions" to the expectations. Also, describe any observed differences in the "style" of play and explain the possible sources for these differences—whether they are perhaps racially based or due to another factor. To explore the social consequences of the racial dimension in sports, describe and explain how athletes from nonwhite ethnic groups were treated off the field, in social settings where sports should not be relevant. Throughout your essay, try to break the "sports taboo" in being honest about *racial* realities, but avoid *racist* stereotyping and bias.

3. Define masculinity *or* femininity, referring to *at least* one of the articles in Chapter 2. Describe the essential traits of "being a man" or of "being a woman." Instead, after giving a brief background about *traditional* gender behaviors, you might focus your essay on defining some version of "alternative masculinity" or "alternative femininity." Who determines the meaning of gender? Is it changeable or fixed? Does it vary across generations? Can its meaning be individual, or is it always shaped by society? How is gender related to social behaviors? Sports? Ethnicity? Work? Many *specific examples* from your observation and experience of *several social contexts* are essential to your definition.

4. Examine a specific *fictional* television or film comedy representing homosexuality, such as the television series *Will and Grace*, or the films *In and Out* (1997) or *My Best Friend's Wedding* (1997). Analyze the depiction of gay and/or lesbian characters, explaining to what extent you think that representation is realistic or relies on stereotypes. To what extent are gay and/or lesbian characters depicted as different from or similar to their heterosexual friends? Does the comedy make fun of both sets of characters equally? Does the comedy evoke sympathy for both straights and gays? Use examples of *specific scenes* as evidence to support your thesis. It is best to view a videotape of the television show or movie so that you can replay scenes for note-taking and interpretation.

Body Modification

University of Oregon folklorist Daniel Wojcik agrees with other researchers that body art, among the 1980s punk rockers, was an oppositional response to what they considered a corrupt and fated social order. However, in *Punk and Neo-Tribal Body Art* (University Press of Mississippi, 1995), he notes a positive, even utopian counter-movement in the subculture of tattooed and pierced people who were striving for a more ideal society through a return to "primitive" customs. Wojcik concludes his book in this way:

> Neo-tribalism . . . tends to emphasize the transformative rather than the destructive aspects of body modification, often expressing a yearning for idealized ways of life imagined to be more fulfilling emotionally, spiritually, and sexually. . . . Pierced, scarred and tattooed, the bodies of neo-tribalists become sites of symbolic control inscribed with primordial power, at a time in which the human body appears increasingly vulnerable, assaulted by the threat of AIDS, environmental destruction, nuclear holocaust, genetic manipulations, the invasive technologies of the medical industry, chemical pollutants, escalating violence and murder, and other forms of bodily exploitation, torment, and annihilation. (36)

Here, Wojcik suggests several metaphors for the body which reiterate some of the concerns of Chapters 1 and 2 and anticipate those of this chapter, as well as of Chapter 5. Recall Jack Kornfield's metaphor for the body as a space where the individual and the universe coincide. Recall, too, Stuart Ewen's metaphor for the machinelike body as a "hard shell"—a site of "social control" achieved through pumping iron, rather than through body art, as

Wojcik discusses. The above passage looks ahead to Chapter 5, "Medicine and Technology," in its metaphor of the body as victim, "assaulted" and exploited by reproductive and genetic technologies, as well as the organ transplant market. Thus, some of the articles in Chapter 5 represent the body as a temple defiled by the unnatural practices of medical science, which operates within a rapacious, wasteful, and destructive commodity-driven capitalism, which stimulates the sale of human body parts.

The readings of Chapter 3 extend the metaphors of the body into new terrain, considering the varieties of body art even as maps and signposts that tell where a changing culture is headed. In the first article, "Marks of Civilization," Arnold Rubin writes from an anthropological and historical perspective to affirm that body art is a "dynamic, cumulative" record of "intense experiences that define the evolving person." In a survey of how tattooing, piercing, and scarification have been used in Africa, Asia, the Pacific Islands, Native America, and contemporary Euro-America, Rubin celebrates these body designs as civilizing marks of cultural tradition, social membership, and religious consciousness. It should be noted here that Rubin's essay originally served as the introduction to a collection of articles based on an academic conference, "Art of the Body," which considered questions of identity, aesthetics, gender formation, spirituality, genealogy, rites of passage, and contemporary subculture. In the original publication, Rubin included thirteen footnotes citing mostly academic journals and books reporting research in natural history, archeology, anthropology, art history, costume, and fashion—mostly from the 1970s and 1980s. In addition, one note cited a 1653 disputation against the "deformations" of body art, and another cited a contemporary popular periodical directed to "piercing fans." In his original essay, Rubin also included sixty-two citations to the articles in the collection he edited; these have been omitted in the reprint to make his work more accessible to readers for whom it is an introduction to the topic of body art, rather than to the specialized scholarship that originally followed it. But as his essay shows, that scholarship embraces cultural relativism and rejects the negative bias in some previous studies of body art, which used such language as "deformation, disfigurement, [and] mutilation." Instead, he and his coauthors adopted the viewpoint of the peoples who have practiced body modification and have considered it a means toward "perfection."

In the second article, "The Body Jigsaw," Philippe Liotard employs two metaphors for the body: as a living "canvas" and as "a space to mix and match physical and cultural elements in defining who or what you want to be," so that the marks of body art come together into a coherent whole, like pieces of an elaborate puzzle. Liotard, writing for a popular publication sponsored by the United Nations, maintains a decidedly international perspective. Still, his article is intended for a general reader, so it cites no scholarship, relying primarily on his own personal observations and interpretations of culture. However, he does cite the opinions of two authorities on the subject: a body artist and an owner of a tattoo-and-piercing chain in the United States. As a journalist, Liotard seems to maintain the objective tone of a neutral reporter.

The third article, "Tattooed: A Participant Observer's Exploration of Meaning," presents the viewpoint of "a heavily tattooed woman" and passionate researcher of this social phenomenon, who presents her findings in a scholarly journal. Therefore, author Shannon Bell follows the expected structure for a social science research report, including a "Works Cited" list of sources; a review of the literature, with the heading "Contextual Background"; her research discoveries, helpfully headed by the interpretive concepts "Subculture" and "Identity"; and a concluding "Discussion" section. What is unusual in this article is the mix of personal testimony and scholarly research, a mix that is quite rare in academic journals. As you read, especially keep in mind her position as "participant" as well as "observer." Also, note her use of the metaphor for the body as a "surface" that can reveal the depth of being, acting as an external manifestation of the internal.

In the fourth article, "Pumped, Pierced, Painted and Pagan," we return to a journalistic perspective in which Joe Woodard incorporates ample sources to give his report authority and credibility. He quotes interviews with several "experts" on the topic of body modification, summarizes one published survey, and includes statistics on plastic surgery (although without naming a specific source). Here, it appears that the journalist's intention is primarily informative, and readers do learn many details about the traditional and contemporary motivations behind the "hot trends in body fashion." However, Woodard also reveals a bias in using the negative terminology of "mutilation"—a use that Rubin criticizes in the first article. In the course of reading Woodard's report, watch for three new metaphors for the body to emerge: as a balloon or ball to be "pumped up," as an on-going art "project," and as an object of atonement for sin.

In the fifth article, "Marks of Shame," Theodore Dalrymple's title suggests that his viewpoint goes beyond reporting to commentary, even editorializing. His ostensible news topic is a bill passed in the U.S. House of Representatives to fund the removal of stigmatizing "anti-social" tattoos in order to help some California residents to "reform" their "criminal" past and to get jobs. While he draws on his own expertise as a doctor and psychiatrist among the poor of Great Britain, Dalrymple relies on no other source except the law itself and the website of the congresswoman who proposed it. His article tends to ostracize what he sees as a violent subculture, but his real attack is against the "liberal" culture, which he blames for indulging criminals and not judging them harshly enough. Finally, he suggests a metaphor for the body as shameless brute.

Marks of Civilization
ARNOLD RUBIN

Until his death in 1988, Arnold Rubin was an associate professor in the Department of Art, Design and Art History at the University of California, Los Angeles. He was a specialist in the arts of sub-Saharan Africa, including architecture, sculpture, and body art, and he also had a special interest in the unconventional arts of southern California, especially the Pasadena Tournament of Roses. Under his direction, a symposium on "Art of the Body" was held at UCLA, January 28–30, 1983, where presentations from the fields of anthropology, sociology, art history, folklore, and medicine formed the basis for the book he later edited, Marks of Civilization: Artistic Transformations of the Human Body *(UCLA Cultural History Museum, 1988). A concluding session of the conference featured the participation of nonacademic practitioners, when outstanding tattoo artists offered comments that were later incorporated into Rubin's chapter introductions and the conference presentations, as revised for the published book.*

As you read, consider how the purpose and interests of the conference itself are expressed in Rubin's opening essay for the conference report. Likewise, consider how the title "Marks of Civilization" predisposes you to read this essay from a particular perspective.

---- ✦ ----

Europeans became aware of the relatively extreme forms of body art practiced by the peoples of Africa, Asia, and the Americas early in the "Age of Exploration," from the late fifteenth century onward. Expanded interest and, in the case of tattoo, actual involvement in body art on a significant scale among Europeans (and Euro-Americans) dates to the late eighteenth and early nineteenth centuries. This interest was one result of the intensified penetration of eastern and southeastern Asia and Oceania by European and American commercial and political interests which took place around that time. In fact, the most likely derivation of the modern term "tattoo" is from one of several Oceanic languages. Sailors and other travellers returned to Europe from Indochina, Indonesia, Japan, Micronesia, and Polynesia with strange and exotic tattoos pricked into their skins, ranging from stark black geometric designs to delicate renderings of fish, flowers and dragons. The stories of their exploits and adventures were usually more lurid than their tattoos, and many subsequently made a comfortable living by recounting their experiences and exhibiting their marks for paying audiences. Early nineteenth-century explorers added their accounts of the strange forms of body art which they had encountered.

Consciousness of these manifestations of the diversity of human culture was further expanded during the second half of the nineteenth century as the major European powers assumed imperial dominion over vast areas of Asia, Africa, Oceania, and Native America. Anthropology emerged as a field of study, by and large, when colonial administrations realized their need to know something of the beliefs and practices of the diverse peoples whom they were charged with governing. Simultaneously, awareness of other cultures on the part of Europeans and Euro-Americans was dramatically expanding through more comfortable, less expensive, and faster travel; the invention of photography; the emergence of mass media through industrialization of the printing industry; expansion of literacy through public education; recreation of the habitats of colonial peoples as features of the great ("World's Fair") expositions; development of national ethnographical collections (usually in conjunction with "natural history" museums); expanding ethnographical and archaeological research and the publication thereof; and a host of other factors.

However, rather than precipitating a sense of the functional equivalence of particular social and cultural systems, of the shared principles ultimately to be found in the nominal diversity of cultural forms, of appreciation for the many and varied ways of being human, the net effect of all this new information was largely to widen rather than narrow the cultural gulf, and to reinforce the European/Euro-American sense of cultural superiority. During the early twentieth century, despite abundant evidence for its invalidity, the stereotype of the naked savage persisted: dark and ominous, with bones in his nose and pierced earlobes, and strange figures incised into his skin. This conceptualization began to be rooted out following World War II, however, as more and more of the peoples so stigmatized gained political independence, increased control of their collective resources, and acknowledgement of their right to seek for themselves the benefits of participation in the modern world.

During the 1960's, two additional developments—in interesting ways complementary—appear to have had a major impact on the evolution of body-art consciousness in the United States and Europe. The Peace Corps and comparable European programs made possible experience of other cultures—particularly of the "Third World"—outside the usual sanitized touristic framework, introducing participants to new attitudes toward the body (including dress and adornment). At about the same time, the "Hippie Movement" accomplished a similar expansion of consciousness, reflected in exposure to (and, in some cases adoption of) a non-European (predominantly Asian or Native American) attitude toward the body. Tattoo was rejuvenated; men began to pierce their ears, women to pierce their ears multiply, and occasionally their nostrils. During the 1970's, Women's Liberation and Gay Liberation asserted—even celebrated—peoples' control over their own bodies, sometimes expressed in previously anathemized [intensely disliked] forms of body art. Subsequent developments, originating among the Punks, further challenged entrenched conventions about the presentation of the self.

5   These gains in information and understanding, this opening up of new possibilities, were accompanied, however, by a kind of cultural homogenization. Although there are a few exceptions, "modernity" has been realized largely at the expense of cultural diversity, particularly as regards the more extreme forms of body art. Beyond more or less subtle educational, religious and "life-style" pressures to conform to more generalized, essentially anonymous "national"—and international—systems of dress and adornment, a number of governments have gone so far as to apply legal sanctions to more traditional modes of body art. There is, in short, a certain irony in the fact that at a time when advanced artists, scholars and theoreticians in Europe and Euro-America are discovering the formal, conceptual, sociological and psychological richness of tattoo and other forms of body art, the forms themselves are disappearing from the cultures which have nurtured and refined them over thousands of years.

Such a statement, of course, begs a very large question: despite their wide distribution, the historical record of irreversible forms of body art is incomplete. Skeletal materials preserve evidence of skull modelling and altered dentition [tooth appearance], and may eventually reveal whether or not a person was tattooed; since skin does not ordinarily survive in archaeological contexts, only through such a breakthrough can the antiquity of the medium be revealed, except for the times and places (such as ancient Egypt, Pre-Columbian Peru, and parts of the Arctic, Central Asia, and Indonesia) where intentional or accidental mummification of human remains took place. The earliest firm evidence for tattooing yet recovered comprises patterns of dots and lines on the body of a priestess of Hathor from the XIth Dynasty of ancient Egypt, around 2200 B.C. The earliest appearances of ear, nose, and lip piercing or of skull modelling or altered dentition have not, to my knowledge, been noted in the archaeological literature.

At another level, determining the ultimate age of body art in human history is essentially of academic interest; given the probability that the few comparatively simple techniques involved were independently discovered more than once, a single origin for any of them is unlikely. Nevertheless, in view of their wide distributions, the major modes and techniques of body art would seem to be very old, and the historical dimensions of body art, particularly in the technical realm, can and should be pursued. Studies of the distribution of particular techniques *may* yield insights into their origins and diffusion. For example, tattooing in parts of the Arctic employs a very distinctive technique: a needle is used to draw a carbon-impregnated thread under the skin to produce linear patterns. Throughout most of Oceania, on the other hand, a small adze-shaped implement with multiple points attached to (or cut into) the blade is tapped with a rod to drive pigment into the skin. In Japan, south, southeast, and western Asia, and North Africa, points set into the end of a rod are pushed directly into the skin. (One may reasonably suspect that the nature and distribution of tattooing changed when, in European and Asian antiquity, metal needles became generally available; this has certainly been the case as electric machines began to replace hand-techniques early in the twentieth century.) Tattooing was not practiced among the dark-skinned peoples of sub-Saharan Africa, south Asia, Melanesia and Australia, since the pigment would not show up; cicatrization or scarification were typical of these areas.

Despite the comparatively simple technology involved, the forms of tattoo range (as noted earlier) from simple patterns made up of dots and lines—typical (for example) of early Egypt and Peru, the Islamic world, and northwestern India—to the highly stylized, stark black geometric shapes of Indonesia, Micronesia and Polynesia, to the large-scale, richly pictorial tradition of Japan. Yet, as is evident in several papers included here, the same technique and conceptual framework can produce strikingly different results, with correspondingly divergent meanings and functions, even among people who share a common heritage. Moreover, the functional contexts within which body art is produced are extremely diverse, and meanings are usually multiple, overlapping and interpenetrating. Tattoos with explicit religious associations, as in Coptic Christianity, are frequent, occurring in some branches of Buddhism and among Hindus and tribal peoples in some parts of India. These religious associations may be coupled with the idea that one's tattoos, inalienable in this life, can be bartered to accomplish the transition to the afterlife. A related tradition encompasses designs intended to protect against illness or other misfortune; tattooed charms to ward off the evil eye are widely distributed in the Islamic world, and Hawaiian warriors wore tattoos to protect them in battle.

Tattoos and piercings also occur as emblems of accomplishment— among Inuit whaling captains and head-takers in Indonesia and Irian Jaya, for example. They may be the hallmarks of a traditional way of life, as with Tiv, Ga'anda, or Nuba women's scars, or Tlingit women's labrets. Or they may reflect modernity, as with Tiv and Baule adoption of letters and numbers—or wristwatches—as scarification motifs, or tattoos of Hindu deities by Gujarati men. From an iconographical point of view, the importance of the lizard motif to Polynesian peoples, but also to Africans is clear. It seems plausible that the jewel-like reticulation of the skins of certain lizards and other reptiles may have represented a paradigm for ornamenting the human skin.

10 Marking of the skin, or some piercings, may indicate group-membership, such as tattooed "caste-marks" among the tribal peoples of Dangs in western India, or tribal scarifications among the Yoruba and other African peoples. Marks may record significant events in the life of an individual, such as initiation into the Butwa Society among the Tabwa, nubility [of marriageable age] among the Ga'anda and their neighbors of northeastern Nigeria, the Nuba, the Tlingit of the northwest coast of North America, or marriage among Ainu women of northern Japan. Distinctive tattoos

were put on to memorialize a deceased relative in traditional Hawaii and among the Yoruba. Tattoos may refer to vocation, as among Japanese firemen or palanquin-bearers, or female musicians, dancers, and courtesans in ancient Egypt. Yoruba women's tattoos, Tabwa, Ga'anda and Nuba scarification, various Tiv forms, and some early Edo (Japanese) tattoos show a willingness to endure pain in order to please a lover; a related idea seems embodied in Newar conceptions that the wounding process—the record of suffering—accrues religious merit. Intriguingly, practically all the African papers indicate the importance of the abdomen—and particularly the navel—in initiating women's programs of body scarification. More or less explicit reference to the woman's childbearing function, to the succession of the generations, seems to be involved in most cases. Whatever else they may embody, the explicitly erogenous content of African women's body scarification—largely, it seems, in tactile terms—is clear. . . .

Body art which signals status—high or low—ranges from the Maori *moko*, the tattoos of the Scythian chief interred Pazyryk, an Inuit whaling captain's labrets, or a Marquesan chief's full-body tattoo, to the pictorial tattoos of a Japanese gangster (*yakuza*) or the markings of a slave or habitual criminal in various cultures. A fundamental aspect of these questions of context relates to the question of visibility. Modern plastic surgery seeks to camouflage its procedures, realizing a "natural" look, whereas traditional forms tend toward ostentation. Depending on prevailing attitudes, visibility may be manipulated in order to accomplish a particular social objective. Conceptualization of the serial development of body art over time as a "work in progress," is opposed to the negative associations of being "incomplete."

As implied by the foregoing, irreversible modes of body art amount to a quintessential imposition of a conceptual—cultural—order upon nature. Given their heavy loading of cultural values, the media of irreversible body art are typically taken for granted by insiders and arouse strong (predominantly negative) feelings among outsiders—usually fascination blended with distaste or even repugnance. Institutionalized repression is one frequent reaction. For present-day Europeans and Euro-Americans such reactions may be seen as a response to the sense of potency associated with body art which has been largely neutralized (by familiarity and facility) in other areas of art-making. Instances of such potency, when the inscription of a line was believed to affect the flow of energy in the universe, survive in the anthropological and art historical record, such as the print by Kuniyoshi showing Nichiren quelling the storm by writing the Buddhist invocation, "Hail to the jewel in the lotus" on a wave. In Nepal, there are traditions of magic writing which could cause or stop earthquakes, tornados, or other natural phenomena; additional examples include Navajo powder-drawings used in healing disease and rock- or ground-paintings by Australian aborigines intended to reactivate the creative centers of the universe. The diversity, apparent antiquity, wide geographical distribution, and artistic potency of irreversible modes of body art as a vehicle of human expression would seem to merit more attention than has previously been paid by students of art and culture.

Discussion Questions

1. Explain what the title "Marks of Civilization" suggests to you.
2. Why do you think wider exposure to different cultures in the nineteenth century tended "to reinforce the European/Euro-American sense of cultural superiority" (paragraph 3)?
3. Briefly describe what you know about the Peace Corps. Then, do a quick Internet search on this volunteer group. Based on what you learn and what you can infer, explain why you think Peace Corps volunteers might be more accepting than average Americans of "non-European" attitudes toward the body?
4. Rubin discusses various reasons that non-Western peoples around the world have for getting tattoos: to prepare for the afterlife; to protect against disease or physical harm; to mark a significant event or accomplishment, specific group membership, or occupation; or to communicate status (paragraphs 8–12). Which of these reasons might apply to contemporary Europeans or Euro-Americans who choose to get tattoos or piercings? Explain.
5. Rubin mentions the "sense of potency associated with body art" that might evoke negative responses from society (paragraph 13). What "potency" or power do you find in the display of tattoos or body piercings in our culture?

The Body Jigsaw
PHILIPPE LIOTARD

A professor of the sociology of sports at the University of Montpellier in southern France, Philippe Liotard is also cofounder of the avant-garde journal Quasimodo. *Researching sports as spectacle, he has analyzed the 1998 World Cup Soccer championship between France and Brazil, an event witnessed by 2 billion fans worldwide. Criticizing the aggressive "us-against-them-attitude" encouraged in the arenas of politics, sports, media, and advertising, he defines the intense national awareness and community building that characterized preparation for the event in France. He has also written on sports medicine, noting that the social goals of elite performance drive most athletes to seek supplements from their doctors, whose ethics should instead focus on sustaining health. In contemporary competitive culture, Liotard concludes, "medicine is turning toward satisfying desires, spurred by images of well-being and youth." He is a regular contributor to the* UNESCO [United Nations Educational, Scientific, and Cultural Organization] Courier, *which originally published the following article in 2001.*

As you read, pay special attention to the international perspective that Liotard assumes as the writer for a UN publication.

———————————— ✦ ————————————

Imagine the body as a canvas, a space to mix and match physical and cultural elements in defining who or what you want to be. Here lies the great paradox. The scarring and piercing of tribal aesthetics are all the rage in rich countries, while in the South, western ideals are coveted by a monied few.

In 1976, the punks barged into the lives of the reserved British with a bang. Disrespect was their word of order, as they went about ranting against the predictable world mapped out by their elders. They insulted the Queen and heaped abuse on nuclear energy, the economy, pollution, work and the media.

For even greater shock value, they tapped the power of the image. They spat on staid English conventions by donning a revolting, yet carefully studied appearance. A skirt could no longer be called a skirt, and punks gleefully paraded in torn, stained and gaudy clothes, marrying colours against all the cannons of good taste. They cut their hair into crests, horns and other shapes, plastered themselves with lurid make-up and wore chains. They covered their arms, faces, necks and heads with tattoos, reinvented piercing using safety-pins, studs and rings in their noses, eyebrows, lips and cheeks, and went so far as to deliberately scar themselves.

With their altered, rebel bodies, the punks quickly gave birth to a charged self-image. Their very own promoters conspired with the media they despised and turned them into symbols of decadence, before exporting their bodily aesthetics throughout Europe, North America and Japan.

5   Now, a quarter of a century later, the punks have spawned a loyal following. Top models, sporting personalities, singers and show-business stars jostle to display original hairstyles and body piercings. In rich countries, teenage girls show off their navel rings and stick out their bejewelled tongues, while boys wear rings in their eyebrows. Twenty-five years on, the socially-scorned practices of piercing or altering one's body have become musts for counting on the fashion scene. Young westerners have appropriated once "underground" practices to gain entry into the trendy but ultimately mainstream club.

There is, however, a paradox in all this. One would expect originality and innovation. In fact, what we are witnessing is a sweeping trend of cultural mix and match, drawing on body-altering techniques long used by non-western cultures for purposes of religion, aesthetics or identity. The American artist Fakir Musafar coined the term "modern primitives," giving rise to a new ideal, a patchwork that "tribalizes" the western body. For the past 50 years, he has explored alternative forms of spirituality incorporating primitive body decoration and rituals.

How did these alternative ways of changing the body travel so far afield? What drives young westerners to have tattoos from the South Sea islands or Japan? What do these "tribal" or "primitive" markings and decorations mean in a western society?

Certainly not a return to the rituals that originally produced them: most of those who go for such adornments know nothing about these distant practices. Moreover, the bodies now being used as models were those that were stigmatized and displayed during colonial exhibitions in Europe and the United States right up to the early 20th century. They were curiosity objects and more significantly, living symbols of the supposed "backwardness" of the colonized peoples. Seen through European eyes, piercing, body scars and elongated lips, necks and ears were evidence of "barbarism," justifying the West's self-appointed duty to civilize. Such practices incarnated the opposite of the ideal "civilized" body.

By way of homage to the civilizations the colonial powers seemingly sought to stamp out, the vanguard of the "modern primitives" set out to investigate these body rituals. The "tribal aesthetics" of Maria Tashjian, who owns a chain of body-alteration shops in the United States, is vaunted as a way to educate people by preserving the memory of extinct cultures and passing on their idea of beauty. Through piercing, stretching the ear-lobe and body scarring, we can thus create a jigsaw of ancient and modern aesthetics.

Others such as Musafar see these practices as the chance to work on one's own profound sense of Self. "Body play," in his words, consists of experimenting with every known body-alteration technique. By willingly going through the initiation ordeals of traditional societies, one actually relives a primal experience that has long been forgotten in the industrialized world. It is the path towards rediscovering an original innocence.

FORGET ABOUT THOSE BLONDE SURFERS

What's important is not the markings left on the body, says Musafar. Instead, what matters is the confrontation with physical pain that takes one toward another plane of consciousness, shunned in western societies where all is done to combat suffering. But unlike the physical and symbolic violence of initiation rites in traditional societies, these bodily alterations are the fruit of a conscious personal choice.

Such discourse, however, will be rarely heard among the millions of people who flirt with body decorating. The vast majority are merely fulfilling the modern-day desire for self-knowledge and recognition from others. They might invoke aesthetics, spirituality, sex games or the desire to belong to a group, but whatever the reason, the process of altering the body and putting it to the test comes down to playing with identity. This reflects a profound cultural shift.

The urge to assert oneself goes hand in hand with a desire to challenge social norms and values, and to advocate different ways of experiencing, feeling and displaying one's body. Many fans of body-art, piercing and tattooing say they can no longer accept the western model of a sanitized, bland, alienated body.

The ideals of the blue-eyed blonde and the Californian surfer with the sleek and muscular bronzed body have to go. In this light, altering one's body becomes a battle against conventional appearance, a quest to give meaning to a life deemed otherwise insignificant.

To this end, it's not enough to go shopping for traditions. Piecing together a body can also be done using modern materials, knowledge and techniques. By inserting foreign objects under their skin, some body artists are creating protuberances on foreheads,

10

15

breastbones and forearms to radically challenge age-old perceptions of the physical self.

A BATTLE AGAINST CREEPING STANDARDIZATION

All these interventions can be seen as a quest to escape a destiny
spelt out in terms of sex, age and social origin. In this sense, they
have political implications. By shattering models, rejecting beauty
standards circulated in the mass media and asserting the right to
do, wear and display what they see fit, this avant-garde is holding
up the body as one of the last bastions where individual freedom
can be expressed.

Faced with the pressure to conform, to discipline one's body
in order to meet economic and social demands, constructing an
appearance becomes the royal road to upsetting normality. Everyone becomes an actor, capable of displaying their body in a
unique way. Rather than sinking into the crowd, they spark a
chain of reactions (grounded or not), from attraction and fascination to rejection and fear.

The refusal to comply with social norms, the awareness that
looking different has an impact, is all part of a battle against
creeping standardization. In this light, such a philosophy stands
at opposite ends from the promise of cosmetic surgery, diets and
the like.

Television and the Internet are giving play to all these trends.
Day after day, we are exposed to a million ways of perceiving the
body, culled from past and present, from the imagination and real
experiments. Such depictions remind us that the body is not
about a static anatomy, and that there is more than one way to
signal membership to a group. They also remind us that culture is
always on the move. What is exotic one day is undesirable the
next and rediscovered later. The globalization of images has
spawned multiple models of the "civilized" body, breaking with
the western standard-bearer.

DRESSED TO KILL IN KINSHASA

20   In developing countries, however, those with money go to no ends
to cling to the most common western model, plucked straight out
of television soap-operas. South American immigrants in the
United States go for breast implants, lighten their skin and bleach

their hair. In southern Africa and among African Americans, skin-lighteners and hair-straightening products are all the rage. The famed sapeurs of Kinshasa, in the Democratic Republic of Congo, make enormous sacrifices to keep up with what they see as the latest in Parisian chic. Cosmetic surgery is as popular in the U.S. as in South America, where women have operations that bring them eerily close to the Barbie doll ideal. In Asia, they ask surgeons to attenuate the "slant" of their eyes. . . . Does a perceived or real context of political and economic domination lead some to hide their specific features? "Westernizing" the human body reads like a strategy to fit in with globalization.

For now, creating a hybrid ideal of the body is a game for the privileged. Among the poor, only a minority is going about removing the stigmas they have historically borne. But popularizing this new ideal is stirring debate. By hijacking appearance codes and adopting body-altering techniques that were originally designed for medical purposes, people are carving in flesh the rules of a new game. Their efforts will likely herald an all-round confusion over what norms, if any, govern the human body.

Discussion Questions

1. Besides the examples of body piercing and tattooing, describe other "underground" fashions or behaviors that you think have become "mainstream."

2. Describe a social "initiation rite" important to your own family, subculture, set of friends, or clique that is accompanied by a dramatic change in appearance. Then explain the meaning of that new "look" or fashion.

3. If, as Liotard states, some body art expresses freedom and identity, compare and contrast such expressions to the bodybuilder's goals in Ewen's article "Hard Bodies" in Chapter 2.

4. Liotard refers to body modifications as expressions of *rebellion against* "the pressure to conform, to discipline one's body in order to meet economic and social demands" (paragraph 17). Compare and contrast this discipline of conformity with the discipline that the bodybuilder practices in Ewen's article. To what extent is being tattooed or pierced a way of "looking different"? To what extent is it another sort of discipline over the body (paragraph 18)?

5. On one hand, tattooing and body piercing may be a way of "rejecting beauty standards circulated in the mass media." On the other hand, since youth are "faced with the pressure to conform," body art may also reflect new standards of desirable behavior. Explain which motivation you think is stronger: rebellion or conformity.

Tattooed: A Participant Observer's Exploration of Meaning

SHANNON BELL

After receiving her B.A. in anthropology from the University of California, Berkeley, Shannon Bell spent three months interning at the Smithsonian Institution's National Museum of American History in the Social History Department's Costume Collection, and another month at the Oakland Museum of California through support from the Costume Society of America. She then moved to New York City to pursue her M.A. in Visual Culture: Costume Studies at New York University and a career in the field of Costume History and Curation, Visual Culture, and the Anthropology of Adornment. In 2000 she served as a curatorial intern at the Guggenheim Museum for the Georgio Armani exhibit, featuring work by the Italian fashion designer.

In her article, Bell admits up front that she is a "heavily tattooed woman." As you read, consider how her personal background might influence her interpretations of the tattooing subculture, how it might help her understand some aspects of this culture, and how it might bias her viewpoint toward other aspects. For example, which section of the article is longest and why?

✦

As a heavily tattooed woman, the depth, complexity and variation of meaning ascribed to tattoos fascinate me. This essay will explore this variation through a discussion of the subculture of tattooed people and the relationship of tattoos to identity. Although the scope of this paper can only scratch the surface of the meaning associated with tattoos, I hope to be able to shed some light on these interpretations through my fifteen years of living with tattoos and tattooed people. I am primarily concerned with American and Western tattoo culture, since aboriginal tattooing has been covered extensively in the anthropological literature and for other reasons which will become clear through the course of this essay. I will begin my discussion with a brief history and overview of tattooing in different cultures to put this intriguing and complex American subculture into context.

CONTEXTUAL BACKGROUND

Tattooing has been widely documented in numerous ancient and aboriginal cultures from the Coptics to the Maoris to the Celts, from Brazil to Africa to Japan. The purpose of the tattoo (customarily done by hand, and not machine, in aboriginal cultures) is usually ornamental, ritual, or identity-oriented in nature. Many tattoos cover a large part of the body and are received during rites of passage to manhood, marriage, or as marks of affiliation, age, and wisdom (Sanders 8). In New Zealand's Maori tribes the *moko*, a facial tattoo, was a direct representation of identity, in that each family had a personal moko that was further personalized for individual family members. In this way, their moko was like a signature, which they actually used when signing documents; that is, instead of signing their names they drew their moko, which was a true representation of self. Aboriginal tattooing is generally abstract; they rarely use literal images per se, their tattoos being primarily composed of geometric shapes, dots, and lines that may have meaning to them but are not always exact representations of *things*.

One of the most artistically advanced forms of tattooing is found in the Japanese culture. For hundreds of years the practice of tattooing has been passed down from *Hori* (tattoo mentor) to student. Japanese tattoos use Japanese mythology as subject matter and are conventionally done as entire *body suits* (covering most of the body). Images are chosen from a prescribed set of imagery although artistic interpretation of the mythological characters may vary. There was a time when warriors and elites were tattooed in Japan, but currently only *Yakuza* (gangsters) and the Japanese youth, who emulate a more American style to be discussed later, take part in this practice. There is an incredible stigma attached to tattoos in Japan today, so much so that the tattooed are segregated from the rest of society and must have their own bath houses, brothels, and bars (Troy Denning, tattoo artist: personal communication 1998).

American tattooing has been evolving since there has been an America to speak of. Its Anglo-Saxon form is thought to have derived from the ancient tribes of the British Isles and is noted to have been practiced at various times throughout history by the aristocracy. As folklore has it, Captain Cook coined the term "tattoo" during his voyage to the South Pacific in 1769; he derived it from the Tahitian word "ta-tu," meaning "to mark," also associated with the sound made by the Tahitian tattoo instrument

(Sanders 14). American tattooing has always been unique, which is why it needs a separate discourse from ancient or aboriginal tattooing. American tattoos are image-oriented, being primarily literal interpretations of *things*, unlike aboriginal tattoos. For the most part, American tattooed people will have a variety of images (or a single image) that stand alone against the skin, unlike the Japanese body suit that is all-encompassing and of a single theme. As a consumer society, it is not surprising that we are attracted to images of *things* and have tattooed ourselves accordingly. Contemporary Japanese youth also tend to have this collage-like, literal, image-oriented type of American tattoos, as opposed to the traditional Japanese type described above. American tattooed people have historically been military personnel, convicts, circus freaks, bikers, and other marginal people, although the current popularity has associated tattoos with celebrities, models, and the middle class.

5   In the following discussion of tattooing in relation to subculture and identity, I work with my belief that, although the act of tattooing may be thought to have meaning that is separate from the chosen image itself, the two are inextricably linked and cannot be analyzed alone.

SUBCULTURE

Tattoos have long been associated with the exotic "other" and are therefore fodder for imagination and use by subcultures of all types. American greasers, bikers, hippies, and punks have all used tattoos as part of their anti-mainstream adornment. Tattoos, as a visual means to separate oneself from the normalized culture, can be thought of as a "loaded choice," a choice that draws attention to oneself intentionally (Hebdige 101). Although Dick Hebdige refers to specific images, clothing, and hairstyles as signs, I believe that the appearance of *any* permanent mark on the body is a sign to the mainstream culture of one's separation, whether one meant it as such or not, regardless of the chosen image. Imagery comes into play where specific and personal identity is concerned, but, in relation to normalization, a tattoo is enough to separate oneself from society at large.

This separation from society is an essential factor in my theory about tattoos and why people get them. Despite one's affiliation with a particular subculture, tattoos are a sure way to dissociate one from the rest of society; a dissociation tattooees themselves sometimes do not fully realize the impact of. A common theme in the literature (Demello, "Not Just for Bikers"; Sanders; Hewitt) is that tattooing is a struggle for individualization in a society that is increasingly impersonal. (This dissociative individuality can be used against you, as in television shows such as *America's Most Wanted*, where a tattoo is used to identify a fugitive.) Tattoos are seen as a physical, visual resistance to the virtual (impermanent) and conservative world that we are now living in. Although I did not appreciate it until well into my 20s, I now enjoy the idea that by having tattoos I assure myself that I will never be part of the "straight" world. To use Vaclav Havel's terminology, being tattooed is synonymous with "living in the truth," one's personal truth, my truth. The tattooed lifestyle will always be resistance-oriented, overlying and encompassing other subcultures because of its basic truthful nature. The act of being tattooed is, in itself, confrontational to the status quo, an idea to be discussed further when I speak about identity.

• • •

IDENTITY

As we have seen, aboriginal cultures have used tattooing to mark themselves with their identity. Japanese Yakuza tattoos can also be thought of as identity markers since one is most likely a gangster if adorned with a *body suit*. Just as clothes and hairstyles allow us to decorate ourselves according to personal aesthetics and identity, choosing how we will be perceived by others, so does the permanent decoration of tattooing.

As an introduction, Paul Willis's theory on *symbolic creativity* is useful for this discussion on identity: "Most young people's lives are not involved with the arts and yet are actually full of expressions, signs, symbols through which individuals and groups seek creatively to establish their presence, identity and meaning" (1). Being tattooed as an act of symbolic creativity in everyday life is part of the common experience of some young people; youth being key to identity formation and when most people get their first tattoos, professionally or on the street (regardless of its illegality under the age of eighteen or total illegality in some states).

Young or old, symbolic creativity concerning the formation of identity is crucial. For some, tattoos are part of this identity and these tattoos can be symbolic of many things. Many choose to honor their family members and lovers by name, display their religious beliefs (ironically, and importantly, despite scripture's words against marking the body) or their association with the military, patriotism being a common theme of tattoos especially in the 1930s and '40s. Increasingly, tattoos have become more personal, with the advent of custom designs discussed above. (An example of extreme personal identity association is a friend of mine who is named "Alien Boy" because his entire upper body is tattooed like H. R. Geiger's biomechanical *Alien* creature of movie fame.) What I propose is that the motivation behind this symbolically creative act and subsequent choice of image varies from person to person, but, to begin my discussion of meaning, can be categorized and analyzed by gender and class.

In terms of gender, tattoos, which have been traditionally associated with men, can be seen as a resistance to the common ideals of female beauty. Tattooing has long been associated with maleness because of the stereotyped imagery of tattooed people and the pain involved in the process. The subject matter for women's tattoos, however, is usually decidedly different from men's. Women tend to choose flowers and softer, more personal images and put them in places like the lower back, shoulder, or ankle. Men, on the other hand, choose more obvious places, of these the most popular being the upper arm. Men often adorn themselves with macho imagery that associates them with a group, such as the Hell's Angels, or they choose decorative but strong imagery such as dragons and the like.

A discussion of class brings us to the inclusion of the most stereotypical, macho, tattooed person, the convict: "(A) person so low in class he is almost unclassifiable." Margo Demello's *Convict Body* clearly stipulates prison tattoos as identity claimers that include group and/or gang associations. The difference between an inmate and convict, according to Demello, is based on how covered with tattoos one is, this being a direct reflection of the acceptance of the convict lifestyle and lifelong marginalization. Demello points out that prison tattoos are technically different from other types of tattooing because of the makeshift technology used while incarcerated. Professional tattoos, done in tattoo parlors or shops, use color, which is unavailable in prison, and are not done with single needles. These differences in tattoo technique and imagery set up visible class markers between prison/street and professional tattooing.

Professional tattooers are thought of as having some sort of artistic talent and are legitimized by the costliness of their time (about $80–$125/hr). These differences make professional tattooing a pastime of the middle class. Because tattooing has had historic association with the lower class and deviant subculture, Demello suggests, in her 1995 article "Not Just for Bikers Anymore" (37), that the media and middle class have worked together to tame the image of tattoos. Before tattoos became trendy, there was an upsurge in the number of regular, "normal," people getting tattoos in the late '80s. At the same time, many books and articles associated current tattoo trends with primitivism of a modern nature (Vale and Juno; Hardy). The recurrent theme was that the urge to be tattooed was *primitive, natural, and universal*. It was, and still is, constantly associated with deep, personal meaning, rites of passage and as a key to spiritual enlightenment through pain (Hewitt 27). Although these associations may be applicable and meaningful for tattooed people of all classes, it is primarily the middle class, customers of artists, which feels the need to emphasize this aspect of tattooing. This ascribed spiritual meaning softens the anti-establishment, crude stereotype of a tattooed person and has paved the way for what we now see as tattoos becoming increasingly popular in the mainstream.

Despite this softening and popularity, I argue that tattoos will never be fully accepted into the mainstream, and to illustrate this point, I would like to further differentiate between two types of tattooed people. Corresponding with the level of dedication to the marginalized lifestyle between inmate and convict, I propose a differentiation between people who *have tattoos* and *tattooed people*. People who "have tattoos" often have only one or two, and they are usually personal images in places easily hidden from view. These people avoid the label of "tattooed person" due to peer or family pressure and the negative societal associations made with tattoos. "Tattooed people," on the other hand, have many bright or bold tattoos in obvious places, closer to the idea of a Japanese body suit in terms of body coverage. These people have decided to cross that point of no return, usually choosing to socialize with tattooists and other tattooed people within the subculture, avoiding the stares and numerous questions of outsiders, fully embracing marginalization.

In addition, I suggest that the recent co-option by the media and trendiness of tattoos as fashion has driven some people who "have tattoos" to the act. These people may not have become tattooed if they did not believe that it was fully accepted by the mainstream. Although I am pleased by the open mindedness of these new recruits, and their recognition of tattoos as identity signifiers similar to clothing, I am concerned that they are being duped into believing that tattoos have lost their stigma. From my personal experience of travel within and outside the United States, this is far

15

from true. The response to tattoos is still very strong and differs from culture to culture and city to city. It takes a strong will and *sense of self* (identity) to withstand the blatant and piercing stares. I feel that many people swept up in the tattoo trend are not always prepared to be separated from society in this way, or may not have thought about its meaning and consequences long enough before-hand (this may explain the rise of tattoo removal services). Being heavily tattooed, even during this trend, is cause for prying questions and mistreatment from curious and overzealous onlookers. Being tattooed is still a "Freak Show."

• • •

DISCUSSION

• • •

In conclusion, I would like to explore the further emphasis on spirituality and primitivism by the middle class mentioned previously. I believe that it may be related to a fear that the American, consumer, visually based society is superficial in nature and to the belief that the act of tattooing must transcend this lack of depth in some way. This adds another dimension to my discussion of meaning and I hope to bring this important point to light. The unique quality of American tattooing, its imagery and literalness, is a product of this surface-oriented society:

> [Surface] is a characteristic of our fast-flowing time, where everything has to communicate fast and move on. . . . Depth is a category that pretends to penetrate surface. . . . First impressions are decisive [and] surface is individuated by apparel. . . . The human body is not very attractive compared to a cheetah, that's why we have fashion. . . . The search for interiority merely creates more surface. (Blonsky 17)

Although Marshall Blonsky is referring to fashion, it is not a far leap to the permanent adornment of tattooing. Tattooing, however, sets up a unique dichotomy of *surface-permanence* unparalleled by other forms of adornment and decoration. Clothes allow people to change their mind, follow the fashion trends, and recreate their identity in a way that tattooing does not. Blonsky goes on: "The nude . . . only creates another garment, one slightly boring after a while. All attempts at depth end up in surface" (18). Perhaps this is why we decorate ourselves, to ease the boredom of the nude, to add visual depth to the common, which only brings us back again to the external and surface that are the images on our skin. Finally, I draw attention to the recurring question, "Is it real?" and the increasing popularity of temporary tattoos and *Henna* (Indian tattoos that wear off). Together, these observations give credence to my disbelief that real tattoos will be accepted by the mainstream in the long term, since it was quickly figured out how to solve the permanence problem. "How much did that cost?" is another frequent question which, although it makes sense in our consumer-based society, boggles me when asked in regards to something that is a permanent mark on your skin, lasting a lifetime. These various questions exemplify the fear of permanence, which is the most common objection to tattoos. This says much to me about society and the unwillingness to commit to identity and accept the consequences. To do something permanent is to be unable to take it back—it is to live in truth for eternity.

Works Cited

Blonsky, Marshall. *American Mythologies*. New York: Oxford UP, 1992.

Demello, Margo. "The Convict Body: Tattooing among Male American Prisoners." *Anthropology Today* 9.6 (Dec. 1993): 10.

———. "Not Just for Bikers Anymore: Popular Representations of American Tattooing." *Journal of Popular Culture* 29.3 (Winter 1995): 37–52.

Hardy, D. E. *Tattoo Time: New Tribalism*. Honolulu: Hardy Marks Publications, 1988.

Havel, Vaclav, and Jan Vladislav, ed. *Living in Truth*. London: Faber and Faber, 1989.

Hebdige, Dick. *Subculture: The Meaning of Style*. New York: Routledge, 1988.

Hewitt, Kim. *Mutilating the Body: Identity in Blood and Ink*. Bowling Green, OH: Bowling Green State University Popular Press, 1997.

Sanders, Clinton R. *Customizing the Body: The Art and Culture of Tattooing*. Philadelphia: Temple UP, 1989.

Vale, V., and Andrea Juno, eds. *Re/Search #12: Modern Primitives*. San Francisco: Re/Search Publications, 1989.

Willis, Paul. *Common Culture: Symbolic Creativity at Play in the Everyday Cultures of the Young*. Buckingham, England: Open UP, 1993.

Discussion Questions

1. Summarize the motivations for "body modification" in Liotard's article and then in Bell's article. Explain the motivations in Bell's article that differ from Liotard's analysis.
2. Liotard seems to write from the viewpoint of a journalist reporting a social phenomenon, while Bell seems to write from the viewpoint of a "participant" in tattooing. Analyze the difference in the two writers' attitudes toward their subject. Quote short phrases from each article to illustrate this difference.
3. Explain the distinction Bell makes between people who have tattoos and "tattooed people." Why is this difference important?
4. Explain how tattooing impacts gender difference, according to Bell. Do you agree or disagree? Explain.
5. Bell suggests that, for women, tattoos may express a macho tolerance of pain (paragraph 11). However, she also advances the theory that pain is, for some, "a key to spiritual enlightenment" (paragraph 13). Do you find these two interpretations of the pain of tattooing incompatible? Why or why not?

Pumped, Pierced, Painted and Pagan
Joe Woodard

After earning a Ph.D. in political philosophy from Claremont Grad-uate School, Canadian journalist Joe Woodard worked for both the U.S. and Canadian governments and taught at colleges and univer-sities in the two countries. Currently religion editor at the Calgary Herald, *Woodard writes book reviews and news stories on religious and ethical issues. He has also reported on Canada's national poli-tics and armed forces, as well as international "peace-keeping" inter-ventions, as in Kosovo and East Timor. In addition, he now serves as vice president of the Canada Family Action Coalition, a citizens' action organization motivated by faith-based Judeo-Christian morality. Before the* Alberta Report *ceased publication in 2003, Woodard was a regular contributor to the magazine, which origi-nally published the following article in 1998.*

Before you read, consider the four elements of the title. What do you anticipate the article to be about? As you read, count the num-ber of times the author refers to body modification as "mutilation,"

not including the three uses quoted from interviews. How does this
term convey his attitude about the topic?

───────────── ✦ ─────────────

Plastic surgeon Benjamin Shore was a little flustered last year
when a 30-something female patient returned to his office, requesting that her breast implants be redone. A year earlier, he had
given her a large set of "double-D cup" saline implants, 500 cubic
centimetres or half-a-litre in size. Now she was back, wanting 800 cc
implants. "She wasn't an exotic dancer," says the Brampton, Ontario, physician. "She was just a woman who wanted to feel good
about herself, and she thought this would do it." But her case also
proved to be the last time he cooperated in such an extravagance.
"Six months later, she was back, wanting the smaller implants,"
he recounts. "With all that weight on her chest, whenever she lay
on her back, she couldn't breathe."

Though plastic surgeons are voicing some discomfort with
the trend, unnaturally large and clearly artificial breasts represent the cutting edge of feminine fashion. The August edition of
the fashion magazine *Allure* surveyed American plastic surgeons,
asking the age-old question, "what do women want?" And according to the doctors, "women today don't want to look natural but
supernatural." The size of the average implant has grown three to
four times, and more telling yet, women are voicing a preference for
high, round implants, over more anatomically-correct teardrop-
shapes. The new ideal has become the gravity-defying "half grape-
fruit" breast, popularized by the chiselled and sculpted former
star of *Baywatch*, Pamela Anderson: absurdly large, firm as a
football, and plainly artificial.

The growth of the breast augmentation industry has clearly
outstripped the needs of mastectomy patients and women genuinely short-changed by nature. During the Dow-Corning implant
fiasco, culminating in the 1992 ban against silicon implants, the
market briefly sagged. But the consumer horror stories about
scarring and supposed links to diseases like fibromyalgia had less
effect than might have been expected. Consumer confidence was
restored by the introduction of alternative saline implants, and
the procedure's popularity again began to soar. In the past six
years, the annual number of breast augmentations has climbed
400%, to over 120,000 in the United States and 10,000 in Canada.

But the desire for unnatural aesthetics is not limited to mam-
moth mammaries; tattooing, body-piercing and scarification are

equally hot trends in body fashion. Experts say all these kinds of cosmetic self-mutilation are unsurprising in our post-Christian culture. In fact, they are the ultimate in retro, a throwback to paganism. Edmontonian Sarai Jorgenson, 23, has accumulated seven tattoos on her breasts, neck, shoulders, back and stomach; and at the moment she has 19 piercings, mostly (though not exclusively) on her face. She wears her naturally blonde hair in green, purple or blue, with black dreadlocks, and people she went to high school with no longer recognize her on the street. She got her first tattoo at 15—a panther she later covered with a butterfly—and her first piercings at 18. "I was a shy person; I had low self-esteem," Ms. Jorgenson recounts. "But I love my body now; I think it's beautiful."

5   Ms. Jorgenson's first youthful forays into body art may have been hesitant; but her intentions now are fully and confidently thought out. "It's like Rufus Camphausen writes in his book, *The Return of the Tribal,* body art is the recovery of a practice 30,000 years old," she says. "We're simply developing modern medical ways of performing a natural human function." She laughs at the suggestion that her purpose is simply attention-seeking. "Like, I do this so people will insult me on the street?" she guffaws, shaking her array of silver rings. "Like, I want to make it really hard to find a job? No. I do this because I think it's beautiful. I look at the women in *Cosmopolitan,* and they look ridiculous. I look at the women in *Savage* magazine, women who look like me, and I think they're beautiful."

The Edmonton waitress just recently began her next body project, stretching her earlobes and nasal septum, and she has already lengthened her lobes three-quarters of an inch. She has no plans to pump up her breasts, both of which she says are adorned with nipple rings. Some time ago, she tried a little scarification, but like most white people, she cannot form the kinds of "keloid scars" that give scarified black people their "gorgeous" lumpy skin patterns. If scars are out for her, she might eventually try the Hindu practice of tongue-splitting, something just now catching on in Los Angeles. "What I'm doing is, I'm taking what I was born with and making it into what I want it to be," she explains patiently. "These are all just different forms of modifying my body. They're no stranger than steroid muscles or silicon breasts."

"The vast majority of women still want breasts that look natural," Dr. Shore reports. "But in the 1970s, that would have meant 100 cc to 120 cc implants. Today, what's considered natural are 375 cc to 450 cc implants. And I'd say about 10% of [Ontario] women now want them so much bigger than that, and so much higher, they're plainly artificial." Despite feminist claims about male oppression, however, he reports that "less than 1%" of women take such leaps into the unnatural from the prompting of husbands or boyfriends. "In almost every case, this is something the woman herself wants to do for herself," he muses. "I'm amazed whenever I have to say to a woman, that would look unnatural, or that would look artificial, and she still says, 'that's okay, that's what I want.' So I just won't take on those patients anymore."

Calgary plastic surgeon Gregory Waslen thinks that demand for "monster breasts" is largely a geographical phenomenon, oddly prevalent in grapefruit-growing states. "We're not California or Florida, here," he argues. "There's always a part of the market that wants something beyond the normal, but I'd guess that's no more than 2% of Alberta patients." In the normal 250 cc to 400 cc (C to D cup) range, breast augmentation now garners a 92% satisfaction rate from its patients, he says. Admittedly, up to 10% of Alberta patients and 50% of American patients subsequently return to their doctors for yet bigger breasts. The trend toward the gargantuan is simply a fad driven by shows like *Baywatch*, in Dr. Waslen's opinion, and it will soon run into its natural upper limit, a limit set by the frequency of "full-figure" backache.

According to the *Allure* survey, however, California's plastic surgeons have some doubts they will be able to hold the line at 1,000 cc implants, or full litre breasts. And magnifying the trend toward the unnatural, a small but growing proportion of women are asking for simultaneous breast implants and the liposuction of their hips, in the attempt to manufacture a body boyishly lean below the ribcage and bovine-bosomy above. They are apparently undeterred by a 3% to 5% complication rate (from internal scarring) for the breast augmentation alone.

New York University psychology professor Paul Vitz, author 10 of *Psychology as Religion*, suspects that monstrous breast augmentation is a fad. However, that sort of fad—cosmetic mutilation—has now been able to enter into the mainstream culture only because of the revival of paganism and the eclipse of the once-dominant Judeo-Christian ethic. "With the exception of [male] circumcision, Orthodox Judaism forbids any alteration of the body, even embalming," he says. "And the Christian tradition has been almost as strict." As the apostle Paul warns in 1 *Corinthians* 3, "Know you not that you are temples of God . . . and if any man defiles the temple of God, him shall God destroy." While modest *pierced* ear studs were traditionally thought permissible, the injunction against "defiling the temple" was understood to forbid everything from tattoos to sexual sterilization.

"There's a different understanding of the body in pagan or animistic cultures," says psychologist Vitz. In Christian cultures, he explains, the physical appetites must be disciplined, but the body is an essential part of human godliness. In pagan cultures, the body is something separate, alien to each person's "inner divinity," yet it belongs entirely to the person or tribe, to do with as they see fit. "As a result, the pagans take a far more extreme and violent attitude toward the domination of the body, as something needing artistic modification or transformation." This "customizing" of the body is not a private activity, however. The tribal group almost always dictates the form of such bodily modifications for anyone who belongs. So the customized bodies are not only painful, but usually highly visible.

"Clearly, all the unnatural breast enhancement today is seeking an effect that is entirely visible," says Dr. Vitz. "Breasts cease to be maternal objects. They even become less and less objects of sexual touch. They've become the 'high kitsch' of an image culture," and primarily signs of status, like the silver rings around an African woman's neck. A century ago, energetic western women might become obsessed with inner moral perfection and fall victim to moral scrupulosity, he continues. Today, however, they seek some vague aesthetic perfection and end up collecting more and more visible abnormalities, like collagen-enhanced lips. "Unnatural breasts aren't the only new cosmetic mutilations," he adds. The new paganism encourages everything from liposuction to body-piercing and scarification.

Tattooing today is almost as common as ear-piercing, says Roman Corkery, an artist with Calgary's "Symbols of Strength" tattoo and body-piercing studio. And as popular as tattooing is, the demand for body piercing has begun to surpass it. "Moms come in with their little 15-year-old daughters, getting little navel rings, then four of their friends come in, then eight more," he marvels. Daily, Mr. Corkery's mid-sized studio averages eight tattoos and a dozen piercings. Body piercing has given tattoos a real race into the mainstream, because its results are less permanent and cheaper. The holes themselves eventually vanish once the jewelry is removed; and piercing runs $20 to $50, while tattoos cost $100 to $500. Scarification and branding, still in the experimental stage in the U.S., have not yet arrived in Alberta.

Good statistics on the growth of these "body arts" are impossible to find, says Caroline Jeffries, owner of the To the Point piercing and Smiling Buddha tattoo studios. But until 15 years ago, Calgary supported only one full-time tattoo parlour; today it boasts a dozen. The first body piercing shop opened in 1991; now there are six. Not accounting for repeat customers, Calgary's 800,000 population may generate as many as 40,000 visits yearly to either sort of establishment.

As tattooing has entered the mainstream, the images of   15
demons, knives and nudes have given way to pictures of dolphins, flowers and Canadian flags, says body artist Corkery. And a high proportion of the women opt for a simple "ankle chain" or "woven armband" pattern. Likewise the majority of piercing enthusiasts opt for multi-earrings or a discreet nose stud. A more adventurous (or randy) minority—roughly 20% of the piercings at "Symbols of Strength"—are on the tongue and 5% to 10% are on the nipples or genitalia. Now available in both Britain and the U.S., but still a fringe interest even there, are the new Teflon and coral "inserts," used primarily to provide "devil's horns" that bond directly onto the customer's skull under the skin.

Anthropologist Claudia Launhardt, who teaches at Trinity Western University in Langley, B.C., agrees that the trend toward cosmetic self-mutilation reflects society's turn toward paganism. The forms of mutilation are consistent with traditional tribal practices the world over. Mutilations can indicate group membership and allegiance, like the tattoos of the Japanese *yakuza* criminal underworld. It can also assert a measure of social dependence. For example, the Manchu Chinese elites of the 19th century bound the feet of female infants almost from birth, partly because small feet were held to be marks of great beauty, but also because it rendered upper-class women almost incapable of walking.

However, there is one crucial difference between traditional tribal mutilations and (at least so far) the modern western equivalents, Prof. Launhardt insists. In tribal societies, the tribe, not the individual, confers the membership, dependence or the status of a particular mutilation.

"Here, so far, what we have is merely fashion or fad, because the individuals decide how they would like to change their bodies," Prof. Launhardt explains. "In a tribal society, the elders or the laws must say whether a warrior, having killed a lion, can now have a particular tattoo, or whether a woman, possessing so many cattle, can wear a certain kind of lip disk. These things are very real and binding marks of a person's status for life." In that sense, breast enhancement is much more tribal than modern body piercing, she argues, because bulbous breasts are an attempt to ape the rich and the famous of Hollywood. In Canada, although medically indicated reconstructive breast surgery is ordinarily covered by medicare, the usual fee for cosmetic work ranges from $4,000 to $4,500.

Cosmetic mutilation has certain repetitive features world-wide that may soon be reproduced in North America. For example, the Haida of the Pacific Northwest, the Kayapo of the Amazon and the Mursi of southern Ethiopia all wore "lip plates," stretching the lower lip either with or without puncturing it. "But the wealth of the material [used in lip plates] was important to the status conveyed, whether it be gold in the Amazon or ivory in Africa." Likewise, from childhood, both the Kikiyu of Africa and the Lao of northern Thailand stretched the necks of their high-born females with silver rings; their necks became so long, they needed the rings to support their heads.

20   Anthropologist Launhardt adds that in primitive cultures, cosmetic mutilation is often a badge of courage and ability to withstand pain. "Having killed a lion, a Dinka tribesman may be allowed a particular, very painful kind of tattoo," she explains. "Having proven his courage, the tattoo becomes the testimony to the pain he can bear." In North America, however, pain is generally something to be avoided at all costs, so mutilation did not become mainstream until modern anaesthesia made it relatively painless. "As our modern mutilations are made less painful," she predicts, "some people will be driven to find ever more extreme forms of mutilation."

And so they are: body artists in Los Angeles and New York are now experimenting with "skin braiding." Three long strips are cut from the flesh and left attached to the body only at the top. The strips are then braided and reattached at the bottom. The result is supposed to heal as a permanent skin braid.

Medical missionary John Patrick of Ottawa, a fellow of the Centre for Renewal in Public Policy, says that he has seen very little cosmetic mutilation during his many recent trips to central Africa. "Most of that has vanished," he reports. "They're new Christians leaving a pagan tradition, just as we're new pagans, leaving a Christian tradition." Yet he marvels at the rapid resurgence of self-mutilation in the West. "It seems to prove that, even when shorn of all hope, human beings still have a natural sense of the necessity of atonement."

For his part, Calgary plastic surgeon Peter Whidden sees little hope of resisting the invasion of the monster breasts. "I'd agree that, so far, maybe only 2% of the women here want huge, unnatural breasts," he says. "But these fads move north a lot faster than we like to think. There's a burlesque subculture developing, and I don't think we can stop it. Still, after 30 years of practice, I'm not going to start deforming little girls, even if they want me to."

Discussion Questions

1. Define "paganism" as discussed by several sources that Woodard quotes. To what extent does contemporary "society's turn toward paganism" (paragraph 16) help explain the popularity of body piercing and tattooing? Give examples of other behaviors or fashions that might indicate this "pagan" trend.
2. Explain how Woodard relates breast implants to other "body fashions."
3. Woodard's article was first published in a Canadian magazine. Which details in the article suggest that he is addressing both Canadian and *American* readers? Which details suggest that he treats the phenomena he reports as representing the same North American culture?
4. Classify the types of "authorities" that Woodard cites to provide examples and evidence about the social phenomena of body modification. For example, he initially quotes a plastic surgeon and then a body art "practitioner"— Sarai Jorgenson. Classify the other sources he incorporates in his article. Which type do you think offers the greatest insight into human behavior?

Marks of Shame: Tattoos and What to Do about Them
THEODORE DALRYMPLE

A physician and psychiatrist in a hospital and prison located in a British slum, Dalrymple is a columnist for London's The Spectator *and a contributing editor of New-York-based* City Journal, *which focuses on such domestic policy issues as school financing, policing strategy, welfare, urban architecture, and family policy. The* Journal *is supported by the conservative Manhattan Institute, "a think tank whose mission is to develop and disseminate new ideas that foster greater economic choice and individual responsibility" (according to their website). His latest book, a collection of his essays from* City Journal, *is titled* Life at the Bottom: The Worldview That Makes the Underclass *(2001). Here, he argues that long-term poverty is caused by liberal values encouraging the notions of victimization and social determinism. While blaming the decline of moral society on the "feel-good," nonjudgmental relativism of the 1960s, he takes a strong position against the lack of standards represented by the British underclass. Consistent with these views, the following article first appeared in* National Review *in 2002.*

———————— ✦ ————————

Rep. Lois Capps, Democrat of California, deserves some praise, however qualified: Her securing of money for the Liberty Tattoo Removal Program of San Luis Obispo County was, at least in theory, a good deed. It meant that she has a genuinely sympathetic appreciation of the plight of some of her poorer constituents.

Contrary to what her detractors and dyed-in-the-wool skeptics say, the social consequences of being tattooed, and therefore of tattoo removal, are by no means trivial or merely aesthetic. One might with justice adapt the old proverb about marriage to the adorning of the skin in this savage fashion: Tattoo in haste, repent at leisure.

Others also argue with the provenance of the funds that she has secured for the program: the Justice Department. To provide public funds for the amelioration of the consequences of private folly might be seen as an encouragement of that very folly. It sets up a perverse incentive. After all, if tattoos can be removed at public expense, why bother to think very carefully about having them done in the first place? Easy come, easy go.

But in fact the proposed terms under which tattoo removal will be performed at public expense are such that this cavalier attitude is unlikely to be promoted. The eligible tattooed will be those who have "gang-related" or "anti-social" tattoos so prominent as to prevent them from obtaining employment. The eligible tattooed will also have to promise not to tattoo themselves again, and to complete 16 hours of public service.

5   In any case, it seems to me highly unlikely that the kind of people who have themselves tattooed in this fashion ever give much thought to the long-term consequences of their decision. They have not hitherto been deterred by the expense of tattoo removal; it is unlikely, therefore, that they will henceforth be encouraged by its cheapness. The problem surely is that people who tattoo themselves in the first place don't think much about the future at all.

There are other, practical objections to the funding, however. The sum of money involved is very small: $50,000. According to a statement on Rep. Capps's website, this money will be used to hire a full-time program coordinator and for education to deter young people from getting tattoos. It is difficult to imagine that there will be much left over for the actual removal of tattoos, which tends to be an expensive business when performed properly. What is presented as tattoo removal is actually an expansion of a health-education bureaucracy of doubtful worth.

The removal of tattoos nevertheless remains a laudable aim, for they are often the visible sign that a man (only recently have women in any numbers had themselves tattooed) belongs to a violent, brutal, antisocial, and criminalized subculture. When a man with such tattoos says he wants them removed, therefore, he is in effect saying that he wants to change his life. He is tired of life among the tattooed.

And what is that life like? It is one of arbitrary and pointless aggression, caused by fragile egos, inflamed by the humiliation of personal failure and insignificance in an age that worships celebrity. It is a world in which a look, a glance, is taken as a challenge and is enough to provoke a vicious attack, for the guilty pursue where no man fleeth.

Several of my patients, for example, have had the words NO FEAR tattooed on the side of their neck, and all of them have been attacked in bars and pubs by other men of the tattooed class. The words are taken as an invitation to such an attack: for if a man says he has no fear, he must mean that he does not find other men fearful. Tough guys regard this as a terrible insult to their manhood, and so launch a preemptive strike. One of my patients thus adorned had had his skull fractured four times as a result.

Many tattooed people—particularly those with the most aggressive tattoos—have themselves tattooed at an early age, the age of indiscretion, when they strongly desire to join the subculture I have described. The consequences for them are long-lasting, however. Recently I met a man with several tattoos, among them one on the palm of his right hand reading, "Pleased to meet you—now f*** off." He had had it done when he was 17 years old. He told me that he now wanted a job in the retail trade, but so far all employers had declined his services.

With the unctuous mealy-mouthedness commonly known as political correctness, Rep. Capps's website explains the rationale of her proposal that such tattoos be removed at public expense:

> People with tattoos often find themselves being unfairly stereotyped in a way that makes it difficult to find employment or be promoted to higher, better paying positions. The Liberty Tattoo

10

Program works with people in our community to help erase this social stigma.

The point about the social stigma is, of course, that it is entirely justified. Indeed, if only it were a little stronger people might not indulge in this primitive behavior to begin with. When a man has "Kill the Pigs" emblazoned on his hands or arms, it is best to assume that he is not an apostle of law and order.

In Britain, for example, the vast majority of white imprisoned criminals (and a growing percentage of darker prisoners too, though their skins are not suited to it) are tattooed. Indeed, the statistical association between tattooing and criminality is far stronger than that between criminality and any other factor, smoking perhaps excepted. While it is not true that all tattooed people are criminals, of course, it is almost true that all criminals are tattooed. Thus the tattooed are grossly "over-represented" in our penal establishments.

The consequences of blithely ignoring the social stigma, on the grounds that one should make no such judgments, are very serious, especially for women. A woman who willfully ignores aggressive tattoos in the selection of her consort is more likely than average to find herself being beaten severely. The refusal to take heed is gradually ascending the social scale. Recently, several nurses in my hospital have consulted me about their "relationships." Indoctrinated during their schooling and their training with the dim ideology of non-judgmentalism, they have ignored the visible signs of the unsuitability of the men they have selected, and have found themselves soon afterwards caught up in a spider's web of insensate jealousy, possessiveness, threats, and violence, from which it is difficult to escape without enormous upheaval. The men who torture them—and torture is hardly too strong a word for it—are all tattooed. If only these nurses had stigmatized as they should have done, their miseries would have been avoided.

15   The insincerity of Rep. Capps's justification is patent and obvious, and indicative of our growing inability to confront obvious truths by speaking of them in simple words. We hide our meaning more delicately than the Victorians covered up piano legs, if in fact they did so (which they didn't). The congresswoman does not suggest, as in other contexts she surely might, that an education program should seek to reduce the stigmatization of the tattooed, to educate our youth not to judge the tattooed adversely, to indoctrinate them into believing that there is nothing intrinsically wrong

with having "F*** the System" indelibly imprinted on one's forehead. She knows perfectly well that the problem is not with the
stigmatization, but with the subculture that is stigmatized.
Why, then can she not say it? It could hardly be from fear of
losing the votes of the tattooed, who even in these times must
constitute a small minority, amongst whom must be many non-
voters. It is because to admit that there is something wrong with
a particular subculture, and not with society's response to it, is to
blow apart one of the liberal pieties of our time, namely multiculturalism. It is to admit that one way of life is better than another,
that some conduct is more civilized than other conduct, that actually we desire standards, and that to pretend otherwise is—well,
a pretense.

But Rep. Capps, herself a former nurse, recognizes (and this
is praiseworthy) that there may come a time in a man's life when
he wishes to reform, or to grow up. The fact is that our prisons
have relatively few men who have committed fresh crimes past
the age of 35. In other words, men grow out of their anti-social
propensities, but may be left with the visible stigmata of them. To
remove their tattoos is to offer them hope and give them encouragement, and this is the reality that Rep. Capps has understood.

Discussion Questions

1. A *summary* of an article should restate the author's major ideas in your own
   words, but *not* introduce any of your own opinions or commentary. After a
   careful reading of "Marks of Shame," write a list of major ideas. Then, setting
   aside the article, write a *summary* of about 250 words that states the *thesis*
   or Dalrymple's central idea and several sentences explaining other major
   points that support this thesis.
2. Describe Dalrymple's attitude toward Capps's proposal for tattoo removal.
3. State what Dalrymple suggests is a problem with "multiculturalism." Do you
   agree or disagree with his definition? Explain.

Topics for Exploration and Writing

You have been reading about and discussing body image and the social psychology of body modification. To explore these ideas, focus on analyzing one
social practice, drawing on examples from your observation and experience.
While most of your content should be original, brief comparisons to *at least
one* of the articles in this chapter are *required* to develop your viewpoint

(refer to authors by last name and to article titles). Your job as a writer is to inform your readers by presenting specific examples that you can explain in detail and then generalizing about these examples by presenting a significant interpretation of a social practice. For any of these topics, if race, ethnicity, gender, sexual preference, age, body size, or disability relates to your analysis, please include these important dimensions in your essay.

1. Explain the individual and social meanings of tattoos and/or body piercing, referring to the text and to your own *personal experience*. To what extent is such body art an expression of creativity, individual identity, rebellion, exhibitionism, masochism, conformity to peer groups, and/or sympathy for punk or rap "subculture"? Explore several possible factors.

2. Answering similar questions as in Topic 1, explain the causes and meaning of one contemporary trend in clothing, shoe wear, hair, or other "fashion."

3. In "The Body Jigsaw," Liotard claims that people's efforts toward body modification "will likely herald an all-round confusion over what norms, if any, govern the human body" (paragraph 21). Consider to what extent you agree with this statement. If you agree, explain why you do. If you disagree, explain what "norms" you believe will always "govern the human body."

4. Compare and contrast Rubin's approach to the topic of body art in "Marks of Civilization" with Dalrymple's approach in "Marks of Shame." Analyze the tone of their language and the differing metaphors for the body that they employ in their discussion of tattooing. Explain the values that you can infer from each author's writing.

5. Compare and contrast body modification and athletic training (or another bodily practice) as two forms of "discipline" over the body, as ways for the mind to "conquer" the body, transcend it, or bring it into harmony; or explain some other metaphor for the mind–body relationship.

Body, Image, Media

Since our individual sense of identity is greatly influenced by our gender, advertising often appeals to socially constructed models of masculinity and femininity in order to promote its products. In *Advertising and Popular Culture* (Sage, 1996), Jib Fowles shows how gender depictions in the media create distinct ideals for masculine and feminine behavior, beginning at an early age. Citing a 1983 study of children's television programming, Fowles suggests that, since boys comprised 78 percent of the characters depicted, young viewers might infer that boys are more important than girls. The same study showed that "female characters were much more likely to have their marital status and family role established, were less often shown as employed, and were typically younger than the male characters—all suggestive of a dependent and diminished status" (Fowles 201). Likewise, a 1989 study of characters younger than 20 on prime-time network broadcasts revealed that boys were shown to be "more active, aggressive, rational and unhappy" than girls, who were generally shown in more domestic roles, playing "dress-up," helping to cook, or talking on the phone (201). Examining representations of adolescents in print ads, two studies (1981 and 1986) found that boys—shown most often engaged in athletics or riding in cars—were depicted as in control of their situations, while girls—shown most often walking or bicycling—were "frequently depicted with infantile traits: soft, wide-eyed, emotional, vulnerable" (Fowles 205). A 1990 comparative analysis of article content in *Seventeen* magazine suggested a progressive shift in some subject matter (perhaps influenced by the feminist movement). While "60% of the copy consistently dealt with beauty, fashion, cooking and decorating," the proportion of articles that promoted "the independence and integrity of the female adolescent" rose between 1961 and 1972, but fell to the former levels by 1985, when "articles treating relations between the genders" were again more numerous (205). Fowles also reviews research on media's depiction of adults, reporting on a 1994 study that found "delimited gender definitions":

> Typically men are portrayed as active, adventurous, powerful, sexually aggressive, and largely uninvolved in human relationships. Just as consistent with cultural views of gender are depictions of women as sex objects who are usually young, thin, beautiful, passive, dependent, and often incompetent and dumb. (Wood qtd. in Fowles 208)

Nonetheless, Fowles is careful to point out that "the young do not adopt in a wholesale fashion the media depictions of maleness and femaleness" (217). For example, Fowles cites a 1988 study of high school students whose own perceptions of social gender roles contradicted the media representations: "Even though television underrepresents the proportion of doctors, lawyers, and police who are female, the students overestimated it" in comparison to census data (220). In fact, Fowles affirms that "gender is increasingly contested territory, with definitions and traits in some degree of flux," revealing internal contradictions and proving "variable over time" (217). Compared to interpersonal contacts in everyday life, media representations have a limited effect, most notably in advertising that shapes adolescents' "ideals of attractiveness" in their own gender, as well as the opposing gender, whose traits are implicitly those to be avoided "in the composition of one's own gender identity" (221–22). More important, such gender ideals may be accepted in order to enhance the social cohesion among peers, satisfying "the need among teenagers for a shared culture and the generational solidarity that it provides" (222). Finally, the relationship of popular culture, especially advertising, to the formation of gender and identity is like a road sign to a driver—suggestive of direction and behavior, but hardly compulsory.

As you read the articles in Chapter 4, keep this relationship in mind. The authors sometimes suggest stronger claims about the media's power than may be confirmed in reality. Even so, these writers believe that the media creates a mirror in which we see ourselves, to some extent, and we may negotiate those images in choosing who we are or want to become. Therefore, the body ideals in ads may reflect the body ideals of society, but the individual can choose to embrace, modify, or reject these ideals.

In the first article, "The Story of My Body," Judith Ortiz Cofer shares a personal narrative in which the body ideals of society changed over space and time, just as her own perceptions of her body changed in response to her social environment. As a Puerto Rican of mixed parentage, she was a "white" child on the island, but became a "brown" child, marked as an ethnic minority, when her family moved to New Jersey. Although as a child she identified with the buxom and powerful Wonder Woman model from mainstream American comics, Ortiz Cofer recalls other changes in her identity and self-perception as she negotiated an alien culture with its own social pecking order and ideals for appearance.

In the second article, "Never Just Pictures: Bodies and Fantasies," Susan Bordo warns against the unhealthy body images promoted in the media, especially in advertisements for clothes and personal care products. What comes across from some of her examples is a metaphor of the body as a clothes rack for the aesthetic display of fashion. Bordo also asks us to analyze "the contradictions of consumer culture," which treats the body as a means of pleasurable self-indulgence, but also as a site of discipline over insatiable appetites and physical vulnerabilities. In developing her own analysis, she cites viewpoints from the popular press, from academic studies, and from an autobiographical novel—thus relying on a variety of sources to support her argument.

In the third article, "Media Mirrors," Carol Moog reviews the history of the Maidenform Bra advertising campaign to show how changes in feminine role models within the ads both reflected and responded to psychological changes in women's self-images from the 1950s through the 1980s. In this work, there is extensive interpretation of the meanings of the ad images and—in the original publication—several reproductions of the ads themselves, which show only young, slim, and attractive women. As a clinical psychologist, Moog opens her article with a passage from her case notes on a client. We can infer from this reference that she is professionally qualified to judge how the unconscious works out its wish fulfillment in dreams and how women might respond to advertising that indulges their fantasies to "try on a new identity" as boldly sexual women in positions of power. However, unlike the social scientists in Chapter 2 or even the popular writers of Chapter 3, Moog makes no attempt to situate her interpretations within a context of viewpoints from experts or other researchers. Basically, her opinions and examples stand on their own merits.

In the fourth article, "A Gentleman and a Consumer," Diane Barthel uses an essentially social science approach to analyze the masculine images in advertising directed to the male audience. The image of the body that emerges from her examples is the athletic ideal of power and performance. It recalls the traditional model of masculinity in Chapter 2—the kind of male who competes against other men and wins for his prize (so the ads imply) the women he desires. The idealized role model is machinelike, so cars in ads become mere extensions of the male body. To support her argument about the changing images of manliness in advertising, Barthel cites and quotes sociologists and cultural critics, besides dozens of passages from the male-directed ads themselves. One novel contribution she makes to the analysis of "masculinity" is her discussion of how ads try to sell such "feminine" personal-care products as permanents and hair sprays, marketed to men as "grooming gear." In contrast to the advertising directed at women, Barthel shows that manly images in ads of the 1980s seem to avoid direct reference to sexuality and, instead, appeal to status and independence.

The Story of My Body
JUDITH ORTIZ COFER

Franklin Professor of English and Creative Writing at the University of Georgia, Judith Ortiz Cofer is the author of several works of fiction, poetry, and memoir that draw richly from her Puerto Rican culture. These titles include Silent Dancing: A Partial Remembrance of a Puerto Rican Childhood *(1990),* An Island Like You: Stories of the Barrio *(1996), and* Woman in Front of the Sun: On Becoming a Writer *(2000). The last work should inspire all writers—working independently or in creative writing classrooms—with its advice for the artist to avidly pursue her craft and realize her creative power despite material and interpersonal struggles. The source of the following selection, her most popular work is* The Latin Deli: Prose and Poetry *(1993), an autobiographical collection of essays, stories, and poems about a New Jersey barrio that comments poignantly on her Puerto Rican heritage, racism, sexism, the Catholic conflict between flesh and spirit, and the challenges of an adolescence spent in "cultural compromise." Nonetheless, this work shows how Ortiz Cofer learned "to survive in two languages and two worlds" through reading and, eventually, through writing.*

*Before reading, consider if you have ever felt "invisible"—
scarcely noticed by other people. Write a paragraph explaining the
experience and your response to it. Then, as you read, compare your
experience with Ortiz Cofer's story.*

———————————— ✦ ————————————

Migration is the story of my body.

—Victor Hernandez Cruz

SKIN

I was born a white girl in Puerto Rico but became a brown girl
when I came to live in the United States: My Puerto Rican relatives called me tall; at the American school, some of my rougher
classmates called me Skinny Bones, and the Shrimp because I
was the smallest member of my classes all through grammar
school until high school, when the midget Gladys was given the
honorary post of front row center for class pictures and score-
keeper, bench warmer, in P.E. I reached my full stature of five feet
in sixth grade.

I started out life as a pretty baby and learned to be a pretty
girl from a pretty mother. Then at ten years of age I suffered one
of the worst cases of chicken pox I have ever heard of. My entire
body, including the inside of my ears and in between my toes, was
covered with pustules which in a fit of panic at my appearance
I scratched off my face, leaving permanent scars. A cruel school
nurse told me I would always have them—tiny cuts that looked as
if a mad cat had plunged its claws deep into my skin. I grew my
hair long and hid behind it for the first years of my adolescence.
This was when I learned to be invisible.

COLOR

In the animal world it indicates danger: the most colorful creatures are often the most poisonous. Color is also a way to attract
and seduce a mate. In the human world color triggers many more
complex and often deadly reactions. As a Puerto Rican girl born
of "white" parents, I spent the first years of my life hearing people
refer to me as *blanca,* white. My mother insisted that I protect
myself from the intense island sun because I was more prone to
sunburn than some of my darker, *trigueno* playmates. People
were always commenting within my hearing about how my black

hair contrasted so nicely with my "pale" skin. I did not think of the color of my skin consciously except when I heard the adults talking about complexion. It seems to me that the subject is much more common in the conversation of mixed-race peoples than in mainstream United States society, where it is a touchy and sometimes even embarrassing topic to discuss, except in a political context. In Puerto Rico I heard many conversations about skin color. A pregnant woman could say, "I hope my baby doesn't turn out *prieto*" (slang for "dark" or "black") "like my husband's grandmother, although she was a good-looking *negra* in her time." I am a combination of both, being olive-skinned—lighter than my mother yet darker than my fair-skinned father. In America, I am a person of color, obviously a Latina. On the Island I have been called everything from a *paloma blanca*, after the song (by a black suitor), to *la gringa*.

My first experience of color prejudice occurred in a supermarket in Paterson, New Jersey. It was Christmastime, and I was eight or nine years old. There was a display of toys in the store where I went two or three times a day to buy things for my mother, who never made lists but sent for milk, cigarettes, a can of this or that, as she remembered from hour to hour. I enjoyed being trusted with money and walking half a city block to the new, modern grocery store. It was owned by three good-looking Italian brothers. I liked the younger one with the crew-cut blond hair. The two older ones watched me and the other Puerto Rican kids as if they thought we were going to steal something. The oldest one would sometimes even try to hurry me with my purchases, although part of my pleasure in these expeditions came from looking at everything in the well-stocked aisles. I was also teaching myself to read English by sounding out the labels on packages: L&M cigarettes, Borden's homogenized milk, Red Devil potted ham, Nestle's chocolate mix, Quaker oats, Bustelo coffee, Wonder bread, Colgate toothpaste, Ivory soap, and Goya (makers of products used in Puerto Rican dishes) everything—these are some of the brand names that taught me nouns. Several times this man had come up to me, wearing his blood-stained butcher's apron, and towering over me had asked in a harsh voice whether there was something he could help me find. On the way out I would glance at the younger brother who ran one of the registers and he would often smile and wink at me.

5   It was the mean brother who first referred to me as "colored." It was a few days before Christmas, and my parents had already told my brother and me that since we were in Los Estados now,

we would get our presents on December 25 instead of Los Reyes, Three Kings Day, when gifts are exchanged in Puerto Rico. We were to give them a wish list that they would take to Santa Claus, who apparently lived in the Macy's store downtown—at least that's where we had caught a glimpse of him when we went shopping. Since my parents were timid about entering the fancy store, we did not approach the huge man in the red suit. I was not interested in sitting on a stranger's lap anyway. But I did covet Susie, the talking schoolteacher doll that was displayed in the center aisle of the Italian brothers' supermarket. She talked when you pulled a string on her back. Susie had a limited repertoire of three sentences: I think she could say: "Hello, I'm Susie Schoolteacher," "Two plus two is four," and one other thing I cannot remember. The day the older brother chased me away, I was reaching to touch Susie's blonde curls. I had been told many times, as most children have, not to touch anything in a store that I was not buying. But I had been looking at Susie for weeks. In my mind, she was my doll. After all, I had put her on my Christmas wish list. The moment is frozen in my mind as if there were a photograph of it on file. It was not a turning point, a disaster, or an earthshaking revelation. It was simply the first time I considered—if naively—the meaning of skin color in human relations.

I reached to touch Susie's hair. It seems to me that I had to get on tiptoe, since the toys were stacked on a table and she sat like a princess on top of the fancy box she came in. Then I heard the booming "Hey, kid, what do you think you're doing!" spoken very loudly from the meat counter. I felt caught, although I knew I was not doing anything criminal. I remember not looking at the man, but standing there, feeling humiliated because I knew everyone in the store must have heard him yell at me. I felt him approach, and when I knew he was behind me, I turned around to face the bloody butcher's apron. His large chest was at my eye level. He blocked my way. I started to run out of the place, but even as I reached the door I heard him shout after me: "Don't come in here unless you gonna buy something. You PR kids put your dirty hands on stuff. You always look dirty. But maybe dirty brown is your natural color." I heard him laugh and someone else too in the back. Outside in the sunlight I looked at my hands. My nails needed a little cleaning as they always did, since I liked to paint with watercolors, but I took a bath every night. I thought the man was dirtier than I was in his stained apron. He was also always sweaty—it showed in big yellow circles under his shirtsleeves. I sat on the front steps of the apartment building where we lived and looked closely at my hands, which showed the only skin I could see, since it was bitter cold and I was wearing my quilted play coat, dungarees, and a knitted navy cap of my father's. I was not pink like my friend Charlene and her sister Kathy, who had blue eyes and light brown hair. My skin is the color of the coffee my grandmother made, which was half milk, *leche con café* rather than *café con leche*. My mother is the opposite mix. She has a lot of café in her color. I could not understand how my skin looked like dirt to the supermarket man.

I went in and washed my hands thoroughly with soap and hot water, and borrowing my mother's nail file, I cleaned the crusted watercolors from underneath my nails. I was pleased with the results. My skin was the same color as before, but I knew I was clean. Clean enough to run my fingers through Susie's fine gold hair when she came home to me.

SIZE

My mother is barely four feet eleven inches in height, which is average for women in her family. When I grew to five feet by age twelve, she was amazed and began to use the word tall to describe me, as in "Since you are tall, this dress will look good on you." As with the color of my skin, I didn't consciously think about my height or size until other people made an issue of it. It is around the preadolescent years that in America the games children play for fun become fierce competitions where everyone is out to "prove" they are better than others. It was in the playground and sports fields that my size-related problems began. No matter how familiar the story is, every child who is the last chosen for a team knows the torment of waiting to be called up. At the Paterson, New Jersey, public schools that I attended, the volleyball or softball game was the metaphor for the battlefield of life to the inner city kids—the black kids versus the Puerto Rican kids, the whites versus the blacks versus the Puerto Rican kids; and I was 4F, skinny, short, bespectacled, and apparently impervious to the blood thirst that drove many of my classmates to play ball as if their lives depended on it. Perhaps they did. I would rather be reading a book than sweating, grunting, and running the risk of pain and injury. I simply did not see the point in competitive sports. My main form of exercise then was walking to the library, many city blocks away from my barrio.

Still, I wanted to be wanted. I wanted to be chosen for the teams. Physical education was compulsory, a class where you were actually given a grade. On my mainly all A report card, the C for compassion I always received from the P.E. teachers shamed me the same as a bad grade in a real class. Invariably, my father would say: "How can you make a low grade for *playing games*? He did not understand. Even if I had managed to make a hit (it never happened) or get the ball over that ridiculously high net, I already had a reputation as a "shrimp," a hopeless nonathlete. It was an area where the girls who didn't like me for one reason or another—mainly because I did better than they in academic subjects—could lord it over me; the playing field was the place where even the smallest girl could make me feel powerless and inferior. I instinctively understood the politics even then; how the *not* choosing me until the teacher forced one of the team captains to call my name was a coup of sorts—there, you little show-off, tomorrow you can beat us in spelling and geography, but this afternoon you are the loser. Or perhaps those were only my own bitter thoughts as I sat or stood in the sidelines while the big girls were grabbed like fish and I, the little brown tadpole, was ignored until Teacher looked over in my general direction and shouted, "Call Ortiz," or, worse, "Somebody's *got* to take her."

No wonder I read Wonder Woman comics and had Legion of   10
Super Heroes daydreams. Although I wanted to think of myself as "intellectual," my body was demanding that I notice it. I saw the little swelling around my once-flat nipples, the fine hairs growing in secret places; but my knees were still bigger than my thighs, and I always wore long- or half-sleeve blouses to hide my bony upper arms. I wanted flesh on my bones—a thick layer of it. I saw a new product advertised on TV. Wate-On. They showed skinny men and women before and after taking the stuff, and it was a transformation like the ninety-seven-pound-weakling-turned-into-Charles-Atlas ads that I saw on the back covers of my comic books. The Wate-On was very expensive. I tried to explain my need for it in Spanish to my mother, but it didn't translate very well, even to my ears—and she said with a tone of finality, eat more of my good food and you'll get fat—anybody can get fat. Right. Except me. I was going to have to join a circus someday as Skinny Bones, the woman without flesh.

Wonder Woman was stacked. She had a cleavage framed by the spread wings of a golden eagle and a muscular body that has become fashionable with women only recently. But since I wanted a body that would serve me in P.E., hers was my ideal. The breasts were an indulgence I allowed myself. Perhaps the daydreams of bigger girls were more glamorous, since our ambitions are filtered through our needs, but I wanted first a powerful body. I daydreamed of leaping up above the gray landscape of the city to where the sky was clear and blue, and in anger and self-pity, I fantasized about scooping my enemies up by their hair from the playing fields and dumping them on a barren asteroid. I would put the P.E. teachers each on their own rock in space too, where they would be the loneliest people in the universe, since I knew they had no "inner resources," no imagination, and in outer space, there would be no air for them to fill their deflated volleyballs with. In my mind all P.E. teachers have blended into one large spiky-haired woman with a whistle on a string around her neck and a volleyball under one arm. My Wonder Woman fantasies of revenge were a source of comfort to me in my early career as a shrimp.

I was saved from more years of P.E. torment by the fact that in my sophomore year of high school I transferred to a school where the midget, Gladys, was the focal point of interest for the people who must rank according to size. Because her height was considered a handicap, there was an unspoken rule about mentioning size around Gladys, but of course, there was no need to say anything. Gladys knew her place: front row center in class photographs. I gladly moved to the left or to the right of her, as far as I could without leaving the picture completely.

LOOKS

Many photographs were taken of me as a baby by my mother to send to my father, who was stationed overseas during the first two years of my life. With the army in Panama when I was born, he later traveled often on tours of duty with the navy. I was a healthy, pretty baby. Recently, I read that people are drawn to big-eyed round-faced creatures, like puppies, kittens, and certain other mammals and marsupials, koalas, for example, and, of course, infants. I was all eyes, since my head and body, even as I grew older, remained thin and small-boned. As a young child I got a lot of attention from my relatives and many other people we met in our barrio. My mother's beauty may have had something to do with how much attention we got from strangers in stores and on the street. I can imagine it. In the pictures I have seen of us together, she is a stunning young woman by Latino standards: long, curly black hair, and round curves in a compact frame. From her I learned how to move, smile, and talk like an attractive woman. I remember going into a bodega for our groceries and being given candy by the proprietor as a reward for being *bonita*, pretty.

I can see in the photographs, and I also remember, that I was dressed in the pretty clothes, the stiff, frilly dresses, with layers of crinolines underneath, the glossy patent leather shoes, and, on special occasions, the skull-hugging little hats and the white gloves that were popular in the late fifties and early sixties. My mother was proud of my looks, although I was a bit too thin. She could dress me up like a doll and take me by the hand to visit relatives, or go to the Spanish mass at the Catholic church, and show me off. How was I to know that she and the others who called me "pretty" were representatives of an aesthetic that would not apply when I went out into the mainstream world of school?

In my Paterson, New Jersey, public schools there were still 15 quite a few white children, although the demographics of the city were changing rapidly. The original waves of Italian and Irish immigrants, silk-mill workers, and laborers in the cloth industries had been "assimilated." Their children were now the middle-class parents of my peers. Many of them moved their children to the Catholic schools that proliferated enough to have leagues of basketball teams. The names I recall hearing still ring in my ears: Don Bosco High versus St. Mary's High, St. Joseph's versus St. John's. Later I too would be transferred to the safer environment of a Catholic school. But I started school at Public School Number 11. I came there from Puerto Rico, thinking myself a pretty girl, and found that the hierarchy for popularity was as follows: pretty white girl, pretty Jewish girl, pretty Puerto Rican girl, pretty black girl. Drop the last two categories; teachers were too busy to have more than one favorite per class, and it was simply understood that if there was a big part in the school play, or any competition where the main qualification was "presentability" (such as escorting a school visitor to or from the principal's office), the classroom's public address speaker would be requesting the pretty and/or nice-looking white boy or girl. By the time I was in the sixth grade, I was sometimes called by the principal to represent my class because I dressed neatly (I knew this from a progress report sent to my mother, which I translated for her) and because all the "presentable" white girls had moved to the Catholic schools (I later surmised this part). But I was still not one of the popular girls with the boys. I remember one incident where I stepped out into the playground in my baggy gym shorts and one Puerto Rican boy said to the other: "What do you think?" The other one answered: "Her face is OK, but look at the toothpick legs." The next best thing to a compliment I got was when my favorite male teacher, while handing out the class pictures, commented that with my long neck and delicate features I resembled the movie star Audrey Hepburn. But the Puerto Rican boys had learned to respond to a fuller figure: long necks and a perfect little nose were not what they looked for in a girl. That is when I decided I was a "brain." I did not settle into the role easily. I was nearly devastated by what the chicken pox episode had done to my self-image. But I looked into the mirror less often after I was told that I would always have scars on my face, and I hid behind my long black hair and my books.

After the problems at the public school got to the point where even nonconfrontational little me got beaten up several times, my parents enrolled me at St. Joseph's High School. I was then a minority of one among the Italian and Irish kids. But I found several good friends there—other girls who took their studies seriously. We did our homework together and talked about the Jackies. The Jackies were two popular girls, one blonde and the other red-haired, who had women's bodies. Their curves showed even in the blue jumper uniforms with straps that we all wore. The blonde Jackie would often let one of the straps fall off her shoulder, and although she, like all of us, wore a white blouse underneath, all the boys stared at her arm. My friends and I talked about this and practiced letting our straps fall off our shoulders. But it wasn't the same without breasts or hips.

My final two and a half years of high school were spent in Augusta, Georgia, where my parents moved our family in search of a more peaceful environment. There we became part of a little community of our army-connected relatives and friends. School was yet another matter. I was enrolled in a huge school of nearly two thousand students that had just that year been forced to integrate. There were two black girls and there was me. I did extremely well academically. As to my social life, it was, for the most part, uneventful—yet it is in my memory blighted by one incident. In my junior year, I became wildly infatuated with a pretty white boy. I'll call him Ted. Oh, he was pretty: yellow hair that fell over his forehead, a smile to die for—and he was a great dancer. I watched him at Teen Town, the youth center at the base where all the military brats gathered on Saturday nights. My father had retired from the navy, and we had all our base privileges—one other reason we had moved to Augusta. Ted looked like an angel to me. I worked on him for a year before he asked me out. This meant maneuvering to be within the periphery of his vision at every

possible occasion. I took the long way to my classes in school just
to pass by his locker, I went to football games, which I detested,
and I danced (I too was a good dancer) in front of him at Teen
Town—this took some fancy footwork, since it involved subtly
moving my partner toward the right spot on the dance floor.
When Ted finally approached me, "A Million to One" was playing
on the jukebox, and when he took me into his arms, the odds suddenly turned in my favor. He asked me to go to a school dance the
following Saturday. I said yes, breathlessly. I said yes, but there
were obstacles to surmount at home. My father did not allow me
to date casually. I was allowed to go to major events like a prom
or a concert with a boy who had been properly screened. There
was such a boy in my life, a neighbor who wanted to be a Baptist
missionary and was practicing his anthropological skills on my
family. If I was desperate to go somewhere and needed a date, I'd
resort to Gary. This is the type of religious nut that Gary was:
when the school bus did not show up one day, he put his hands
over his face and prayed to Christ to get us a way to get to school.
Within ten minutes a mother in a station wagon, on her way to
town, stopped to ask why we weren't in school. Gary informed
her that the Lord had sent her just in time to find us a way to get
there in time for roll call. He assumed that I was impressed. Gary
was even good-looking in a bland sort of way, but he kissed me
with his lips tightly pressed together. I think Gary probably ended
up marrying a native woman from wherever he may have gone to
preach the Gospel according to Paul. She probably believes that
all white men pray to God for transportation and kiss with their
mouths closed. But it was Ted's mouth, his whole beautiful self,
that concerned me in those days. I knew my father would say no
to our date, but I planned to run away from home if necessary.
I told my mother how important this date was. I cajoled and
pleaded with her from Sunday to Wednesday. She listened to my
arguments and must have heard the note of desperation in my
voice. She said very gently to me: "You better be ready for disappointment." I did not ask what she meant. I did not want her
fears for me to taint my happiness. I asked her to tell my father
about my date. Thursday at breakfast my father looked at me
across the table with his eyebrows together. My mother looked at
him with her mouth set in a straight line. I looked down at my
bowl of cereal. Nobody said anything. Friday I tried on every
dress in my closet. Ted would be picking me up at six on
Saturday: dinner and then the sock hop at school. Friday night I
was in my room doing my nails or something else in preparation

for Saturday (I know I groomed myself nonstop all week) when the telephone rang. I ran to get it. It was Ted. His voice sounded funny when he said my name, so funny that I felt compelled to ask: "Is something wrong?" Ted blurted it all out without a preamble. His father had asked who he was going out with. Ted had told him my name. "Ortiz? That's Spanish, isn't it?" the father had asked. Ted had told him yes, then shown him my picture in the yearbook. Ted's father had shaken his head. No. Ted would not be taking me out. Ted's father had known Puerto Ricans in the army. He had lived in New York City while studying architecture and had seen how the spics lived. Like rats. Ted repeated his father's words to me as if I should understand his predicament when I heard why he was breaking our date. I don't remember what I said before hanging up. I do recall the darkness of my room that sleepless night and the heaviness of my blanket in which I wrapped myself like a shroud. And I remember my parents' respect for my pain and their gentleness toward me that weekend. My mother did not say "I warned you," and I was grateful for her understanding silence.

In college, I suddenly became an "exotic" woman to the men who had survived the popularity wars in high school, who were now practicing to be worldly: they had to act liberal in their politics, in their lifestyles, and in the women they went out with. I dated heavily for a while, then married young. I had discovered that I needed stability more than social life. I had brains for sure and some talent in writing. These facts were a constant in my life. My skin color, my size, and my appearance were variables—things that were judged according to my current self-image, the aesthetic values of the times, the places I was in, and the people I met. My studies, later my writing, the respect of people who saw me as an individual person they cared about, these were the criteria for my sense of self-worth that I would concentrate on in my adult life.

Discussion Questions

1. Review your paragraph (see prereading, page 125) about having the experience of being "invisible." Then, write another paragraph comparing your experience with Ortiz Cofer's story.
2. In a well-developed paragraph, describe the experiences of prejudice that Ortiz Cofer recounts in "The Story of My Body."

3. Recall your own childhood and adolescence. Relate a brief story that resembles one of Ortiz Cofer's experiences. What do you believe was the reason for the prejudice or ill-feeling against you? To what extent was race, class, or family background a factor? To what extent did the response of another person make you feel like an outsider?

4. Ortiz Cofer admits that she "did not see the point of competitive sports" (paragraph 8) and found her "sense of self-worth" (paragraph 18) through her studies in school. Comparing and contrasting with her experience, describe your own source of "self-worth" in grade school or high school.

Never Just Pictures: Bodies and Fantasies

Susan Bordo

Susan Bordo earned her Ph.D. from the State University of New York at Stony Brook. She is now the Singletary Chair in Humanities and Professor of English and Women's Studies at the University of Kentucky, where she teaches and researches such topics as contemporary culture and the body, eating disorders, cosmetic surgery, masculinity, and the social impacts of the media. Her first popular book was Unbearable Weight: Feminism, Western Culture, and the Body *(1993), which argues that many problems of contemporary Western societies derive from the mind–body dualism of Plato, as established in modern science by Descartes. Here she also critiques the socially constructed association between women and instinct, nature, or the body, in which the "manly" mind or soul is supposedly trapped. More recent work includes* The Male Body: A New Look at Men in Public and in Private *(1999), an analysis of the male nude as it reveals attitudes about sexuality in popular culture. Citing examples from movies, television, art, fashion, celebrity culture, pop psychology, social science, literature, and medicine, Bordo explores the notions of masculinity expressed by the image of the "lean, fit body that virtually everyone . . . now aspires to." Interestingly, she explains the recent influence of African American and gay cultures, whose attitudes about public display of the male body were first popularized in Calvin Klein ads. The following essay is from her 1997 book,* Twilight Zones: The Hidden Life of Cultural Images from Plato to O. J. Simpson.*

◆

When Alicia Silverstone, the svelte nineteen-year-old star of *Clueless*, appeared at the Academy Awards just a smidge more substantial than she had been in the movie, the tabloids ribbed her cruelly, calling her "fatgirl" and "buttgirl" (her next movie role is Batgirl) and "more *Babe* than babe."[1] Our idolatry of the trim, tight body shows no signs of relinquishing its grip on our conceptions of beauty and normality. Since I began exploring this obsession it seems to have gathered momentum, like a spreading mass hysteria. Fat is the devil, and we are continually beating him—"eliminating" our stomachs, "busting" our thighs, "taming" our tummies—pummeling and purging our bodies, attempting to make them into something other than flesh. On television, infomercials hawking miracle diet pills and videos promising to turn our body parts into steel have become as commonplace as aspirin ads. There hasn't been a tabloid cover in the past few years that didn't boast of an inside scoop on some star's diet regime, a "fabulous" success story of weight loss, or a tragic relapse. (When they can't come up with a current one, they scrounge up an old one; a few weeks ago the *National Inquirer* ran a story on Joan Lunden's fifty-pound weight loss fifteen years ago!) Children in this culture grow up knowing that you can never be thin enough and that being fat is one of the worst things one can be. One study asked ten- and eleven-year-old boys and girls to rank drawings of children with various physical handicaps; drawings of fat children elicited the greatest disapproval and discomfort, over pictures of kids with facial disfigurements and missing hands.

Psychologists commonly believe that girls with eating disorders suffer from "body image disturbance syndrome": they are unable to see themselves as anything but fat, no matter how thin they become. If this is a disorder, it is one that has become a norm of cultural perception. Our ideas about what constitutes a body in need of a diet have become more and more pathologically trained on the slightest hint of excess. This ideal of the body beautiful has largely come from fashion designers and models. (Movie stars, who often used to embody a more voluptuous ideal, are now modeling themselves after the models.) They have taught us "to love a woman's pelvis, her hipbones jutting out through a bias-cut grown . . . the clavicle in its role as a coat hanger from which clothes are suspended."[2] (An old fashion industry justification for skinniness in models was that clothes just don't "hang right" on heftier types.) The fashion industry has taught us to regard a perfectly healthy, nonobese body . . . as an unsightly "before" ("Before CitraLean, no wonder they wore swimsuits like that" [a loose-cut two-piece]). In fact, those in the business have admitted that models have been getting thinner since 1993, when Kate Moss first repopularized the waif look. British models Trish Goff and Annie Morton make Moss look well fed by comparison,[3] and recent ad campaigns for Jil Sander go way beyond the thin body-as-coat-hanger paradigm to a blatant glamorization of the cadaverous, starved look itself. More and more ads featuring anorexic-looking young men are appearing too.

The main challenge to such images is a muscular aesthetic that *looks* more life-affirming but is no less punishing and compulsion-inducing in its demands on ordinary bodies. During the 1996 Summer Olympics—which were reported with unprecedented focus and hype on the fat-free beauty of muscular bodies—commentators celebrated the "health" of this aesthetic over anorexic glamour. But there is growing evidence of rampant eating disorders among female athletes, and it's hard to imagine that those taut and tiny Olympic gymnasts—the idols of preadolescents across the country—are having regular menstrual cycles. Their skimpy level of body fat just won't support it. During the Olympics I heard a commentator gushing about how great it was that the 1996 team was composed predominantly of eighteen- and nineteen-year-old women rather than little girls. To me it is far more disturbing that these nineteen-year-olds still *look* (and talk) like little girls! As I watched them vault and leap, my admiration for their tremendous skill and spirit was shadowed by thoughts of what was going on *inside* their bodies—the hormones unreleased because of insufficient body fat, the organ development delayed, perhaps halted.

Is it any wonder that despite media attention to the dangers of starvation dieting and habitual vomiting, eating disorders have spread throughout the culture?[4] In 1993 in *Unbearable Weight* I argued that the old clinical generalizations positing distinctive class, race, family, and "personality" profiles for the women most likely to develop an eating disorder were being blasted apart by the normalizing power of mass imagery. Some feminists complained that I had not sufficiently attended to racial and ethnic "difference" and was assuming the white, middle-class experience as the norm. Since then it has been widely acknowledged among medical professionals that the incidence of eating and body-image problems among African American, Hispanic, and Native American women has been grossly underestimated and is on the increase.[5] Even the gender gap is being narrowed, as more and more men are developing eating disorders and exercise compulsions too. (In the mid-eighties the men in my classes used to yawn and pass notes when we discussed the pressure to diet; in 1996 they are more apt to protest if the women in the class talk as though it's their problem alone.)

5   The spread of eating disorders, of course, is not just about images. The emergence of eating disorders is a complex, multilayered cultural "symptom," reflecting problems that are historical as well as contemporary, arising in our time because of the confluence of a number of factors.[6] Eating disorders are overdetermined in this culture. They have to do not only with new social expectations of women and ambivalence toward their bodies but also with more general anxieties about the body as the source of hungers, needs, and physical vulnerabilities not within our control. These anxieties are deep and long-standing in Western philosophy and religion, and they are especially acute in our own time. Eating disorders are also linked to the contradictions of consumer culture, which is continually encouraging us to binge on our desires at the same time as it glamorizes self-discipline and scorns fat as a symbol of laziness and lack of willpower. And these disorders reflect, too, our increasing fascination with the possibilities of reshaping our bodies and selves in radical ways, creating new bodies according to our mind's design.

The relationship between problems such as these and cultural images is complex. On the one hand, the idealization of certain kinds of bodies foments and perpetuates our anxieties and insecurities, that's clear. Glamorous images of hyperthin models certainly don't encourage a more relaxed or accepting attitude toward the body, particularly among those whose own bodies are far from that ideal. But, on the other hand, such images carry fantasized solutions to our anxieties and insecurities, and that's part of the reason why they are powerful. They speak to us not just about how to be beautiful or desirable but about how to get control of our lives, get safe, be cool, avoid hurt. When I look at the picture of a skeletal and seemingly barely breathing young woman in [some advertising], for example, I do not see a vacuous fashion ideal. I see a visual embodiment of what novelist and ex-anorexic Stephanie Grant means when she says in her autobiographical novel, *The Passion of Alice*, "If I had to say my anorexia was about any single thing, I would have said it was about living without desire. Without longing of any kind.[7]

Now, this may not seem like a particularly attractive philosophy of life (or a particularly attractive body, for that matter). Why would anyone want to look like death, you might be asking. Why would anyone want to live without desire? But recent articles in both *The New Yorker* and the *New York Times* have noted a new aesthetic in contemporary ads, in which the models appear dislocated and withdrawn, with chipped black nail polish and greasy hair, staring out at the viewer in a deathlike trance, seeming to be "barely a person." Some have called this wasted look "heroin chic": ex-model Zoe Fleischauer recalls that "they wanted models that looked like junkies. The more skinny and fucked-up you look, the more everybody thinks you're fabulous."[8]

Hilton Als, in *The New Yorker*, interprets this trend as making the statement that fashion is dead and beauty is "trivial in relation to depression."[9] I read these ads very differently. Although the photographers may see themselves as ironically "deconstructing" fashion, the reality is that no fashion advertisement can declare fashion to be dead—it's virtually a grammatical impossibility. Put that frame around the image, whatever the content, and we are instructed to find it glamorous. These ads are not telling us that beauty is trivial in relation to depression, they are telling us that depression is beautiful, that being wasted is *cool*. The question then becomes not "Is fashion dead?" but "Why has death become glamorous?"

Freud tells us that in the psyche death represents not the destruction of the self but its return to a state prior to need, thus freedom from unfulfilled longing, from anxiety over not having one's needs met. Following Freud, I would argue that ghostly pallor and bodily disrepair, in "heroin chic" images, are about the allure, the safety, of being beyond needing, beyond caring, beyond desire. Should we be surprised at the appeal of being without desire in a culture that has invested our needs with anxiety, stress, and danger, that has made us craving and hungering machines, creatures of desire, and then repaid us with addictions, AIDS, shallow and unstable relationships, and cutthroat competition for jobs and mates? To have given up the quest for fulfillment, to be unconcerned with the body or its needs—or its vulnerability—is much wiser than to care.

So, yes, the causes of eating disorders are "deeper" than just obedience to images. But cultural images themselves *are* deep. And the way they become imbued and animated with such power is hardly mysterious. Far from being the purely aesthetic inventions that designers and photographers would like to have us believe they are—"It's just fashion, darling, nothing to get all politically steamed up about"—they reflect the designers' cultural savvy, their ability to sense and give form to flutters and quakes in the cultural psyche.

10

These folks have a strong and simple motivation to hone their skills as cultural Geiger counters. It's called the profit motive. They want their images and the products associated with them to sell.

The profit motive can sometimes produce seemingly "transgressive" wrinkles in current norms. Recently designers such as Calvin Klein and Jil Sander have begun to use rather plain, ordinary-looking, un-madeup faces in their ad campaigns. Unlike the models in "heroin chic" ads, these men and women do not appear wasted so much as unadorned, unpolished, stripped of the glamorous veneer we have come to expect of fashion spreads. While many of them have interesting faces, few of them qualify as beautiful by any prevailing standards. They have rampant freckles, moles in unbeautiful places, oddly proportioned heads. Noticing these ads, I at first wondered whether we really were shifting into a new gear, more genuinely accepting of diversity and "flaws" in appearance. Then it suddenly hit me that these imperfect faces were showing up in clothing and perfume ads only and the bodies in these ads were as relentlessly normalizing as ever—not one plump body to complement the facial "diversity."

I now believe that what we are witnessing here is a commercial war. Clothing manufacturers, realizing that many people—particularly young people, at whom most of these ads are aimed—have limited resources and that encouraging them to spend all their money fixing up their faces rather than buying clothes is not in their best interests, are reasserting the importance of body over face as the "site" of our fantasies. In the new codes of these ads a too madeup look signifies a lack of cool, too much investment in how one looks. "Just Be," Calvin Klein tells us in a recent CK One ad. But looks—a lean body—still matter enormously in these ads, and we are still being told how to be—in the mode which best serves Calvin Klein. And all the while, of course, makeup and hair products continue to promote their own self-serving aesthetics of facial perfection.

Endnotes

1. I give great credit to Alicia Silverstone for her response to these taunts. In *Vanity Fair* she says, "I do my best. But it's much more important to me that my brain be working in the morning than getting up early and doing exercise. . . . The most important thing for me is that I eat and that I sleep and that I get the work done, but unfortunately . . . it's the perception that women in film should look a certain way" ("Hollywood Princess," September 1996, pp. 292–294). One wonders how long she will manage to retain such a sane attitude!

2. Holly Brubach, "The Athletic Esthetic," *The New York Times Magazine*, June 23, 1996, p. 51.

3. In early 1996 the Swiss watch manufacturer Omega threatened to stop advertising in British *Vogue* because of *Vogue's* use of such hyperthin models, but it later reversed this decision. The furor was reminiscent of boycotts that were threatened in 1994 when Calvin Klein and Coca-Cola first began to use photos of Kate Moss in their ads. In neither case has the fashion industry acknowledged any validity to the charge that their imagery encourages eating disorders. Instead, they have responded with defensive "rebuttals."

4. Despite media attention to eating disorders, an air of scornful impatience with "victim feminism" has infected attitudes toward women's body issues. Christina Hoff-Sommers charges Naomi Wolf (*The Beauty Myth*) with grossly inflating statistics on eating disorders and she poo-poos the notion that women are dying from dieting. Even if some particular set of statistics is inaccurate; why would Hoff-Sommers want to deny the reality of the problem, which as a teacher she can surely see right before her eyes?

5. For the spread of eating disorders in minority groups, see, for example, "The Art of Integrating Diversity: Addressing Treatment Issues of Minority Women in the 90's," in *The Renfrew Perspective*, Winter 1994; see also Becky Thompson, *A Hunger So Wide and So Deep* (Minneapolis: University of Minnesota Press, 1994).

6. See my *Unbearable Weight* (Berkeley: University of California Press, 1993).

7. Stephanie Grant, *The Passion of Alice* (New York: Houghton Mifflin, 1995), p. 58.

8. Zoe Fleischauer quoted in "Rockers, Models, and the New Allure of Heroin, *Newsweek*, August 26, 1996.

9. Hilton Als, "Buying the Fantasy," *The New Yorker*, October 10, 1996, p. 70.

Discussion Questions

1. Paraphrase Bordo's reasons for the rise of eating disorders in American culture. To what extent do you think that "cool" body and facial images have changed since 1997, when her article was published?

2. Bordo suggests that eating disorders have social origins in women's "ambivalence toward their bodies" and "anxieties about the body as a source of hungers, needs and physical vulnerabilities not within our control" (paragraph 5). First, explain why women would feel ambivalent or contradictory attitudes about their bodies? To what extent do men also feel this way?

Second, explain some of the bodily needs or weaknesses that might create anxieties in women and/or men. From your personal experience or observation, describe some behaviors—besides eating disorders—that seem to be responses to such anxieties.

3. Bordo argues that glamorous body images in advertising offer solutions for us "to get control of our lives" (paragraph 6). To what extent do you feel in control of your life and to what extent do you not feel in control? If you can control your eating and/or exercise habits, describe the satisfaction that this control brings you.

Media Mirrors
CAROL MOOG

With a Ph.D. in clinical psychology, Carol Moog has practiced as a therapist treating women who often reflect on how the media shape their desires and sense of self. She has written about how tobacco and alcohol ads, in particular, appeal to women's ambitions for "heightened independence and self-fulfillment," while depicting them as childlike creatures of leisure and pleasure. Besides working as an active critic of advertising, Moog is also president of Creative Focus, a Philadelphia consulting firm advising ad agencies on the design of their campaigns. The following selection is from her book "Are They Selling Her Lips?": Advertising and Identity (1990).

——————————— ✦ ———————————

Breasts.
Philip Roth yearned for them.
Hef built an empire on them.
But Maidenform made the fortune from them.

Sharon, the forty-seven-year-old wife of a dentist with two grown children, is telling me about the dream she had three nights before:

Richard and I were in a restaurant. I think it was the Citadel, where we ate about a month ago—I don't know. But it was different. There were all these men around, and I felt uncomfortable. But they weren't alone. They were there with some old women—like their mothers or grandmothers or something. And I was very angry at Richard. I remember fighting with him there before too. He kept telling me to shut up, that I was drinking too much. Suddenly, I realized I didn't have anything on and he was mad at me because everyone was staring. I thought, I've got to get out of here. I panicked. But I couldn't move. No one at the other tables seemed to pay any attention. And here's where it got really strange. I started to relax. I felt beautiful. And Richard smiled.

Sharon's dream has triggered a thought in my mind that starts to crystallize into an image that helps me understand what she's thinking about. I'm imagining Bea Coleman and her mother, Ida Rosenthal, and the brilliant campaign they launched more than thirty years ago. A campaign so brilliant that it touched the most potent fantasies of a woman's dreams.

It was the Maidenform fantasy. The "I dreamed I was . . . in my Maidenform bra" campaign ran for twenty years and made Bea Coleman and Ida Rosenthal rich beyond their wildest dreams.

The original Maidenform ads were created by the agency of Norman, Craig and Kummel Advertising, and showed women acting out fantasies (frequently controversial fantasies), that fully displayed their Maidenform bras. Ads like the lady lawyer who "dreamed I swayed the jury in my Maidenform bra" unleashed and exposed the secret fantasizes of traditional women of the fifties and invited them to step brazenly into dreams of power and influence. What the ads had women "dream" was that they could go ahead and be exhibitionistic, but not just about their bodies; about their capabilities. Clearly, a psychological chord was struck with this campaign. Women sent scores of unsolicited photos of themselves in endless scenes of "I dreamed I was . . . in my Maidenform bra." In terms of how the campaign portrayed women, it was a real set-breaker. The campaign put the company on the map and gave cultural approval to powerful wishes women certainly harbored but rarely advertised.

What was going on in the women who responded so posi- 5 tively to the Maidenform campaign? This was pre-women's lib, when gender roles were still plainly spelled out: Females were Devoted Housewives and males were Preoccupied Breadwinners. Then along comes Maidenform with full-color photos of poised, clear-eyed, confident women unabashedly exposing their fantasies along with their chests. They're not in the least self-conscious. They're relaxed and composed. The campaign offered a sensational subconscious release for the duty-bound women of that period. It was enormously gratifying to identify with the courage of the Maidenform woman daring to show herself as fully developed to anyone interested in looking. Interested persons included parents, husbands, clergymen, and teachers. The fifties woman got to vicariously thumb her nose at all the right people. She got to break out of the socially appropriate straitjacket she'd willingly donned—ostensibly for the good of family and cultural stability—and try on a new identity.

Psychologically, that's what dreams are about anyway. They're what the unconscious produces, busily fulfilling wishes that our rational selves have deemed too outrageous to express in real life. There's something else about dreams. They show us images of ourselves that we've already accepted internally but that we haven't risked trying out yet.

• • •

Here was a landmark campaign that came at precisely the right time to rivet women's attention. A piece of anatomical support empowered their dreams, permitting them to become "Maidenform women," in control of themselves, their circumstances, and their future. The Maidenform campaign was a strong one, largely because it reflected one advertiser's personal convictions. Bea Coleman, Maidenform's dynamic CEO, always admired her entrepreneurial mother, Ida Rosenthal, who founded the company with her physician-husband, William. Ida was a powerhouse. Mother and daughter both dared to dream big and do more. The "I dreamed..." concept was turned down by another lingerie company but embraced by Maidenform, perhaps because it was consistent with both Bea's and Ida's perceptions of women. Bea seemed to use her mother as a positive role model, and Ida may have unintentionally modeled aspects of herself through the endless permutations of the dream campaign. She persuaded women not just to buy $100 million worth of underwear, but to see themselves as more capable people.

But the dream campaign hit social forces beyond its control—and turned with the tide of change. By the late sixties, the younger women who should have been buying Maidenform bras had begun to associate "I dreamed..." images with their mothers—and bras themselves with the constraints of traditional female roles and functions. When young women started ditching their bras along with their mothers' ideas as they reached for autonomy, the advertiser responded to the psychological climate by ditching the "I dreamed . . ." campaign. (Interestingly, Bea Coleman's own story runs a close parallel to the course of the campaign—this was just about the time that she shocked the male-dominated intimate-apparel industry in 1968 by taking over the company as president after her husband's death.)

What happened? Like Bea Coleman herself, women weren't just acknowledging their dreams of power, they were out there making them happen. The dream campaign symbolized the exciting but frustrated longings of the past. These were fantasy ads meant for the women they were trying to escape in their mothers and in themselves. The ads no longer had their initial freeing effect. Instead, they waved a red flag. Women like my old friend Phyllis were burning their bras, not dreaming about showing them off.

The Maidenform woman was mothballed for eleven years. 10
When she reappeared, she launched the greatest controversy in bra history. In a reincarnation created by the Daniel & Charles advertising agency, she was still depicted doing active, even aggressive things, like commuting to work, reading *The Wall Street Journal*, going to the theater, or being a lawyer. She was daringly clad in her matching bra and panties. But now *there were men in the picture!* They appeared disinterested, oblivious to the delectable spectacle of "The Maidenform Woman. You never know where she'll turn up." The men were shot slightly out of focus. They were deeply absorbed, eyes discreetly everywhere else but you-know-where.

Here was a real twist, and the campaign ended up generating the kind of hot attention that left feminists seething and Maidenform sales soaring. Completely unanticipated! Maidenform didn't intend (as many advertisers do) to create a potentially explosive campaign. The agency just thought it had a great new approach for a new age. Advertiser and agency were equally surprised when the campaign got scorching reviews from angered members of women's movements. It also put Maidenform in the painful position of having to reevaluate the "success" of a campaign that, without question, was a success in terms of sales.

What ticked off women when Maidenform tried to turn them on? As the advertiser sees it, the campaign was inadvertently suggesting that the Maidenform woman had achieved her enviable position, such as tiger tamer, strictly on the basis of her sexuality rather than her actual competence. The most noteworthy clunker, the one that finally deep-sixed the "You never know where she'll turn up" campaign, was the white-coated lady doctor piece. Everyone (male or female) who had ever worn a white coat—nurses, lab technicians, beauticians, the American Medical Association—bombarded Maidenform with calls and letters of protest.

• • •

What was really most offensive were the self-indulgent, narcissistic posturings of the *men* in the picture. For the woman wearing a Maidenform bra, the experience was no longer a good dream. It was a bad dream. It is humiliating on the deepest levels, where our feelings of self-worth are most fragile, for any of us to expose ourselves at our most naked and vulnerable . . . and make no impact whatsoever. Women can easily identify with the Maidenform image in the ads, put themselves in her position and feel the angry confusion of someone who dolls herself up but still gets ignored.

There's more. Despite being pictured in the trappings of power, this Maidenform woman ended up looking weak and vulnerable. Look at the contrast between the unblinking confidence and forward-thrusting body posture of the lady pool-shark and check out the demure, downcast glance and tight-kneed toe-tipped stance of the tiger tamer. Maidenform tried to tell women that it was listening, that it respected their hard-won accomplishments, but it sent some subtle messages that undercut the communication. Women bought the bras but were left with images of themselves as "sweet nothings"—ironically the name of one of Maidenform's best-selling lines.

15   After four years of profitable (although sometimes uncomfortable) campaigning, Maidenform pulled back from its big-strong-pretty-young-things-turning-up-half-naked-in-front-of-self-involved-men approach. Romance, Maidenform perceived, was coming back. It was time to turn from power to syrup. Women were beginning to gag on advertisers' endless portraits of them as superhuman jugglers of kids, career, hubby, and housework.

Stripped of any power cues, the next Maidenform Woman was one who "Dares to Dream." And what are her daring dreams about now? Sitting around wearing underwear and a wistful, vacant expression, she boldly fantasizes about going out on a date. Here is a woman with no pretensions of being anything other than the lovely, compliant, and ever-so-feminine creature her mother modeled in the fifties. She's straight out of the whistle-clean Harlequin Romance series, right down to the quasi-book-jacket logo in the corner. And like these little stories, Maidenform declares that its "Delectables" will "make your life as soft and smooth as your dreams."

At this stage of the game, all of us, women especially, have gotten to be fairly sophisticated cynics. We know that advertisers run various images of us to see whether they can stir a ripple of salesworthy responses. The "Dares to Dream" campaign reached out to women who had been feeling like miserable failures for fantasizing about guys. While everybody else was out there self-actualizing into steel-plated CEOs, Maidenform gave the new romantics permission to go ahead and dream the dreams of adolescent girls if they wanted.

Sales proved that many women wanted just that. Enough battling against male indifference and resistance. Maidenform was tired of trying to tickle the fancies of feminists; the campaign regressed to the lowest-risk imagery for the masses—woman as a glowworm for love.

• • •

Following this purely saccharine retreat from Maidenform's gutsy heritage, the sixty-five-year-old lingerie company set out in pursuit of the Holy Grail of advertising—a new image. After a grueling selection process, Levine, Huntley, Schmidt & Beaver won the account—and the opportunity to sweat its way toward a singularly brilliant advertising idea.

What Levine, Huntley, Schmidt & Beaver created, and what   20
the advertiser had the courage to appreciate, is a radical departure for lingerie ads.

No women, no product—just male movie-star-types like Omar Sharif, Michael York, and Corbin Bernsen. The campaign has been noticed by the media, by competitors, and apparently by women, who've written comments to the advertiser like "I don't normally watch commercials—however, your Michael York commercial is fantastic! So much so I've switched to Maidenform." "Your commercial will be shown at our annual meeting . . . as a prime example of excellent advertising. It appeals to women as adults, not children . . . keep up the good work." And "This is the type of commercial that instills a need in me to purchase your product."

Now just what is driving these ads? What happens when women see someone like Omar Sharif shot in deep shadows, murmuring, "Lingerie says a lot about a woman. I listen as often as possible"? There's an edge of the forbidden, the dangerous, to Sharif's exotic, rakish seductiveness that is a psychological turn-on to the dainty dreamers of Maidenform's recent past. They can rebel against the sweet-young-thing image, and run away (in their fantasies) with a sexy devil. No one has to take the modesty of a woman publicly displayed in her underwear. Sharif's appeal is also clearly to a mature market; he's not exactly the current heart-throb of younger women. So the advertiser moved away from charming vignettes of moody little models and is effectively hook-ing grown-ups with male bait.

With Corbin Bernsen of *L.A. Law*, the psychological lure isn't just juicy evil. Here's a recognizably competent lady-killer, who enters the mysterious realm of a lingerie department and finds it "a little embarrassing. A little intimidating." What a gift to the fe-male ego! If Maidenform can give women a way to embarrass and intimidate the likes of Mr. Bernsen, even "a little," it's not just un-derwear anymore—it's personal power.

• • •

The trouble with the advertising mirror is that we never really see ourselves reflected; we only see reflections of what advertisers want us to think their products will do for us. If the image of who we might be if we used the advertiser's product resonates with where we secretly, or not so secretly, wish we were then there we are, consciously or unconsciously, measuring up to Madison Av-enue. Sometimes that's not such a bad thing, but sometimes whatever insecurities we have get exacerbated by advertisers' im-age-making and by our own intense desires to make it—to win first prize in Madison Avenue's perpetual lookalike contest.

Discussion Questions

1. Moog claims that the Maidenform bra ads in the 1950s conveyed a feminist message that frustrated housewives could assume positions of "power and influence" (paragraph 4). Are such appeals to women present in advertising today? Describe some relevant examples in television commercials or magazine ads.

2. Moog suggests that most ads operate as a kind of wish fulfillment—as pleasant answers to our own fantasies for a better image of ourselves. Recall some examples of advertising that do *not* work, psychologically, in this way—providing a desirable role model for us to assume. For what types of products would this appeal *not* be effective?

3. Can you recall a print advertisement or television commercial to which you responded strongly? If not, flip through a popular magazine or view a few commercials on television and select one that gets under your skin. Explain exactly how you responded to the ad's or commercial's pitch for the product.

Was your response positive or negative? Why? Did your feelings relate only to the presentation, the scene created by the ad or commercial, or to the product itself? Explain how you think the advertisers worked on you, psychologically, to create desires or even to offend you in some way.

4. In a brief paragraph, describe how "the feminine" is represented by Moog in "Media Mirrors."

A Gentleman and a Consumer
Diane Barthel

With a Ph.D. from Harvard, Diane Barthel is a professor of sociology at the State University of New York at Stony Brook, where her research focuses on the sociology of art, nonprofit organizations, symbolic communities, and gender issues. Of interest to historians, museum curators, and other sociologists, her recent publications include Historic Preservation: Collective Memory and Historical Identity *(1996). The following selection is from her 1988 book* Putting On Appearances: Gender and Advertising.

As you read, notice the two major headings that separate the second and third sections of the article from the beginning section. Consider how the headings might help you to understand the information contained in the later sections. What heading would you give the first section that would announce its major concerns?

———————— ✦ ————————

There are no men's beauty and glamour magazines with circulations even approaching those of the women's magazines. . . . The very idea of men's beauty magazines may strike one as odd. In our society men traditionally were supposed to make the right appearance, to be well groomed and neatly tailored. What they were *not* supposed to do was to be overly concerned with their appearance, much less vain about their beauty. That was to be effeminate, and not a "real man." Male beauty was associated with homosexuals, and "real men" had to show how red-blooded they were by maintaining a certain distance from fashion.

Perhaps the best-known male fashion magazine is *GQ* founded in 1957 and with a circulation of 446,000 in 1986. More recently, we have seen the launching of *YMF* and *Young Black Male*, which in 1987 still have few advertising pages. *M* magazine, founded in 1983, attracts an audience "a cut above" that of *GQ*.

Esquire magazine, more venerable (founded in 1933), is classified as a general interest magazine. Although it does attract many women readers, many of the columns and features and much of the advertising are definitely directed toward attracting the attention of the male readers, who still make up the overwhelming majority of the readership.

As mentioned in the introduction, the highest circulations for men's magazines are for magazines specializing either in sex (*Playboy*, circulation 4.1 million; *Penthouse*, circulation nearly 3.8 million; and *Hustler*, circulation 1.5 million) or sports (*Sports Illustrated*, circulation 2.7 million). That these magazines share an emphasis on power—either power over women or over other men on the playing field—should not surprise. In fact, sociologist John Gagnon would argue that sex and sports now represent the major fields in which the male role, as defined by power, is played out, with physical power in work, and even in warfare, less important than it was before industrialization and technological advance.

5   If we are looking for comparative evidence as to how advertisements define gender roles for men and women, we should not then see the male role as defined primarily through beauty and fashion. This seems an obvious point, but it is important to emphasize how different cultural attitudes toward both the social person and the physical body shape the gender roles of men and women. These cultural attitudes are changing, and advertisements are helping to legitimate the use of beauty products and an interest in fashion for men, as we shall see. As advertisements directed toward women are beginning to use male imagery, so too advertisements for men occasionally use imagery resembling that found in advertisements directed toward women. We are speaking of two *modes*, then. As [French social critic] Baudrillard writes, these modes "do not result from the differentiated nature of the two sexes, but from the differential logic of the system. The relationship of the Masculine and the Feminine to real men and women is relatively arbitrary." Increasingly today, men and women use both modes. The two great terms of opposition (Masculine and Feminine) still, however, structure the forms that consumption takes; they provide identities for products and consumers.

Baudrillard agrees that the feminine model encourages a woman to please herself, to encourage a certain complacency and even narcissistic solicitude. But by pleasing herself, it is understood that she will also please others, and that she will be chosen.

"She never enters into direct competition. . . . If she is beautiful, that is to say, if this woman is a woman, she will be chosen. If the man is a man, he will choose his woman as he would other objects/signs (HIS car, HIS woman, HIS eau de toilette)." Whereas the feminine model is based on passivity, complacency, and narcissism, the masculine model is based on exactingness and choice.

> All of masculine advertising insists on rule, on choice, in terms of rigor and inflexible minutiae. He does not neglect a detail. . . . It is not a question of just letting things go, or of taking pleasure in something, but rather of distinguishing himself. To know how to choose, and not to fail at it, is here the equivalent of the military and puritanical virtues: intransigence, decision, "virtus."

This masculine model, these masculine virtues, are best reflected in the many car advertisements. There, the keywords are masculine terms: *power, performance, precision.* Sometimes the car is a woman, responding to the touch and will of her male driver, after attracting him with her sexy body. "Pure shape, pure power, pure Z. It turns you on." But, as the juxtaposition of shape and power in this advertisement suggest, the car is not simply other; it is also an extension of the owner. As he turns it on, he turns himself on. Its power is his power; through it, he will be able to overpower other men and impress and seduce women.

> How well does it perform?
> How well can you drive? (Merkur XR4Ti)

> The 1987 Celica GT-S has the sweeping lines and aggressive stance that promise performance. And Celica keeps its word.
> Renault GTA: Zero to sixty to zero in 13.9 sec.
> It's the result of a performance philosophy where acceleration and braking are equally important.
> There's a new Renault sports sedan called GTA. Under its slick monochromatic skin is a road car with a total performance attitude. . . . It's our hot new pocket rocket.

In this last example, the car, like the driver, has a total performance attitude. That is what works. The slick monochromatic skin, like the Bond Street suit, makes a good first impression. But car, like owner, must have what it takes, must be able to go the distance faster and better than the competition. This point is explicitly made in advertisements in which the car becomes a means through which this masculine competition at work is extended in leisure. Some refer directly to the manly sport of autoracing: "The Mitsubishi Starion ESI-R. Patiently crafted to ignite your imagination. Leaving little else to say except . . . gentlemen, start your engines." Others refer to competition in the business world: "To move ahead fast in this world, you've got to have connections. The totally new Cordolia FX 16 GT-S has the right ones." Or in life in general. "It doesn't take any [Japanese characters] from anyone. It won't stand for any guff from 300ZX. Or RX-7. Introducing Conquest Tsi, the new turbo sport coupe designed and built by Mitsubishi in Japan." Or Ferrari, which says simply, "We are the competition." In this competition between products, the owners become almost superfluous. But the advertisements, of course, suggest that the qualities of the car will reflect the qualities of the owner, as opposed to the purely abstract, a personal quality of money needed for purchase. Thus, like the would-be owner, the BMW also demonstrates a "relentless refusal to compromise." It is for "those who thrive on a maximum daily requirement of high performance." While the BMW has the business attitude of the old school ("aggression has never been expressed with such dignity"), a Beretta suggests what it takes to survive today in the shark-infested waters of Wall Street. In a glossy three-page cover foldout, a photograph of a shark's fin cutting through indigo waters is accompanied by the legend "Discover a new species from today's Chevrolet." The following two pages show a sleek black Beretta similarly cutting through water and, presumably, through the competition: "Not just a new car, but a new species . . . with a natural instinct for the road . . . Aggressive stance. And a bold tail lamp. See it on the road and you won't soon forget. Drive it, and you never will."

10 And as with men, so with cars. "Power corrupts. Absolute power corrupts; absolutely" (Maserati). Not having the money to pay for a Maserati, to corrupt and be corrupted, is a source of embarrassment. Advertisements reassure the consumer that he need not lose face in this manly battle. Hyundai promises, "It's affordable. (But you'd never know it.)"

> On first impression, the new Hyundai Excel GLS Sedan might seem a trifle beyond most people's means. But that's entirely by design. Sleek European design, to be exact.

Many advertisements suggest sexual pleasure and escape, as in "Pure shape, pure power, pure Z. It turns you on." Or "The all-new Chrysler Le Baron. Beauty . . . with a passion for driving." The Le Baron may initially suggest a beautiful female, with its "image of arresting beauty" and its passion "to drive. And drive it does!" But it is "Le Baron," not "La Baronness." And the advertisement continues to emphasize how "it *attacks* [emphasis mine] the road with a high torque, 2.5 liter fuel-injected engine. And its turbo option can blur the surface of any passing lane." Thus the object of the pleasure hardly has to be female if it is beautiful or sleek. The car is an extension of the male that conquers and tames the (female) road: "Positive-response suspension will calm the most demanding roads." The car becomes the ultimate lover when, like the Honda Prelude, it promises to combine power, "muscle," with finesse. Automobile advertisements thus play with androgyny and sexuality; the pleasure is in the union and confusion of form and movement, sex and speed. As in any sexual union, there is ultimately a merging of identities, rather than rigid maintenance of their separation. Polymorphous perverse? Perhaps. But it sells.

• • •

This is a world of patriarchal order in which the individual male can and must challenge the father. He achieves identity by breaking loose of the structure and breaking free of the pack. In the process he recreates the order and reaffirms the myth of masculine independence. Above all, he demonstrates that he knows what he wants; he is critical, demanding, and free from the constraints of others. What he definitely does not want, and goes to some measure to avoid, is to appear less than masculine, in any way weak, frilly, feminine.

AVOIDING THE FEMININE

Advertisers trying to develop male markets for products previously associated primarily with women must overcome the taboo that only women wear moisturizer, face cream, hair spray, or perfume. They do this by overt reference to masculine symbols, language, and imagery, and sometimes by confronting the problem head-on.

There is not so much of a problem in selling products to counteract balding—that traditionally has been recognized as a male problem (a bald woman is a sexual joke that is not particularly amusing to the elderly). But other hair products are another story, as the March 1987 *GQ* cover asks, "Are you man enough for mousse?" So the advertisements must make their products seem manly, as with S-Curl's "wave and curl kit" offering "The Manly Look" on its manly model dressed in business suit and carrying a hard hat (a nifty social class compromise), and as in college basketball sportscaster Al McGuire's testimonial for Consort hair spray:

> "Years ago, if someone had said to me, 'Hey Al, do you use hair spray?' I would have said, 'No way, baby!'"
> "That was before I tried Consort Pump."
> "Consort adds extra control to my hair without looking stiff or phony. Control that lasts clean into overtime and post-game interviews. . . ."
> Grooming Gear for Real Guys. *Consort*.

15   Beside such "grooming gear" as perms and hair sprays, Real Guys use "skin supplies" and "shaving resources." They adopt a "survival strategy" to fight balding, and the "Fila philosophy"— "products with a singular purpose: performance"—for effective "bodycare." If they wear scent, it smells of anything *but* flowers: musk, woods, spices, citrus, and surf are all acceptable. And the names must be manly, whether symbolizing physical power ("Brut") or financial power ("Giorgio VIP Special Reserve," "The Baron. A distinctive fragrance for men," "Halston—For the privileged few.")

• • •

Men's products connect status and success; the right products show that you have the right stuff, that you're one of them. In the 1950s C. Wright Mills described what it took to get ahead, to become part of the "power elite":

> The fit survive, and fitness means, not formal competence . . . but conformity with the criteria of those who have already succeeded. To be compatible with the top men is to act like them, to look like them, to think like them: to be of and for them—or at least to display oneself to them in such a way as to create that impression. This, in fact, is what is meant by "creating"—a well-chosen word—"a good impression." This is what is meant—and nothing else—by being a "sound man," as sound as a dollar.

Today, having what it takes includes knowing "the difference between dressed, and well dressed" (Bally shoes). It is knowing that "what you carry says as much about you as what you put inside it" (Hartmann luggage). It is knowing enough to imitate Doug Fout, "member of one of the foremost equestrian families in the country."

> Because of our adherence to quality and the natural shoulder tradition, Southwick clothing was adopted by the Fout family years ago. Clearly, they have as much appreciation for good lines in a jacket as they do in a thoroughbred.

There it is, old money. There is no substitute for it, really, in business or in advertising, where appeals to tradition form one of the mainstays guaranteeing men that their choices are not overly fashionable or feminine, not working class or cheap, but, rather, correct, in good form, above criticism. If, when they achieve this status of gentlemanly perfection, then, the advertisement suggests, they may be invited to join the club.

• • •

MASCULINE HOMILIES

A homily is a short sermon, discourse, or informal lecture, often on a moral topic and suggesting a course of conduct. Some of the most intriguing advertisements offer just that, short statements and bits of advice on what masculinity is and on how real men should conduct themselves. As with many short sermons, many of the advertising homilies have a self-congratulatory air about them; after all, you do not want the consumer to feel bad about himself.

What is it, then, to be a man? It is to be *independent*. "There are some things a man will not relinquish." Among them, says the advertisement, his Tretorn tennis shoes. 20

It is to *savor freedom*. "Dress easy, get away from it all and let Tom Sawyer paint the fence," advises Alexander Julian, the men's designer. "Because man was meant to fly, we gave him wings" (even if only on his sunglasses).

It is to live a life of *adventure*. KL Homme cologne is "for the man who lives on the edge." Prudential Life Insurance preaches, "If you can dream it, you can do it." New Man sportswear tells the reader, "Life is more adventurous when you feel like a New Man."

It is to *keep one's cool.* "J & B Scotch. A few individuals know how to keep their heads, even when their necks are on the line." And it is to stay one step *ahead of the competition.* "Altec Lansing. Hear what others only imagine." Alexander Julian again: "Dress up a bit when you dress down. They'll think you know something they don't."

25   What is it, then, to be a woman? It is to be *dependent.* "A woman needs a man," reads the copy in the Rigolletto advertisement showing a young man changing a tire for a grateful young woman.

The American cowboy as cultural model was not supposed to care for or about appearances. He was what he was, hardworking, straightforward, and honest. He was authentic. Men who cared "too much" about how they looked did not fit this model; the dandy was effete, a European invention, insufficient in masculinity and not red-blooded enough to be a real American. The other cultural model, imported from England, was the gentleman. A gentleman did care about his appearance, in the proper measure and manifestation, attention to tailoring and to quality, understatement rather than exaggeration.

From the gray flannel suit of the 1950s to the "power look" of the 1980s, clothes made the man fit in with his company's image. Sex appeal and corporate correctness merged in a look that spelled success, that exuded confidence.

Whether or not a man presumed to care about his appearance, he did care about having "the right stuff," as Tom Wolfe and *Esquire* call it, or "men's toys," as in a recent special issue of *M* magazine. Cars, motorcycles, stereos, sports equipment: these are part of the masculine appearance. They allow the man to demonstrate his taste, his special knowledge, his affluence: to extend his control. He can be and is demanding, for only the best will do.

He also wants to be loved, but he does not want to appear needy. Advertisements suggest the magic ability of products ranging from cars to hair creams to attract female attention. With the right products a man can have it all, with no strings attached: no boring marital ties, hefty mortgages, corporate compromises.

30   According to sociologist Barbara Ehrenreich, *Playboy* magazine did much to legitimate this image of male freedom. The old male ethos, up to the postwar period, required exchanging bachelor irresponsibility for married responsibility, which also symbolized entrance into social adulthood. The perennial bachelor, with his flashy cars and interchangeable women, was the object of both envy and derision; he had fun, but and because he was not

fully grown up. There was something frivolous in his lack of purpose and application.

This old ethos has lost much of its legitimacy. Today's male can, as Baudrillard suggests, operate in both modes: the feminine mode of indulging oneself and being indulged and the masculine mode of exigency and competition. With the right look and the right stuff, he can feel confident and manly in boardroom or suburban backyard. Consumer society thus invites both men and women to live in a world of appearances and to devote ever more attention to them.

Discussion Questions

1. To what extent do you believe that, in American culture, "the feminine model is based on passivity, complacency and narcissism" (paragraph 7)?
2. Describe the ways in which advertising directed to men changed in the 1980s, according to Barthel.
3. Analyze the image of "the perennial bachelor, with his flashy cars and interchangeable women . . . , not fully grown up . . . , frivolous in his lack of purpose" (paragraph 30). To what extent is this image relevant today? If not, describe an alternate image of bachelorhood. In what ways is remaining unmarried seen as a responsible choice for men? Compare and contrast with social images of the married man.
4. Compare and contrast how "masculinity" is represented in Moog's article, "Media Mirrors"; in Barthel's article, "A Gentleman and a Consumer"; and in Ewen's article, "Hard Bodies" (in Chapter 2).
5. Review your response to Question 4 above. Presenting examples from your own experience or observation, explain the ways in which you agree and/or disagree with the three authors' views of "masculinity."

Topics for Exploration and Writing

You have been reading about and discussing various relationships among body image, masculine and feminine characteristics, ethnicity, and popular culture. To explore these ideas, analyze one "cultural text"—a concrete expression of American popular culture (advertisement, comic book, film, toy, game)—that reveals our assumptions and beliefs about body image. In some ways, your analysis will resemble a close reading and interpretation of a short story, except that your "story" consists not only of words, but also of images and perhaps social practices, such as how girls or boys play with dolls. Your essay must first *describe* the "text," especially if it may be unfamiliar to some members of your class. Also, to provide evidence for your interpretation, your essay must include quotations or examples. While most of your content should be original, make brief comparisons to *at least one* of the articles in this chapter to develop your viewpoint (referring to authors by last name and to article titles). If your text is fairly brief, such as an ad or comic, you should attach it to your essay as a supporting document.

1. Examine a specific *fictional* film representing cross-dressing, such as *Some Like It Hot* (1959), *Tootsie* (1982), or *Mrs. Doubtfire* (1993). Analyze the characteristics that are depicted as "masculine" and "feminine," explaining to what extent you think that representation is realistic or relies on stereotypes. To what extent does the cross-dressing character possess both "masculine" and "feminine" characteristics? Explain the point that you think the film makes about gender and socially determined gender roles. Use examples of *specific scenes* as evidence to support your thesis. It is best to view a videotape of the film so that you can replay scenes for note-taking and interpretation.

2. Analyze the role models projected by the Susie Schoolteacher doll and Wonder Woman in Ortiz Cofer's "The Story of My Body." Explain why and how these mainstream American cultural models appealed to her as a child from a "minority" culture. That is, explain the meanings of the doll and the comic book image in Ortiz Cofer's own growing-up process. You may also want to compare her experience to your own childhood experience if you identified with a particular toy or pop culture role model from comics, books, movies, or cartoons.

3. Instead of focusing on Ortiz Cofer's article as in Topic 2, you may explain it briefly as a starting point and then develop most of your essay as an analysis of the meaning of a particular doll, toy, or game in your personal childhood experience or among the siblings in your family. For instance, you might explain how you played with a particular doll, a doll house, a train set, tinker toys, a cowboy or cowgirl outfit, or an "action figure" (such as GI Joe). Whatever single "cultural text" you select, analyze its importance in shaping your ideas of *body image*, behavior, and identity, especially as a boy or a girl. If the toy or doll appealed equally to both girls and boys in your family, explain what values each child found in playing with it. If you recall name-calling that labeled you a "sissy" or a "tomboy" because of your interest in this doll or activity, explain the context and interpret how you felt about your own choices. You will probably analyze gender issues raised by this cultural practice, but also consider issues of ethnicity and social class if relevant.

4. Select a popular magazine with a clear audience (such as *Seventeen*, *Hot Rod*, *GQ*, *Rolling Stone*, *Self*, *Muscle*, *Esquire*, or *Glamour*) and find a fullpage, color ad that provides good descriptive details and a lengthy

text (30+ words) to interpret. Recalling the readings in this chapter, approach your essay as a *cultural criticism* of the particular ad you select. Consider this manifestation of popular culture in terms of its social meanings; its models for readers' individual identities; its depiction of particular races, classes, genders, or sexual preferences; its implied commentary on American values, beliefs, and treasured myths. Above all, select an ad that represents the *human body* or promotes a personal product related to appearance or image.

Of course, to write such an essay seems to make much more of a picture or a product slogan than maybe even an ad agency intended. But the point of this exercise is to get beneath the surface and try to understand the complexity of media messages that we normally take for granted and accept at face value as somewhat trivial. To assist you in developing this critical perspective, incorporate some insight from one of the Chapter 4 articles in your analysis.

You can generalize or discover a thesis only by citing specific examples and details from the data (pictures and words) in your chosen subject, working from individual cases to create a perspective that synthesizes or integrates ideas. To *interpret* the ad, you must explain how the ad appeals to the reader. Discuss its representation of society and its psychology—what assumptions it makes about men or women or students or people in general; what social practices or cultural values it assumes or takes advantage of; how it "exploits" the desires of the reader; what it takes for granted about the reader's attitudes on such topics as sexuality and gender, economic class and notions of "success," ethnicity and diversity, political awareness or preferences. You can structure your analysis by separately considering the following elements of the ad, but you should also write introductory and concluding paragraphs:

- Based on the magazine itself, analyze the "ideal" audience or readers. Consider how their interests, concerns, gender, race, likely economic class, roles in society, and purposes for reading the magazine might affect its content and advertising. How are these interests and backgrounds represented in the magazine? Explain associations between keywords, hot topics, and repeated visual images (in both articles and advertising) and their subjective meanings.
- In your particular ad, "read" the picture and explain the dramatic "scene" or action the picture tries to create. Point out details and suggest their purpose and their relation to the product or its image. What kind of person or society does the picture represent? What gender and race are the people you see? What sort of people are not represented? Identify cultural values that the picture assumes and explain whether the values are fairly or legitimately associated with the

product. To gain some critical perspective on the visual material, consider those values you share, those that you resist or cannot believe in, and those that you can negotiate or believe in to some extent.

- Interpret the text of the ad. Focus on the language and explain the key terms. What concerns or values does it assume to be important? Discuss the level of diction—formal, educated, conversational, casual, or slang. Does the ad appear to use the vocabulary of the audience? Does the ad's language make legitimate associations with the product itself? How do you respond to the cultural values of the ad? How can you explain your pleasure, excitement, disgust, or apathy?

- Explain the ad's rhetorical appeals; decide which appeal dominates the ad: *logical*—orderly reasoning from facts, numbers, "scientific" details; *emotional*—the feeling the ad tries to invoke in the audience or readers; *ethical*—the self-image (*ethos*) that the speaker of the ad represents, the role model that the reader is asked to believe in and identify with. Explain to what extent you accommodate, resist, and/or negotiate this role model.

5. Instead of focusing on a single advertisement, as in Topic 4, analyze several ads for the same product selected over an extended period of time (five years or even three decades). Review the above guidelines for analysis, but rather than analyzing the entire text and imagery of one ad in detail, explain the *changes* in the advertising strategy or psychological appeals to the potential customer. Use Moog's article as a model for your social analysis. Explain how these changes in psychological and rhetorical appeals to sell a product actually reflect changes in American society or culture over the time period of your ad samples.

6. Instead of focusing on a single advertisement, as in Topic 4, analyze several ads in one sports magazine to reveal how the body images of men and women are represented. Review the above guidelines for analysis, but rather than analyzing the entire text and imagery of one ad in detail, analyze selected ads, especially for products that claim to enhance body image or appearance. Explain to what extent the images of men and women in the ads are similar or different. Explain the psychological appeals to men and to women, especially if they differ. To what extent are women's needs (for fitness, strength, muscles, lean appearance, etc.) represented as similar to or different from men's needs for the product. Are there, in fact, "masculine" and "feminine" versions of the product? As much as possible, explain how body images in the sports ads reflect both realities and myths of gender differences in American culture. Besides referring to one of the articles in Chapter 4, you may want to incorporate viewpoints from Ewen's article, "Hard Bodies," in Chapter 2.

Medicine and Technology

Neurology's favorite word is 'deficit,' denoting an impairment or incapacity of neurological function," writes Oliver Sacks in the opening sentence of *The Man Who Mistook His Wife for a Hat* (Summit, 1985). He asserts that his profession has been misled by the research locating particular neurological powers—of speech or mathematical reasoning, for example—in particular centers in the left hemisphere of the brain. Neurology sustains misperceptions, Sacks suggests, because its deficit model of disease neglects the reality that excesses of function—such as the massive electrical discharges in the brain that trigger an epileptic seizure—can also cause neurological "dysfunction." Furthermore, "the rather rigid and mechanical neurology of the past" (6) has been limited by its neglect of syndromes in the right hemisphere, where "the physical foundations of the *persona*, the self" are located. Sacks advises neurologists, and physicians in general, to assist their patients in their assertive struggle toward wholeness in mind, body and self. "A disease is never a mere loss or excess," he affirms. "There is always a reaction, on the part of the affected organism or individual, to restore, to replace, to compensate for and to preserve its identity" (6).

The real danger of the deficit model of medicine is that we may "pathologize" a normal range of behaviors. If a boy cannot sit still to focus on school work, he is often diagnosed with Attention Deficit Disorder (ADD) and dosed with psychoactive prescription drugs for several years. Likewise, the deficit model encourages us to emphasize the dysfunctions or defects of disabled people, rather than the activities and contributions they are capable of. The deficit model also encourages women to correct the "pathology" of infertility through the heroic efforts and expensive technologies of artificial insemination.

Most of the articles in Chapter 5 respond to Oliver Sacks's challenge to rethink the deficit model that pervades our technocratic health care system. The first article, "Pandora's Baby," challenges our faith in technology that has enabled the birth of a million artificially inseminated babies. Robin Marantz Henig argues that in vitro fertilization, despite its success with women who could not otherwise conceive, should provide a lesson for how U.S. society might govern the future of cloning research. In making her science-based argument to the educated readers of *Scientific American*, her cited authorities include the British magazine *Nova*, a University of Chicago biologist, and the *New England Journal of Medicine*. Though she warns of the dangers inherent in unleashing "entrepreneurial scientists" to develop cloning for profit, she also uses the language of "birth defects," thereby marking those children who are born with dysfunction as humans who have suffered a loss.

In the second article, "Choosing Disability," Laura Hershey argues against such a model, affirming from her own experience that life—however limited by physical constraints—is worth all the efforts of her parents and all her ongoing efforts to cope with her own limitations. In her journalistic writing, she is less concerned with scientific facts than with the social implications of medical science, so she cites such sources as activists for disability rights and health care, civil rights lawyers, a Time/CNN survey about abortion, and officials of the National Abortion and Reproductive Rights Action League. Like the participant-observer model of Shannon Bell's research in "Tattooed" from Chapter 3, Hershey makes no claim to be impartial, but writes passionately in support of social justice for the disabled, rejecting society's "assumptions about our inabilities" and affirming, like Sacks, the individual's struggle toward wholeness and identity.

In the third article, "Cloning for Medicine," we return to a more scientific model of writing since Ian Wilmut is the researcher who successfully bred the sheep named Dolly, "the first mammal to be cloned from an adult" in 1997. Since most of his evidence is based on his own laboratory studies, Wilmut's sources are limited to one other *Scientific American* article. Even though he is adamantly in favor of biomedical research in cloning, his work raises ethical questions similar to those that Henig raises in the first article. However, Wilmut tries to allay the fears of his readers by presuming that embryos are not persons, by negotiating cloning research policy through the review of a public advisory committee, and by rejecting the cloning of human embryos as tissue donors. Finally, he writes as a scientist, confident that medical technology will master the biological body in order to improve human lives.

In the fourth article, "Keeping an Eye on the Global Traffic in Human Organs," Nancy Scheper-Hughes reports on the international studies she and another medical anthropologist have done with the help of postgraduate research assistants. In her report, "desperate kidney buyers" certainly accept the deficit model of medicine because they consider that their own dysfunction—the lack of a healthy kidney—can be remedied by replacement with a "spare" kidney from a paid donor. This trading of human organs in the marketplace also invokes the metaphor of the body as a machine, which can be repaired by interchangeable parts. And due to the power of immunosuppressant drugs that prevent the rejection of a transplanted kidney, this is true to some extent. Scheper-Hughes examines the economic exploitation of the transaction, governed as it is by supply and demand, vastly different standards of living, and the rates of currency exchange. But she also criticizes the human and social impacts of this new "slave trade," blaming surgeons for the "mutilation" of paid donors, who are often stigmatized in their communities as "prostitutes." This idea introduces yet another metaphor for the body as a "commodity."

In the fifth article, "America's Altered States," Joshua Wolf Shenk presents the most thoroughly documented research, even though this work was originally published in a popular magazine. He cites psychiatrists, a psychologist, a senator, pharmacologists, the director of the National Institutes of Mental Health (NIMH), a drug policy "think tank," a federal antidrug ad campaign, the Pharmaceutical Research and Manufacturer's Association, prescription medication ads, and four books, including the Aldous Huxley classics *Brave New World* and *The Doors of Perception*. Shenk also uses an impressive array of statistics, but does not identify their source. Throughout his writing on the "drug wars," he considers the big business and the medical science of psychopharmacology, but also reports on his own experience. Despite their promises of health, he finds that the psychoactive drugs his doctors prescribed have never alleviated his depression or cured his presumed detachment of mind and body. Again, the deficit model of modern medicine fails with psychiatric treatment because the doctors cannot seem to find the deficit, the missing piece in the psyche without which mental balance is upset and mental disease arises. Finally, Shenk questions not only the medical treatments for presumed psychological disorders, but also the socioeconomic system that considers the mind as an entity separate from the body to be manipulated and regulated for the enhancement of social order and maximum profit.

Pandora's Baby
ROBIN MARANTZ HENIG

For twenty-five years Robin Marantz Henig has been a freelance writer, specializing in science and medicine. Her articles have appeared in such publications as the New York Times Magazine, Civilization, Scientific American, *and* Discover. *She has also had an active lecture and teaching schedule, including a seminar at the Santa Fe Science Writing Workshop. Over her career, she has written seven books, including* The Monk in the Garden: The Lost and Found Genius of Gregor Mendel, the Father of Genetics *(2000). Her honors include a nomination for a National Book Critics Circle Award. She lives in New York City with her husband, Jeff Henig, a political science professor at Columbia University; they have two nearly grown daughters. Her most recent book, incorporating the following selection, is entitled* Pandora's Baby: How the First Test Tube Babies Sparked the Reproductive Revolution *(2004).*

Before you read, consider whether what you know of cloning inspires fear or hope for medical breakthroughs. As you read, consider how the three headings help you to understand the reading: "Then and Now," "IVF Unbound," and "IVF Risks Revealed."

---------------- ✦ ----------------

On July 25, [2003], a once unique person will turn 25. This nursery school aide in the west of England seems like an average young woman, a quiet, shy blonde who enjoys an occasional round of darts at the neighborhood pub. But Louise Brown's birth was greeted by newspaper headlines calling her the "baby of the century." Brown was the world's first test tube baby.

Today people may remember Brown's name, or that she was British, or that her doctors, Steptoe and Edwards, sounded vaguely like a vaudeville act. But the past quarter of a century has dimmed the memory of one of the most important aspects of her arrival: many people were horrified by it. Even some scientists feared that Patrick Steptoe and Robert Edwards might have brewed pestilence in a petri dish. Would the child be normal, or would the laboratory manipulations leave dreadful genetic derangements? Would she be psychologically scarred by the knowledge of how bizarrely she had been created? And was she a harbinger of a race of unnatural beings who might eventually be fashioned specifically as a means to nefarious ends?

Now that in vitro fertilization (IVF) has led to the birth of an estimated one million babies worldwide, these fears and speculations may seem quaint and even absurd. But the same concerns once raised about IVF are being voiced, sometimes almost verbatim, about human cloning. Will cloning go the way of IVF, morphing from the monstrous to the mundane? And if human cloning, as well as other genetic interventions on the embryo, does someday become as commonplace as test tube baby-making, is that to be feared—or embraced? The lessons that have been learned from the IVF experience can illuminate the next decisions to be made.

THEN AND NOW

As IVF moved from the hypothetical to the actual, some considered it to be nothing more than scientists showing off: "The development of test tube babies," one critic remarked, "can be compared to the perfecting of wing transplants so that pigs might fly." But others thought of IVF as a perilous insult to nature. The British magazine *Nova* ran a cover story in the spring of 1972 suggesting that test tube babies were "the biggest threat since the atom bomb" and demanding that the public rein in the unpredictable scientists. "If today we do not accept the responsibility for directing the biologist," the *Nova* editors wrote, "tomorrow we may pay a bitter price—the loss of free choice and, with it, our humanity. We don't have much time left."

A prominent early enemy of IVF was Leon Kass, a biologist at   5
the University of Chicago who took a professional interest in the emerging field of bioethics. If society allowed IVF to proceed, he wrote shortly after Louise Brown's birth, some enormous issues were at stake: "the idea of the humanness of our human life and the meaning of our embodiment, our sexual being, and our relation to ancestors and descendants."

Now read Kass, a leading detractor of every new form of reproductive technology for the past 30 years, in 2003: "[Cloning] threatens the dignity of human procreation, giving one generation unprecedented genetic control over the next," he wrote in the *New York Times*. "It is the first step toward a eugenic world in which children become objects of manipulation and products of will." Such commentary coming from Kass is particularly noteworthy because of his unique position: for the past two years he has been the head of President George W. Bush's Council on Bioethics, whose first task was to offer advice on how to regulate human cloning.

Of course, IVF did not wind up creating legions of less than human children, nor did it play a role in the disintegration of the nuclear family, consequences that people like Kass feared. And so many newer, more advanced methods of assisted reproduction have been introduced in the past decade that the "basic IVF" that produced Louise Brown now seems positively routine. One early prediction, however, did turn out to contain more than a kernel of truth. In the 1970s critics cautioned that IVF would set us tumbling down the proverbial slippery slope toward more sophisticated and, to some, objectionable forms of reproductive technology—and that once we opened the floodgates by allowing human eggs to be fertilized in the laboratory, there would be no stopping our descent.

If you consider all the techniques that might soon be available to manipulate a developing embryo, it could appear that the IVF naysayers were correct in their assessment of the slipperiness of the slope. After all, none of the genetic interventions now being debated—prenatal genetic diagnosis, gene insertions in sex cells or embryos to correct disease, the creation of new embryonic stem cell lines and, the elephant in the living room, cloning— would even be potentialities had scientists not first learned how to fertilize human eggs in a laboratory dish.

But does the existence of a such a slippery slope mean that present reproductive technology research will lead inevitably to developments that some find odious, such as embryos for tissue harvesting, or the even more abhorrent manufacture of human-nonhuman hybrids and human clones? Many people clearly fear so, which explains the current U.S. efforts to curtail scientists' ability to manipulate embryos even before the work gets under way. But those efforts raise the question of whether science that has profound moral and ethical implications should simply never be done. Or should such science proceed, with careful attention paid to the early evolution of certain areas of research so that society can make informed decisions about whether regulation is needed?

IVF UNBOUND

The frenzy to try to regulate or even outlaw cloning is in part a   10
deliberate attempt not to let it go the way of IVF, which has been
a hodgepodge of unregulated activities with no governmental or
ethical oversight and no scientific coordination. Ironically, the
reason IVF became so ubiquitous and uncontrolled in the U.S.
was that its opponents, particularly antiabortion activists, were
trying to stop it completely. Antiabortion activists' primary objection to IVF was that it involved the creation of extra embryos that
would ultimately be unceremoniously destroyed—a genocide
worse than at any abortion clinic, they believed. Accordingly, they
thought that their best strategy would be to keep the federal government from financing IVF research.

A succession of presidential commissions starting in 1973 debated the ethics of IVF but failed to clarify matters. Some of the
commissions got so bogged down in abortion politics that they
never managed to hold a single meeting. Others concluded that
IVF research was ethically acceptable as long as scientists honored the embryo's unique status as a "potential human life," a
statement rather than a practical guideline. In 1974 the government banned federal funding for fetal research. It also forbade
funding for research on the human embryo (defined as a fetus
less than eight weeks old), which includes IVF. In 1993 President
Bill Clinton signed the NIH Revitalization Act, which allowed federal funding of IVF research. (In 1996, however, Congress again
banned embryo research.) The bottom line is that despite a series
of recommendations from federal bioethics panels stating that
taxpayer support of IVF research would be acceptable with certain safeguards in place, the government has never sponsored a
single research grant for human IVF.

This lack of government involvement—which would also have
served to direct the course of IVF research—led to a funding vacuum, into which rushed entrepreneurial scientists supported by private money. These free agents did essentially whatever they wanted
and whatever the market would bear, turning IVF into a cowboy science driven by the marketplace and undertaken without guidance.
The profession attempted to regulate itself—in 1986, for example,
the American Fertility Society issued ethical and clinical guidelines
for its members—but voluntary oversight was only sporadically effective. The quality of clinics, of which there were more than 160 by
1990, remained spotty, and those seeking IVF had little in the way of
objective information to help them choose the best ones.

Today, in what appears to be an effort to avoid the mistakes made with IVF, the federal government is actively involved in regulating cloning. With the announcement in 1997 of the birth of Dolly, the first mammal cloned from an adult cell, President Clinton established mechanisms, which remain in place, to prohibit such activities in humans. Congress has made several attempts to outlaw human cloning, most recently with a bill that would make any form of human cloning punishable by a $1 million fine and up to 10 years in prison. (The House of Representatives passed this bill this past winter, but the Senate has yet to debate it.) Politicians thus lumped together two types of cloning that scientists have tried to keep separate: "therapeutic," or "research," cloning, designed to produce embryonic stem cells that might eventually mature into specialized human tissues to treat degenerative diseases; and "reproductive" cloning, undertaken specifically to bring forth a cloned human being. A second bill now before the Senate would explicitly protect research cloning while making reproductive cloning a federal offense.

IVF RISKS REVEALED

One result of the unregulated nature of IVF is that it took nearly 25 years to recognize that IVF children are at increased medical risk. For most of the 1980s and 1990s, IVF was thought to have no effect on birth outcomes, with the exception of problems associated with multiple births: one third of all IVF pregnancies resulted in twins or triplets, the unintended consequence of the widespread practice of implanting six or eight or even 10 embryos into the womb during each IVF cycle, in the hope that at least one of them would "take." (This brute-force method also leads to the occasional set of quadruplets.) When early studies raised concerns about the safety of IVF—showing a doubling of the miscarriage rate, a tripling of the rate of stillbirths and neonatal deaths, and a fivefold increase in ectopic pregnancies—many people attributed the problems not to IVF itself but to its association with multiple pregnancies.

15   By last year, however, IVF's medical dark side became undeniable. In March 2002 the *New England Journal of Medicine* published two studies that controlled for the increased rate of multiple births among IVF babies and still found problems. One study compared the birth weights of more than 42,000 babies conceived through assisted reproductive technology, including IVF, in the U.S. in 1996 and 1997 with the weights of more than three million babies conceived naturally. Excluding both premature

births and multiple births, the test tube babies were still two and a half times as likely to have low birth weights, defined as less than 2,500 grams, or about five and a half pounds. The other study looked at more than 5,000 babies born in Australia between 1993 and 1997, including 22 percent born as a result of IVF. It found that IVF babies were twice as likely as naturally conceived infants to have multiple major birth defects, in particular chromosomal and musculoskeletal abnormalities. The Australian researchers speculate that these problems may be a consequence of the drugs used to induce ovulation or to maintain pregnancy in its early stages. In addition, factors contributing to infertility may increase the risk of birth defects. The technique of IVF itself also might be to blame. A flawed sperm injected into an egg, as it is in one IVF variation, may have been unable to penetrate the egg on its own and is thus given a chance it would otherwise not have to produce a baby with a developmental abnormality.

Clearly, these risks could remain hidden during more than two decades of experience with IVF only because no system was ever put in place to track results. "If the government had supported IVF, the field would have made much more rapid progress," says Duane Alexander, director of the National Institute of Child Health and Human Development. "But as it is, the institute has never funded human IVF research of any form"—a record that Alexander calls both incredible and embarrassing.

Although the medical downsides of IVF are finally coming to light, many of the more alarmist predictions about where IVF would lead never came to pass. For example, one scenario was that it would bring us "wombs for hire," an oppressed underclass of women paid to bear the children of the infertile rich. But surrogate motherhood turned out to be expensive and emotionally complex for all parties, and it never became widespread.

Human cloning, too, might turn out to be less frightening than we currently imagine. Market forces might make reproductive cloning impractical, and scientific advancement might make it unnecessary. For example, people unable to produce eggs or sperm might ponder cloning to produce offspring. But the technology developed for cloning could make it possible to create artificial eggs or sperm containing the woman's or man's own DNA, which could then be combined with the sperm or egg of a partner. In the future, "cloning" might refer only to what is now being called therapeutic cloning, and it might eventually be truly therapeutic: a laboratory technique for making cells for the regeneration of damaged organs, for example. And some observers believe that the most common use of cloning technology will ultimately not involve human cells at all: the creature most likely to be cloned may wind up being a favorite family dog or cat.

The history of IVF reveals the pitfalls facing cloning if decision making is simply avoided. But despite similarities in societal reactions to IVF and cloning, the two technologies are philosophically quite different. The goal of IVF is to enable sexual reproduction in order to produce a genetically unique human being. Only the site of conception changes, after which events proceed much the way they normally do. Cloning disregards sexual reproduction, its goal being to mimic not the process but the already existing living entity. Perhaps the biggest difference between IVF and cloning, however, is the focus of our anxieties. In the 1970s the greatest fear related to in vitro fertilization was that it would fail, leading to sorrow, disappointment and possibly the birth of grotesquely abnormal babies. Today the greatest fear about human cloning is that it may succeed.

Discussion Questions

1. To what extent do you believe that in vitro fertilization represents another instance of scientists "playing God"? To what extent do you consider this reproductive technology a reasonable option to parents who can afford it? Does your opinion change when those parents are a lesbian couple, rather than heterosexual married partners? Explain.

2. To what extent do you consider test-tube babies and cloning to be similar technologies? Explain in several sentences outlining your position.

Choosing Disability
LAURA HERSHEY

A freelance writer and disability rights activist in Denver, Laura Hershey has published in Progressive, Women's Studies Quarterly, *and* Off Our Backs: The Feminist News Journal. *Her work certainly supports the mission of the latter journal: "to serve as a forum for feminist ideas and theory; to be an information resource on feminist, women's and lesbian culture; and to seek social justice and equality for women worldwide" (as stated on the publication's Web page). She not only writes about, but also advocates for, disabled women struggling to gain greater independence through greater access to support services, among other initiatives. The following selection first appeared in* Ms. *magazine in 1994.*

As you read, consider your own position on "reproductive freedom." What limits do you believe should be imposed on a woman's choice of abortion at a reasonable cost? Admitting your own prejudice, consider at what points you agree with and disagree with Hershey's viewpoint.

—————————— ✦ ——————————

In 1983, when I was in college, local antiabortion protesters commemorated the tenth anniversary of *Roe v. Wade* with a rally. Our student feminist organization held a small counter-demonstration. Frantic in their zeal, anti-choice protesters assailed us with epithets like "slut" and "bitch." But the most hostile remark was directed at me. I was confronted by an angry nun whose "Abortion Is Murder" sign hung tiredly at her side. She stopped in front of me and aimed a pugnacious finger. "You see?" she announced. "God even let you be born!"

I'm not sure the sister realized that I had been part of the pro-choice demonstration. All she saw in me was a poster child for her holy crusade. I must have seemed to her an obvious mistake of nature: a severely disabled person, who, through a combination of divine intervention and legal restrictions, had been born anyway.

That was my first inkling of how attitudes about disability function in the volatile debate over reproductive rights. I understood that the nun and her co-crusaders were no friends of mine. To her, I was a former fetus who had escaped the abortionists. No room in that view for my identity as an adult woman; no room for the choices I might make. Now, more than a decade later, anti-abortion groups are courting the disability community. The approach has become less clumsy, emphasizing respect for the lives of people with disabilities, and some activists have accepted the anti-choice message because they find it consistent with the goals of the disability rights movement. As a feminist, however, I recoil at the "pro-life" movement's disregard for the lives and freedom of women.

But I cannot overlook the fact that when a prenatal test reveals the possibility of a "major defect," as the medical profession puts it, the pregnancy almost always ends in "therapeutic abortion." The prospect of bearing a child with disabilities causes such anxiety that abortion has become the accepted outcome even among people who oppose abortion rights in general.

Indeed, fear of disability played a key role in the legalization of abortion in the United States in the 1960s. When thousands of
5

pregnant women who had taken thalidomide (a drug used in tranquilizers) or had contracted rubella (German measles) gave birth to children with "defects," doctors called for easing abortion laws.

Today, despite three decades of activism by the disability community, and substantial disability rights legislation, avoiding disability is an important factor in the use and regulation of abortion. In a 1992 Time/CNN survey, for example, 70 percent of respondents favored abortion if a fetus was likely to be born deformed.

This is the quandary we face: the choices we all seek to defend—choices individual women make about childbirth—can conflict with efforts to promote acceptance, equality, and respect for people with disabilities. I am inseparably committed to the empowerment of both people with disabilities and women. Therefore, my pro-choice stance must lie somewhere in the common ground between feminism and disability rights. I want to analyze social and scientific trends, and to vocalize my troubled feelings about where all of this may lead. I want to defy patriarchy's attempts to control women, and also to challenge an age-old bias against people with disabilities. I want to discuss the ethics of choice—without advocating restrictions on choice. To draw a parallel, feminists have no problem attacking sex-selective abortion used to guarantee giving birth to a child of the "right" sex (most often male), but we try to educate against the practice, rather than seek legislation.

In an effort to clarify my own thinking about these complex, interlocking issues, I have been reading and listening to the words of other disabled women. Diane Coleman, a Nashville-based disability rights organizer, is deeply concerned about the number of abortions based on fetal disability: Coleman sees this as "a way that society expresses its complete rejection of people with disabilities, and the conviction that it would be better if we were dead." I find myself sharing her indignation.

Julie Reiskin, a social worker in Denver who is active in both disability rights and abortion rights, tells me, "I live with a disability, and I have a hard time saying, 'This is great.' I think that the goal should be to eliminate disabilities." It jars me to hear this, but Reiskin makes a further point that I find helpful. "Most abortions are not because there's something wrong with the fetus," she says. "Most abortions are because we don't have decent birth control." In other words, we should never have to use fetal disability as a reason to keep abortion legal: "It should be because women have the right to do what we want with our bodies, period," says Reiskin.

We are a diverse community, and it's no surprise to find divergent opinions on as difficult an issue as abortion. Our personal histories and hopes, viewed through the lens of current circumstances, shape our values and politics. Like all women I interviewed, I must be guided by my own experiences of living with disability. At two years old, I still could not walk. Once I was diagnosed—I have a rare neuromuscular condition—doctors told my parents that I would live only another year or two. Don't bother about school, they advised; just buy her a few toys and make her comfortable until the end.

My parents ignored the doctors' advice. Instead of giving up on me, they taught me to read. They made sure I had a child-size wheelchair and a tricycle. My father built a sled for me, and when the neighborhood kids went to the park to fly downhill in fresh snow, he pulled me along. My mother performed much of my physical care, but was determined not to do all of it; college students helped out in exchange for housing. She knew that her own wholeness and my future depended on being able to utilize resources outside our home.

Now my life is my own. I have a house, a career, a partner, and a community of friends with and without disabilities. I rely on a motorized wheelchair for mobility, a voice-activated computer for my writing, and the assistance of Medicaid-funded attendants for daily needs—dressing, bathing, eating, going to the bathroom. I manage it all according to my own goals and needs.

My life contradicts society's stereotypes about how people with disabilities live. Across the country, thousands of other severely disabled people are working, loving, and agitating for change. I don't mean to paint a simplistic picture. Most of us work very hard to attain independence, against real physical and/or financial obstacles. Too many people are denied the kind of daily in-home assistance that makes my life possible. Guaranteeing such services has become a top priority for the disability rights movement.

Changes like these, amounting to a small revolution, are slow to reach the public consciousness. Science, on the other hand, puts progress into practice relatively quickly. Prenatal screening seems to give pregnant women more power—but is it actually asking women to ratify social prejudices through their reproductive "choices"? I cannot help thinking that in most cases, when a woman terminates a previously wanted pregnancy expressly to avoid giving birth to a disabled child, she is buying into obsolete assumptions about that child's future. And she is making a statement about the desirability of the relative worth of such a child. Abortion based on disability results from, and in turn strengthens, certain beliefs: children with disabilities (and by implication adults with disabilities) are a burden to family and society; life with a disability is scarcely worth living; preventing the birth is an act of kindness; women who bear disabled children have failed.

15   Language reinforces the negativity. Terms like "fetal deformity" and "defective fetus" are deeply stigmatizing, carrying connotations of inadequacy and shame. Many of us have been called "abnormal" by medical personnel, who view us primarily as "patients," subject to the definitions and control of the medical profession. "Medical professionals often have countless incorrect assumptions about our lives," says Diane Coleman. "Maybe they see us as failures on their part." As a result, doctors who diagnose fetuses with disabilities often recommend either abortion or institutionalization. "I really haven't heard very many say, 'It's O.K. to have a disability, your family's going to be fine,'" Coleman says.

The independent living movement, which is the disabled community's civil rights movement, challenges this medical model. Instead of locating our difficulties within ourselves, we identify our oppression within a society that refuses to accommodate our disabilities. The real solution is to change society—to ensure full accessibility, equal opportunity, and a range of community support services—not to attempt to eliminate disabilities.

The idea that disability might someday be permanently eradicated—whether through prenatal screening and abortion or through medical research leading to "cures"—has strong appeal for a society wary of spending resources on human needs. Maybe there lurks, in the back of society's mind, the belief—the hope?— that one day there will be no people with disabilities. That attitude works against the goals of civil rights and independent living. We struggle for integration, access, and support services, yet our existence remains an unresolved question. Under the circumstances, we cannot expect society to guarantee and fund our full citizenship.

My life of disability has not been easy or carefree. But in measuring the quality of my life, other factors—education, friends, and meaningful work, for example—have been decisive.

If I were asked for an opinion on whether to bring a child into the world, knowing she would have the same limitations and opportunities I have had, I would not hesitate to say, "Yes." I know that many women do not have the resources my parents had. Many lack education, are poor, or are without the support of friends and family. The problems created by these circumstances are intensified with a child who is disabled. No woman should have a child she can't handle or doesn't want. Having said that, I must also say that all kinds of women raise healthy, self-respecting children with disabilities, without unduly compromising their own lives. Raising a child with disabilities is difficult, but raising any child is difficult; just as you expect any other child to enrich your life, you can expect the same from a child with disabilities. But the media often portray raising a child with disabilities as a personal martyrdom. Disabled children, disabled *people*, are viewed as misfortunes.

I believe the choice to abort a disabled fetus represents a rejection of children who have disabilities. Human beings have a deep-seated fear of confronting the physical vulnerability that is part of being human. This terror has been dubbed "disabiliphobia" by some activists. I confront disabiliphobia every day: the usher who gripes that I take up too much room in a theater lobby; the store owner who insists that a ramp is expensive and unnecessary because people in wheelchairs never come in; the talk-show host who resents the money spent to educate students with disabilities. These are the voices of an age-old belief that disability compromises our humanity and requires us to be kept apart and ignored.

Disabiliphobia affects health care reform too. In the proposed Clinton health plan only people disabled through injury or illness—not those of us with congenital disabilities—will be covered. Is this exclusion premised on the assumption that those of us born with disabilities have lesser value and that our needs are too costly?

People with severe disabilities do sometimes require additional resources for medical and support services. But disabiliphobia runs deeper than a cost-benefit analysis. Witness the ordeal of Bree Walker, a Los Angeles newscaster with a mild physical disability affecting her hands and feet. In 1990, when Walker became pregnant with her second child, she knew the fetus might inherit her condition, as had the first. She chose to continue the pregnancy, which led talk-show hosts and listeners to feel they

20

had the right to spend hours debating whether Walker should have the child (most said no). Walker received numerous hostile letters. The callers and letter writers seemed to be questioning her right to exist, as well as her child's.

Walker's experience also pointed out how easily disabiliphobia slips from decisions about fetuses with disabilities to decisions about people with disabilities. That's why abortion is an area where we fear that the devaluation of our lives could become enshrined in public policy. Pro-choice groups must work to ensure that they do not support legislation that sets different standards based on disability.

A case in point is Utah's restrictive 1991 anti-abortion law (which has since been declared unconstitutional). The law allowed abortions only in cases of rape, incest, endangerment of the woman's life, a profound health risk to the woman—or "fetal defect." According to Susanne Millsaps, director of Utah's NARAL [National Abortion and Reproductive Rights Action League] affiliate, some disability rights activists wanted NARAL and other pro-choice groups to join in opposing the "fetal defect" exemption. The groups did not specifically take a stand on the exemption; instead they opposed the entire law. I would agree that the whole statute had to be opposed on constitutional and feminist grounds. But I would also agree that there should have been a stronger response to the fetal disability exemption.

25   To group "fetal defect" together with rape, incest, and life-endangering complications is to reveal deep fears about disability. As Barbara Faye Waxman, an expert on the reproductive rights of women with disabilities, says: "In this culture, disability, in and of itself, is perceived as a threat to the welfare of the mother. I find that to be troublesome and offensive."

There is more at stake here than my feelings, or anyone else's, about a woman's decision. Rapidly changing reproductive technologies, combined with socially constructed prejudices, weigh heavily on any decision affecting a fetus with possible disabilities. While some women lack basic prenatal and infant care, huge amounts of money are poured into prenatal screening and genetic research. Approximately 450 disorders can now be predicted before birth. In most cases the tests reveal only the propensity for a condition, not the condition itself. The Human Genome Project aims to complete the DNA map, and to locate hundreds more physical and developmental attributes. There is little public debate about the worth or ultimate uses of this federally funded multibillion dollar program. But there are issues with regard to abortion that we can no longer afford to ignore:

- Does prenatal screening provide more data for women's informed choices, or does it promote the idea that no woman should risk having a disabled child?
- Who decides whether a woman should undergo prenatal screening, and what she should do with the results?
- Are expensive, government-funded genetic research projects initiated primarily for the benefit of a society unwilling to support disability-related needs?
- Is society attempting to eradicate certain disabilities? Should this ever be a goal? If so, should all women be expected to cooperate in it?

The January/February 1994 issue of *Disability Rag & Resource*, a publication of the disability rights movement, devoted several articles to genetic screening. In one, feminist lawyer Lisa Blumberg argues that women are being coerced into accepting prenatal tests, and then pressured to terminate their pregnancies when disabling conditions appear likely. "Prenatal testing has largely become the decision of the doctor," Blumberg writes, and "the social purpose of these tests is to reduce the incidence of live births of people with disabilities."

A woman faced with this choice usually feels pressure from many directions. Family, friends, doctors, and the media predict all kinds of negative results should her child be disabled. At the same time, she is unlikely to be given information about community resources; nor is she encouraged to meet individuals who have the condition her child might be born with. This lack of exposure to real-life, nonmedical facts about living with a disability should make us wonder whether women are really making "informed" choices about bearing children with disabilities.

Few outside the disability community have dealt with these issues in any depth. "We are all aware of the potential for abuses in reproductive technology and in genetic testing," says Marcy Wilder, legal director for NARAL's national office in Washington, D.C. "I don't see that there have been widespread abuses— but we're certainly concerned." That concern has not led to any coalition-building with disability rights groups, however.

Many feminist disability rights activists report chilly responses when they attempt to network with pro-choice groups. Too often, when we object to positions that implicitly doubt the   30 humanity of children born disabled, we are accused of being anti-choice. One activist I know recently told me about her experience speaking at a meeting of a National Organization for Women chapter. She mentioned feeling discomfort about the widespread abortion of disabled fetuses—and was startled by the members' reactions. "They said, 'How could you claim to be a feminist and pro-choice and even begin to think that there should be any limitations?' I tried to tell them I don't think there should be limitations, but that our issues need to be included."

On both sides, the fears are genuine, rational, and terrifying—if not always articulated. For the pro-choice movement, the fear is that questioning the motives and assumptions behind any reproductive decision could give ammunition to anti-abortionists. Defenders of disability rights fear that the widespread use of prenatal testing and abortion for the purpose of eliminating disability could inaugurate a new eugenics movement. If we cannot unite and find ways to address issues of reproductive screening and manipulation, we all face the prospect that what is supposed to be a private decision—the termination of a pregnancy—might become the first step in a campaign to eliminate people with disabilities.

I am accusing the pro-choice movement not of spurring these trends, but of failing to address them. Most pro-choice organizations do not favor the use of abortion to eliminate disabilities, but their silence leaves a vacuum in which fear of disability flourishes.

Disabiliphobia and the "genetics enterprise," as activist Adrienne Asch calls it, have also had legal implications for the reproductive rights of all women. The tendency to blame social problems such as poverty and discrimination on individuals with disabilities and their mothers has made women vulnerable to the charge that they are undermining progress toward human "perfectibility"—because they insist on a genuine choice. Some legal and medical experts have developed a concept called "fetal rights," in which mothers can be held responsible for the condition of their unborn or newborn children. According to Lisa Blumberg, "fetal rights" could more accurately be called "fetal quality control." For women with hereditary disabilities who decide to have children this concept is nothing new. Society and medical professionals have often tried to prevent us from bearing and raising children. Disabled women know, as well as anyone, what it means to be deprived of reproductive choice. More broadly, decisions involving our health care, sexuality, and parenting have been made by others based on assumptions about our inabilities and/or our asexuality.

The right to control one's body begins with good gynecological care. Low income, and dependence on disability "systems," restrict access to that care. Like many women of disability, my health care choices are limited by the accessibility of medical facilities, and by providers' attitudes toward disability and their willingness to accept the low reimbursement of Medicaid. And Medicaid will not cover most abortions, a policy that discriminates against poor women and many women with disabilities.

Paradoxically, policy is often undermined by practice. Although   35
public funding rarely pays for abortions, many women with disabilities are encouraged to have them—even when they would prefer to have a child. Doctors try to convince us an abortion would be best for "health reasons"—in which case, Medicaid will pay for it after all. "Abortions are easier for disabled women to get," says Nancy Moulton, a health care advocate in Atlanta, "because the medical establishment sees us as not being fit parents." Most women grow up amid strong if subtle pressures to become mothers. For those of us with disabilities, there is an equal or greater pressure to forgo motherhood. This pressure has taken the form of forced sterilization, lost custody battles, and forced abortion.

Consequently, for women with disabilities, reproductive freedom means more than being able to get an abortion. It is hard for many of us to relate to those in the reproductive rights movement whose primary concern is keeping abortions legal and available. But I believe our different perspectives on reproductive freedom are fundamentally compatible, like variations on a single theme.

Whatever the reason, feminist organizations seem inclined to overlook disability concerns. Feminist speakers might add "ableism" to their standard list of offensive "isms," but they do little to challenge it. Now more than ever, women with disabilities need the feminist movement's vigorous support. We need you to defend our rights as if they were your own—which they are. Here are a few suggestions:

- Recognize women with disabilities' equal stake in the pro-choice movement's goals. That means accepting us as women, not dismissing us as "other," or infirm, or genderless.
- Recognize us as a community of diverse individuals whose health needs, lifestyles, and choices vary.
- Defend all our reproductive rights: the right to appropriate education about sexuality and reproduction; to gynecological care, family planning services, and birth control; the right to be sexually active; to have children and to keep and raise those children, with assistance if necessary; and the right to abortion in accessible facilities, with practitioners who are sensitive to our needs.

- Remove the barriers that restrict the access of women with disabilities to services. Help to improve physical accessibility, arrange disability awareness training for staff and volunteers, and conduct outreach activities to reach women with disabilities.
- Continue struggling to build coalitions around reproductive rights and disability issues. There is plenty of common ground, although we may have to tiptoe through dangerous, mine-filled territory to get to it.
- Question the assumptions that seem to make bearing children with disabilities unacceptable.

Despite our rhetoric, abortion is not strictly a private decision. Individual choices are made in a context of social values; I want us to unearth, sort out, and appraise those values. I wouldn't deny any woman the right to choose abortion. But I would issue a challenge to all women making a decision whether to give birth to a child who may have disabilities.

The challenge is this: consider all relevant information, not just the medical facts. More important than a particular diagnosis are the conditions awaiting a child—community acceptance, access to buildings and transportation, civil rights protection, and opportunities for education and employment. Where these things are lacking or inadequate, consider joining the movement to change them. In many communities, adults with disabilities and parents of disabled children have developed powerful advocacy coalitions. I recognize that, having weighed all the factors, some women will decide they cannot give birth to a child with disabilities. It pains me, but I acknowledge their right and their choice. Meanwhile, there is much work still to be done.

Discussion Questions

1. Explain your personal opinion about abortion to avoid "fetal disability."
2. To what extent do you believe that "life with a disability is scarcely worth living" (paragraph 14) and to what extent do you believe this to be a misconception?
3. If you have ever witnessed or experienced an instance of "disabiliphobia" (paragraph 20), describe the circumstances.
4. In "Pandora's Baby," Henig implies that after twenty-five years of in vitro fertilization (IVF), medical science has only recently recognized its dangers: "low birth weight" babies and higher incidence of "birth defects." Explain

how Hershey, in "Choosing Disability," answers the critics of IVF who wish to protect the health of the fetus through prenatal screening. Write a well-developed paragraph fully considering her argument.

Cloning for Medicine
Ian Wilmut

Famous for successfully cloning the first mammal (Dolly) from an adult in 1997, Professor Ian Wilmut continues to pursue research on the genetic engineering of livestock at the Roslin Institute in Scotland. After obtaining a Ph.D. from the University of Cambridge for research on methods of freezing boar semen, he did postdoctoral work at Cambridge on techniques for freezing animal embryos. Later Wilmut identified the developmental and physiological causes of prenatal death in sheep and pigs, before turning to studies of ways to improve economically important animals. The following report—including both scientific details and ethical speculation—was first published in Scientific American.

———————— ✦ ————————

In the summer of 1995 the birth of two lambs at my institution, the Roslin Institute near Edinburgh in Midlothian, Scotland, heralded what many scientists believe will be a period of revolutionary opportunities in biology and medicine. Megan and Morag, both carried to term by a surrogate mother, were not produced from the union of a sperm and an egg. Rather their genetic material came from cultured cells originally derived from a nine-day-old embryo. That made Megan and Morag genetic copies, or clones, of the embryo.

Before the arrival of the lambs, researchers had already learned how to produce sheep, cattle and other animals by genetically copying cells painstakingly isolated from early-stage embryos. Our work promised to make cloning vastly more practical, because cultured cells are relatively easy to work with. Megan and Morag proved that even though such cells are partially specialized, or differentiated, they can be genetically reprogrammed to function like those in an early embryo. Most biologists had believed that this would be impossible.

We went on to clone animals from cultured cells taken from a 26-day-old fetus and from a mature ewe. The ewe's cells gave rise to Dolly, the first mammal to be cloned from an adult. Our announcement of Dolly's birth in February 1997 attracted enormous press interest, perhaps because Dolly drew attention to the theoretical possibility of cloning humans. This is an outcome I hope never comes to pass. But the ability to make clones from cultured cells derived from easily obtained tissue should bring numerous practical benefits in animal husbandry and medical science, as well as answer critical biological questions.

HOW TO CLONE

Cloning is based on nuclear transfer, the same technique scientists have used for some years to copy animals from embryonic cells. Nuclear transfer involves the use of two cells. The recipient cell is normally an unfertilized egg taken from an animal soon after ovulation. Such eggs are poised to begin developing once they are appropriately stimulated. The donor cell is the one to be copied. A researcher working under a high-power microscope holds the recipient egg cell by suction on the end of a fine pipette and uses an extremely fine micropipette to suck out the chromosomes, sausage-shaped bodies that incorporate the cell's DNA. (At this stage, chromosomes are not enclosed in a distinct nucleus.) Then, typically, the donor cell, complete with its nucleus, is fused with the recipient egg. Some fused cells start to develop like a normal embryo and produce offspring if implanted into the uterus of a surrogate mother.

5   In our experiments with cultured cells, we took special measures to make the donor and recipient cells compatible. In particular, we tried to coordinate the cycles of duplication of DNA and those of the production of messenger RNA, a molecule that is copied from DNA and guides the manufacture of proteins. We chose to use donor cells whose DNA was not being duplicated at the time of the transfer. To arrange this, we worked with cells that we forced to become quiescent by reducing the concentration of nutrients in their culture medium. In addition, we delivered pulses of electric current to the egg after the transfer, to encourage the cells to fuse and to mimic the stimulation normally provided by a sperm.

After the birth of Megan and Morag demonstrated that we could produce viable offspring from embryo-derived cultures, we filed for patents and started experiments to see whether offspring could be produced from more completely differentiated cultured cells. Working in collaboration with PPL Therapeutics, also near

Edinburgh, we tested fetal fibroblasts (common cells found in connective tissue) and cells taken from the udder of a ewe that was three and a half months pregnant. We selected a pregnant adult because mammary cells grow vigorously at this stage of pregnancy, indicating that they might do well in culture. Moreover, they have stable chromosomes, suggesting that they retain all their genetic information. The successful cloning of Dolly from the mammary-derived culture and of other lambs from the cultured fibroblasts showed that the Roslin protocol was robust and repeatable.

All the cloned offspring in our experiments looked, as expected, like the breed of sheep that donated the originating nucleus, rather than like their surrogate mothers or the egg donors. Genetic tests prove beyond doubt that Dolly is indeed a clone of an adult. It is most likely that she was derived from a fully differentiated mammary cell, although it is impossible to be certain because the culture also contained some less differentiated cells found in small numbers in the mammary gland. Other laboratories have since used an essentially similar technique to create healthy clones of cattle and mice from cultured cells, including ones from nonpregnant animals.

Although cloning by nuclear transfer is repeatable, it has limitations. Some cloned cattle and sheep are unusually large, but this effect has also been seen when embryos are simply cultured before gestation. Perhaps more important, nuclear transfer is not yet efficient. John B. Gurdon, now at the University of Cambridge, found in nuclear-transfer experiments with frogs almost 30 years ago that the number of embryos surviving to become tadpoles was smaller when donor cells were taken from animals at a more advanced developmental stage. Our first results with mammals showed a similar pattern. All the cloning studies described so far show a consistent pattern of deaths during embryonic and fetal development, with laboratories reporting only 1 to 2 percent of embryos surviving to become live offspring. Sadly, even some clones that survive through birth die shortly afterward.

CLONES WITH A DIFFERENCE

The cause of these losses remains unknown, but it may reflect the complexity of the genetic reprogramming needed if a healthy offspring is to be born. If even one gene inappropriately expresses or fails to express a crucial protein at a sensitive point, the result might be fatal. Yet reprogramming might involve regulating thousands of genes in a process that could involve some randomness. Technical improvements, such as the use of different donor cells, might reduce the toll.

10   The ability to produce offspring from cultured cells opens up relatively easy ways to make genetically modified, or transgenic, animals. Such animals are important for research and can produce medically valuable human proteins.

The standard technique for making transgenic animals is painfully slow and inefficient. It entails microinjecting a genetic construct—a DNA sequence incorporating a desired gene—into a large number of fertilized eggs. A few of them take up the introduced DNA so that the resulting offspring express it. These animals are then bred to pass on the construct (see "Transgenic Livestock as Drug Factories," by William H. Velander, Henryk Lubon and William N. Drohan; *Scientific American*, January 1997).

In contrast, a simple chemical treatment can persuade cultured cells to take up a DNA construct. If these cells are then used as donors for nuclear transfer, the resulting cloned offspring will all carry the construct. The Roslin Institute and PPL Therapeutics have already used this approach to produce transgenic animals more efficiently than is possible with microinjection.

We have incorporated into sheep the gene for human factor IX, a blood-clotting protein used to treat hemophilia B. In this experiment we transferred an antibiotic-resistance gene to the donor cells along with the factor IX gene, so that by adding a toxic dose of the antibiotic neomycin to the culture, we could kill cells that had failed to take up the added DNA. Yet despite this genetic disruption, the proportion of embryos that developed to term after nuclear transfer was in line with our previous results.

The first transgenic sheep produced this way, Polly, was born in the summer of 1997. Polly and other transgenic clones secrete the human protein in their milk. These observations suggest that once techniques for the retrieval of egg cells in different species have been perfected, cloning will make it possible to introduce precise genetic changes into any mammal and to create multiple individuals bearing the alteration.

15   Cultures of mammary gland cells might have a particular advantage as donor material. Until recently, the only practical way to assess whether a DNA construct would cause a protein to be secreted in milk was to transfer it into female mice, then test their milk. It should be possible, however, to test mammary cells in

culture directly. That will speed up the process of finding good constructs and cells that have incorporated them so as to give efficient secretion of the protein.

Cloning offers many other possibilities. One is the generation of genetically modified animal organs that are suitable for transplantation into humans. At present, thousands of patients die every year before a replacement heart, liver or kidney becomes available. A normal pig organ would be rapidly destroyed by a "hyperacute" immune reaction if transplanted into a human. This reaction is triggered by proteins on the pig cells that have been modified by an enzyme called alpha-galactosyl transferase. It stands to reason, then, that an organ from a pig that has been genetically altered so that it lacks this enzyme might be well tolerated if doctors gave the recipient drugs to suppress other, less extreme immune reactions.

Another promising area is the rapid production of large animals carrying genetic defects that mimic human illnesses, such as cystic fibrosis. Although mice have provided some information, mice and humans have very different genes for cystic fibrosis. Sheep are expected to be more valuable for research into this condition, because their lungs resemble those of humans. Moreover, because sheep live for years, scientists can evaluate their long-term responses to treatments.

Creating animals with genetic defects raises challenging ethical questions. But it seems clear that society does in the main support research on animals, provided that the illnesses being studied are serious ones and that efforts are made to avoid unnecessary suffering.

The power to make animals with a precisely engineered genetic constitution could also be employed more directly in cell-based therapies for important illnesses, including Parkinson's disease, diabetes and muscular dystrophy. None of these conditions currently has any fully effective treatment. In each, some pathological process damages specific cell populations, which are unable to repair or replace themselves. Several novel approaches are now being explored that would provide new cells—ones taken from the patient and cultured, donated by other humans or taken from animals.

To be useful, transferred cells must be incapable of transmit- 20
ting new disease and must match the patient's physiological need closely. Any immune response they produce must be manageable. Cloned animals with precise genetic modifications that minimize

the human immune response might constitute a plentiful supply of suitable cells. Animals might even produce cells with special properties, although any modifications would risk a stronger immune reaction.

Cloning could also be a way to produce herds of cattle that lack the prion protein gene. This gene makes cattle susceptible to infection with prions, agents that cause bovine spongiform encephalitis (BSE), or mad cow disease. Because many medicines contain gelatin or other products derived from cattle, health officials are concerned that prions from infected animals could infect patients. Cloning could create herds that, lacking the prion protein gene, would be a source of ingredients for certifiable prion-free medicines.

The technique might in addition curtail the transmission of genetic disease. Many scientists are now working on therapies that would supplement or replace defective genes in cells, but even successfully treated patients will still pass on defective genes to their offspring. If a couple was willing to produce an embryo that could be treated by advanced forms of gene therapy, nuclei from modified embryonic cells could be transferred to eggs to create children who would be entirely free of a given disease.

Some of the most ambitious medical projects now being considered envision the production of universal human donor cells. Scientists know how to isolate from very early mouse embryos undifferentiated stem cells, which can contribute to all the different tissues of the adult. Equivalent cells can be obtained for some other species, and humans are probably no exception. Scientists are learning how to differentiate stem cells in culture, so it may be possible to manufacture cells to repair or replace tissue damaged by illness.

MAKING HUMAN STEM CELLS

Stem cells matched to an individual patient could be made by creating an embryo by nuclear transfer just for that purpose, using one of the patient's cells as the donor and a human egg as the recipient. The embryo would be allowed to develop only to the stage needed to separate and culture stem cells from it. At that point, an embryo has only a few hundred cells, and they have not started to differentiate. In particular, the nervous system has not begun to develop, so the embryo has no means of feeling pain or sensing the environment. Embryo-derived cells might be used to treat a variety of serious diseases caused by damage to cells, perhaps including AIDS as well as Parkinson's, muscular dystrophy and diabetes.

Scenarios that involve growing human embryos for their cells 25 are deeply disturbing to some people, because embryos have the potential to become people. The views of those who consider life sacred from conception should be respected, but I suggest a contrasting view. The embryo is a cluster of cells that does not become a sentient being until much later in development, so it is not yet a person. In the U.K., the Human Genetics Advisory Commission has initiated a major public consultation to assess attitudes toward this use of cloning.

Creating an embryo to treat a specific patient is likely to be an expensive proposition, so it might be more practical to establish permanent, stable human embryonic stem-cell lines from cloned embryos. Cells could then be differentiated as needed. Implanted cells derived this way would not be genetically perfect matches, but the immune reaction would probably be controllable. In the longer term, scientists might be able to develop methods for manufacturing genetically matched stem cells for a patient by "dedifferentiating" them directly, without having to utilize an embryo to do it.

Several commentators and scientists have suggested that it might in some cases be ethically acceptable to clone existing people. One scenario envisages generating a replacement for a dying relative. All such possibilities, however, raise the concern that the clone would be treated as less than a complete individual, because he or she would likely be subjected to limitations and expectations based on the family's knowledge of the genetic "twin." Those expectations might be false, because human personality is only partly determined by genes. The clone of an extrovert could have a quite different demeanor. Clones of athletes, movie stars, entrepreneurs or scientists might well choose different careers because of chance events in early life.

Some pontificators have also put forward the notion that couples in which one member is infertile might choose to make a copy of one or the other partner. But society ought to be concerned that a couple might not treat naturally a child who is a copy of just one of them. Because other methods are available for the treatment of all known types of infertility, conventional therapeutic avenues seem more appropriate. None of the suggested uses of cloning for making copies of existing people is ethically acceptable to my way of thinking, because they are not in the interests of the resulting child. It should go without saying that

I strongly oppose allowing cloned human embryos to develop so that they can be tissue donors.

It nonetheless seems clear that cloning from cultured cells will offer important medical opportunities. Predictions about new technologies are often wrong: societal attitudes change; unexpected developments occur. Time will tell. But biomedical researchers probing the potential of cloning now have a full agenda.

Discussion Questions

1. Based on Wilmut's descriptions, which of the medical applications of cloning do you support and which do you consider unethical? Explain your viewpoint for each case.
2. Explain your position on the use of human embryos in developing stem cells for medical treatments. Comment on the science, as you understand it, and on the ethics of such research.

Keeping an Eye on the Global Traffic in Human Organs

NANCY SCHEPER-HUGHES

Professor of medical anthropology at the University of California, Berkeley, Nancy Scheper-Hughes directs the doctoral program in Critical Studies in Medicine, Science, and the Body. Denying the model of positivist science, she views anthropologists "as hunters and gatherers of human values." She has conducted research and been politically engaged in such issues as AIDS and human rights in Cuba, death squads and the extermination of street kids in Brazil, the Catholic Church and clerical celibacy, politics in South Africa, and child sex abuse. She may be best known for her books Saints, Scholars and Schizophrenics: Mental Illness in Rural Ireland *(1979) and* Death without Weeping: The Violence of Everyday Life in Brazil *(1992). Reflecting on the latter work, Scheper-Hughes recalled a friend and informant who had been abandoned by three men and seen several of her children die, and yet she was "putting on a short skirt and getting ready to dance carnival." In reply to the researcher's surprise, the woman answered, "That's my strength, that I still will dance, even in the face of death." The following article presents ongoing research that is part of her forthcoming book,*

The Ends of the Body: The Global Traffic in Organs. *An accomplished academic, Scheper-Hughes also plays an activist role as cofounder and director of Organs Watch, a medical human rights project, and as an advisor to the World Health Organization (WHO).*

As you read, consider the author's tone in her writing. How does she suggest her concern for the problem she investigates? How would you describe her attitude toward the victims and the facilitators of the organ transplant market?

───────── ✦ ─────────

If a living donor can do without an organ, why shouldn't the donor profit and medical science benefit?
—RADCLIFFE-RICHARDS J., ET AL., *LANCET* 1998; **351**: 1951.

• • •

The kidney as a commodity has emerged as the gold standard in the new body trade, representing the poor person's ultimate collateral against hunger, debt, and penury. Thus, I refer to the bartered kidney as the organ of last resort. Meanwhile, transplant tourism has become a vital asset to the medical economies of poorer countries from Peru, South Africa, India, the Philippines, Iraq, China, and Russia to Turkey. In general, the circulation of kidneys follows established routes of capital from South to North, from East to West, from poorer to more affluent bodies, from black and brown bodies to white ones, and from female to male or from poor, low status men to more affluent men. Women are rarely the recipients of purchased organs anywhere in the world.

In the face of this postmodern dilemma, my colleague Lawrence Cohen and I—both medical anthropologists with wide experience and understanding of poverty and sickness in the third world—founded Organs Watch in 1999 as an independent research and medical human rights project at the University of California, Berkeley, as a stop-gap measure in the presence of an unrecognised global medical emergency, and in the absence of any other organisation of its kind. We have since undertaken original fieldwork on the changing economic and cultural context of organ transplant in 12 countries across the globe.

With the help of our postgraduate and medical student research assistants we have followed desperate kidney buyers and their equally desperate kidney sellers, their surgeons, and their brokers and intermediaries. We have gone to all the places where the economically and politically dispossessed—the homeless, refugees, undocumented workers, prisoners, soldiers who are absent without leave, ageing prostitutes, cigarette smugglers, petty thieves, and other marginalised people—are lured (and sometimes tricked) into selling their organs. We have followed patients from dialysis clinics to meetings with organ brokers in shopping malls, tea shops, and coffee houses, to illicit surgeries in operating rooms of hospitals—some resembling five-star hotels, others reminiscent of clandestine back alley abortion clinics. We have observed and interviewed hundreds of transplant surgeons who practise or facilitate, or who simply condone illicit surgeries with purchased organs; we have met with organ brokers and their criminal links; and we have communicated some of our findings to medical ethics and licensing boards and to Ministries of Health as well as to US congressional hearings and to special meetings of the Council of Europe.

In all, we have begun to map the routes and the international medical and financial connections that make possible the new traffic in human beings, a veritable slave trade that can bring together parties from three or more countries. In one well travelled route, small groups of Israeli transplant patients go by charter plane to Turkey where they are matched with kidney sellers from rural Moldova and Romania and are transplanted by a team of surgeons—one Israeli and one Turkish. Another network unites European and North American patients with Philippine kidney sellers in a private episcopal hospital in Manila, arranged through an independent internet broker who advertises via the web site Liver4You. Brokers in Brooklyn, New York, posing as a non-profit organisation, traffic in Russian immigrants to service foreign patients from Israel who are transplanted in some of the best medical facilities on the east coast of the USA. Wealthy Palestinians travel to Iraq where they can buy a kidney from poor Arabs coming from Jordan. The kidney sellers are housed in a special ward of the hospital that has all the appearances of a kidney motel. A Nigerian doctor/broker facilitates foreign transplants in South Africa or Boston, USA (patient's/buyer's choice), with a ready supply of poor Nigerian kidney sellers, most of them single women. The purchase agreement is notarised by a distinguished law firm in Lagos, Nigeria.

5   Despite widespread knowledge about these new practices and official reports made to various governing bodies, few surgeons have been investigated and none have lost their credentials. The procurement of poor people's body parts, although illegal in almost

every country of the world, is not recognised as a problem about which something must be done—even less is it viewed as a medical human rights abuse. There is empathy, of course, for the many transplant patients whose needs are being partly met in this way, but there is little concern for the organ sellers who are usually transient, socially invisible, and generally assumed to be making free, informed, and self-interested choices.

From an exclusively market oriented supply and demand perspective—one that is obviously dominant today—the problem of black-markets in human organs can best be solved by regulation rather than by prohibition. The profoundly human and ethical dilemmas are thereby reduced to a simple problem in medical management. In the rational choice language of contemporary medical ethics, the conflict between non-malfeasance (do no harm) and beneficence (the moral duty to do good acts) is increasingly resolved in favour of the libertarian and consumer-oriented principle that those able to broker or buy a human organ should not be prevented from doing so. Paying for a kidney donation is viewed as a potential win-win situation that can benefit both parties. Individual decision making and patient autonomy have become the final arbiters of medical and bioethical values. Social justice and notions of the good society hardly figure at all in these discussions.

Rational arguments for regulation are, however, out of touch with the social and medical realities pertaining in many parts of the world where kidney selling is most common. In poorer countries the medical institutions created to monitor organ harvesting and distribution are often underfunded, dysfunctional, or readily compromised by the power of organ markets, the protection supplied by criminal networks, and by the impunity of outlaw surgeons who are willing to run donor-for-dollars programmes, or who are merely uninterested in where the transplant organ originates.

Surgeons who themselves (or whose patients) take part in transplant tourism have denied the risks of kidney removal in the absence of any published, longitudinal studies of the effects of nephrectomy on the urban poor living in dangerous work and health conditions. Even in the best social and medical circumstances living kidney and part liver donors do sometimes die after the surgical procedure, or are themselves in need of a kidney or liver transplant at a later date. The usual risks multiply when the buyers and sellers are unrelated because the sellers are likely to be extremely poor, often in poor health, and trapped in environments in which the everyday risks to their survival are legion.

Kidney sellers face exposure to urban violence, transportation and work related accidents, and infectious diseases that can compromise their remaining kidney. If and when that spare part fails, most kidney sellers we have interviewed would have no access to dialysis let alone to transplantation.

The few published studies of the social, psychological, and medical effects of nephrectomy on kidney sellers in India, Iran, the Philippines, and Moldova are unambiguous. Kidney sellers subsequently experience (for complicated medical, social, economic, and psychological reasons) chronic pain, ill health, unemployment, reduced incomes, serious depression and sense of worthlessness, family problems, and social isolation (related to the sale).

10   Even with such attempts as in Iran to regulate and control an official system of kidney selling, the outcomes are troubling. One of our Organs Watch researchers has reported directly from Iran that kidney sellers there are recruited from the slums by wealthy kidney activists. They are paid a pittance for their body part. After the sale (which is legal there) the sellers feel profound shame, resentment, and family stigma. In our studies of kidney sellers in India, Turkey, the Philippines, and Eastern Europe, the feelings toward the doctors who removed their kidney can only be described as hostile and, in some cases, even murderous. The disappointment, anger, resentment, and hatred for the surgeons and even for the recipients of their organs—as reported by 100 paid kidney donors in Iran—strongly suggests that kidney selling is a serious social pathology.

Kidney sellers in the Philippines and in Eastern Europe frequently face medical problems, including hypertension, and even kidney insufficiency, without having access to necessary medical care. On returning to their villages or urban shantytowns, kidney sellers are often unemployed because they are unable to sustain the demands of heavy agricultural or construction work, the only labour available to men of their skills and backgrounds. Several kidney sellers in Moldova reported spending their kidney earnings (about US$2,700) to hire labourers to compensate for the heavy agricultural work they could no longer do.

Moldovan sellers are frequently alienated from their families and co-workers, excommunicated from their local Orthodox churches, and, if single, they are excluded from marriage. "No young woman in this village will marry a man with the tell-tale scar of a kidney seller," the father of a kidney seller in Mingir (Moldova) told me. Sergei, a young kidney seller from Chisinau

(Moldova), said that only his mother knew the real reason for the large, sabre-like scar on his abdomen. Sergei's young wife believed his story that he had been injured in a work-related accident in Turkey. Some kidney sellers have disappeared from their families and loved ones, and one is reported to have committed suicide. "They call us prostitutes," Niculae Bardan, a 27-year-old kidney seller from the village of Mingir told me sadly. Then he added: "Actually, we are worse than prostitutes because we have sold something we can never get back. We are disgrace to our families and to our country." Their families often suffer from the stigma of association with a kidney seller. In Turkey, the children of kidney sellers are ridiculed in village schools as one-kidneys.

Despite frequent complaints of pain and weakness, none of the recent kidney sellers we interviewed in Brazil, Turkey, Moldova, and Manila had seen a doctor or been treated in the first year after their operations. Some who looked for medical attention had been turned away from the very same hospitals where their operations were done. One kidney seller from Bagon Lupa shantytown in Manila was given a consultation at the hospital where he had sold his organ, and he was given a prescription for antibiotics and painkillers that he could not afford. Because of the shame associated with their act, I had to coax young kidney sellers in Manila and Moldova to submit to a basic clinical examination and sonogram at the expense of Organs Watch. Some were ashamed to appear in a public clinic because they had tried to keep the sale (and their ruined bodies) a secret. Others were fearful of receiving a bad report because they would be unable to pay for the treatments or medications. Above all, the kidney sellers I interviewed avoided getting medical attention for fear of being seen and labelled as weak or disabled by their potential employers, their families, and their co-workers, or (for single men) by potential girl friends.

If regulation, rather than more effective prohibition, is to be the norm, how can a government set a fair price on the body parts of its poorer citizens without compromising national pride, democratic values, or ethical principles? The circulation of kidneys transcends national borders, and international markets will co-exist with any national, regulated systems. National regulatory programmes—such as the Kid-Net programme (modelled after commercial blood banks), which is currently being considered in the Philippines—would still have to compete with international black markets, which adjust the local value of kidneys according to consumer prejudices. In today's global market an Indian or an

African kidney fetches as little as $1,000, a Filipino kidney can get $1,300, a Moldovan or Romanian kidney yields $2,700, whereas a Turkish or an urban Peruvian kidney can command up to $10,000 or more. Sellers in the USA can receive up to $30,000.

15   Putting a market price on body parts—even a fair one— exploits the desperation of the poor, the mentally weak, and dependent classes. Servants, agricultural workers, illegal workers, and prisoners are pressured by their employers and guardians to enter the kidney market. In Argentina, Organs Watch visited a large asylum for the mentally deficient that had provided blood, cornea, and kidneys to local hospitals and eye banks, until the corrupt hospital director was caught in a web of criminal intrigue that brought him to jail and the institution put under government receivership. In Tel Aviv, Israel, I encountered a mentally deficient prisoner, a common thief, who had sold one of his kidneys to his own lawyer and then tried to sue him in small claims court because he was paid half what he was promised. In Canada a businessman recently received a kidney from his domestic worker, a Philippine woman, who argued that Filipinos are a people "who are anxious to please their bosses." Finally, surgeons, whose primary responsibility is to protect and care for vulnerable bodies, should not be advocates of paid mutilation even in the interest of saving lives at the expense of others.

Bioethical arguments about the right to buy or sell an organ or other body part are based on Euro-American notions of contract and individual choice. But these create the semblance of ethical choice in an intrinsically unethical context. The choice to sell a kidney in an urban slum of Calcutta or in a Brazilian *favela* or a Philippine shantytown is often anything but a free and autonomous one. Consent is problematic, with the executioner— whether on death row or at the door of the slum resident— looking over one's shoulder, and when a seller has no other option left but to sell a part of himself. Asking the law to negotiate a fair price for a live human kidney goes against everything that contract theory stands for.

Although many individuals have benefited from the ability to purchase the organs they need, the social harm produced to the donors, their families, and their communities gives sufficient reason for pause. Does the life that is teased out of the body of the one and transferred into the body of the other bear any resemblance to the ethical life of the free citizen? But neither Aristotle nor Aquinas is with us. Instead, we are asked to take counsel from the new discipline of bioethics that has been finely calibrated to meet the needs of advanced biomedical technologies and the desires of postmodern medical consumers.

What goes by the wayside in these illicit transactions are not only laws and longstanding medical regulations but also the very bedrock supporting medical ethics—humanist ideas of bodily holism, integrity, and human dignity. Amidst the tensions between organ givers and organ recipients, between North and South, between the illegal and the so-called merely unethical, clarity is needed about whose values and whose notions of the body are represented. Deeply held beliefs in human dignity and bodily integrity are not solely the legacy of Western Enlightenment.

• • •

The division of the world into organ buyers and organ sellers is a medical, social, and moral tragedy of immense and not yet fully recognised proportions.

Discussion Questions

1. The author describes the organ market as "transplant tourism." Explain the term, comparing the consequences of conventional international tourism and of organ transplants on the native population. To what extent do you believe this comparison is fair or accurate?

2. Summarize the social, psychological, and medical effects on kidney sellers (paragraphs 9–13).

3. To what extent do you believe that the doctors are responsible for the abuses of the kidney market? To what extent are the sick buyers responsible due to their willingness to pay for a "donated" organ?

America's Altered States
Joshua Wolf Shenk

Publishing widely on advertising, public education, celebrity journalism, and Disney World, Joshua Wolf Shenk has written for Mother Jones, The New York Times, Washington Monthly, U.S. News and World Report, The Economist, *and the online 'zine* Salon. *He is also a regular book reviewer and has written a memoir about his Orthodox Jewish upbringing. Because of his own lifelong struggle with depression, he returns periodically to the topics of drug policy, mental illness, and pharmacology. The following selection first appeared in 1999 in* Harper's *magazine.*

As you read, take note of the three separate sections marked by Roman numerals. Try to identify the focus of each section. After you finish reading the article, write a label for each section that summarizes its main focus.

———————— ✦ ————————

My soul was a burden, bruised and bleeding. It was tired of the man who carried it, but I found no place to set it down to rest. Neither the charm of the countryside nor the sweet scents of a garden could soothe it. It found no peace in song or laughter, none in the company of friends at table or in the pleasures of love, none even in books or poetry. . . . Where could my heart find refuge from itself? Where could I go, yet leave myself behind?

—St. Augustine

To suffer and long for relief is a central experience of humanity. But the absence of pain or discomfort or what Pablo Neruda called "the infinite ache" is never enough. Relief is bound up with satisfaction, pleasure, happiness—the pursuit of which is declared a right in the manifesto of our republic. I sit here with two agents of that pursuit: on my right, a bottle from Duane Reade pharmacy; on my left, a bag of plant matter, bought last night for about the same sum in an East Village bar from a group of men who would have sold me different kinds of contraband if they hadn't sniffed cop in my curiosity and eagerness. This being Rudy Giuliani's New York, I had feared *they* were undercover. But my worst-case scenario was a night or two in jail and theirs a fifteen-year minimum. As I exited the bar, I saw an empty police van idling, waiting to be filled with people like me but, mostly, people like them, who are there only because I am.

Fear and suspicion, secrecy and shame, the yearning for pleasure, and the wish to avoid men in blue uniforms. This is (in rough, incomplete terms) an emotional report from the front. The drug wars which, having spanned more than eight decades, require the plural—are palpable in New York City. The mayor blends propaganda, brute force, and guerrilla tactics, dispatching undercover cops to call "smoke, smoke" and "bud, bud"—and to arrest those who answer. In Washington Square Park, he erected ten video cameras that sweep the environs twenty-four hours a day. Surveillance is a larger theme of these wars, as is the notion that cherished freedoms are incidental. But it is telling that such an extreme manifestation of these ideas appears in a public park, one of the very few common spaces in this city not controlled by, and an altar to, corporate commerce. Several times a month, I walk through that park to the pharmacy, where a doctor's slip is my passport to another world. Here, altering the mind and body with powders and plants is not only legal but even patriotic. Among the souls wandering these aisles, I feel I have kin. But I am equally at home, and equally ill at ease, among the outlaws. I cross back and forth with wide eyes.

What I see is this: From 1970 to 1998, the inflation-adjusted revenue of major pharmaceutical companies more than quadrupled to $81 billion, 24 percent of that from drugs affecting the central nervous system and sense organs. Sales of herbal medicines now exceed $4 billion a year. Meanwhile, the war on Other drugs escalated dramatically. Since 1970 the federal antidrug budget has risen 3,700 percent and now exceeds $17 billion. More than one and a half million people are arrested on drug charges each year, and 400,000 are now in prison. These numbers are just a window onto an obvious truth: We take more drugs and reward those who supply them. We punish more people for taking drugs and especially punish those who supply them. On the surface, there is no conflict. One kind of drugs is *medicine*, righting wrongs, restoring the ill to a proper, natural state. These drugs have the sheen of corporate logos and men in white coats. They are kept in the room where we wash grime from our skin and do the same with our souls. Our conception of illegal drugs is a warped reflection of this picture. Offered up from the dirty underworld, they are hedonistic, not curative. They induce artificial pleasure, not health. They harm rather than help, enslave rather than liberate.

There is some truth in each of these extreme pictures. But   5
with my dual citizenship, consciousness split and altered many times over, I come to say this: The drug wars and the drug boom are interrelated, of the same body. The hostility and veneration, the punishment and profits, these come from the same beliefs and the same mistakes.

I

Before marijuana, cocaine, or "Ecstasy," before nitrous oxide or magic mushrooms, before I had tried any of these, I poked through the foil enclosing a single capsule of fluoxetine hydrochloride. My drug story begins at this point, at the end of a devastating first year of college. For years, I had wrapped myself in an illusion that my lifelong troubles—intense despair, loneliness, anxiety, a relentless inner soundtrack of self-criticism—would dissolve if I could only please the gatekeepers of the Ivy League. By the spring of freshman year, I had been skinned of this illusion and plunged into a deep darkness. From a phone booth in a library basement, I resumed contact with a psychiatrist I'd begun seeing in high school.

I told him how awful I felt, and, after a few sessions, he suggested I consider medication. By now our exchange is a familiar one. This was 1990, three years after Prozac introduced the country to a new class of antidepressants, called selective serotonin reuptake inhibitors. SSRIs were an impressive innovation chemically but a stunning innovation for the market, because, while no more effective than previous generations of antidepressants, SSRIs had fewer side effects and thus could be given to a much broader range of people. (At last count, 22 million Americans have used Prozac alone.) When my doctor suggested I take Prozac, it was with a casual tone. Although the idea of "altering my brain chemistry" unsettled me at first, I soon absorbed his attitude. When I returned home that summer, I asked him how such drugs worked. He drew a crude map of a synapse, or the junction between nerve cells. There is a neurotransmitter called serotonin, he told me, that is ordinarily released at one end of the synapse and, at the other end, absorbed by a sort of molecular pump. Prozac inhibits this pumping process and therefore increases serotonin's presence in the brain. "What we don't understand," he said, looking up from his pad, "is why increased levels of serotonin alleviate depression. But that's what seems to happen."

I didn't understand the importance of this moment until years later, after I had noticed many more sentences in which the distance between the name of a drug—Prozac, heroin, Ritalin, crack cocaine—and its effects had collapsed. For example, the phrase "Prozac eases depression," properly unpacked, actually represents this more complicated thought: "Prozac influences the serotonin patterns in the brain, which for some unknown reason is found to alleviate, more often than would a placebo, a collection of symptoms referred to as depression." What gets lost in abbreviation—Prozac cures! Heroin kills!—is that drugs work because the human body works, and they fail or hurt us because the body and spirit are vulnerable. When drugs spark miracles—prolonging the lives of those with HIV, say, or dulling the edges of a potentially deadly manic depression—we should be thankful.[1] But many of these processes are mysteries that might never yield to science. The psychiatric establishment, for example, still does not understand why serotonin affects mood. According to Michael Montagne of the Massachusetts College of Pharmacy, 42 percent of marketed drugs likewise have no proven mechanism of action. In *Listening to Prozac*, Peter Kramer quotes a pharmacologist explaining the problem this way: "If the human brain were simple enough for us to understand, we would be too simple to understand it." Yet pharmaceutical companies exude certainty. "Smooth and powerful depression relief," reads an ad for Effexor in a recent issue of *The American Journal of Psychiatry*. "Antidepressant efficacy that brings your patients back." In case this message is too subtle, the ad shows an ecstatic mother and child playing together, with a note written in crayon: "I got my mommy back."

The irony is that our *faith* in pharmaceuticals is based on a model of consciousness that science is slowly displacing. "Throughout history," chemist and religious scholar Daniel Perrine writes in *The Chemistry of Mind-Altering Drugs*, "the power that many psychoactive drugs have exerted over the behavior of human beings has been variously ascribed to gods or demons." In a sense, that continues. "We ascribe magical powers to substances," says Perrine, "as if the joy is inside the bottle. Our culture has no sacred realm, so we've assigned a sacred power to these drugs. This is what [Alfred North] Whitehead would call the 'fallacy of misplaced concreteness.' We say 'The good is in that Prozac powder,' or 'The evil is in that cocaine powder.' But evil and good are not attributes of molecules."

This is a hard lesson to learn. In my gut, where it matters, I still haven't learned it. Back in 1990, I took the Prozac and, eventually, more than two dozen other medications: antidepressants, antipsychotics, antianxiety agents, and so on. The sample pills would be elegantly wrapped. Handing them to me, the doctors would explain the desired effect: this drug might quiet the voices in my head; this one might make me less depressed and less anxious; this combination might help my concentration and ease my repetitive, obsessive thoughts. Each time I swelled with hope. I've spent many years in therapy and have looked for redemption in literature, work, love. But nothing quite matches the expectancy of putting a capsule on my tongue and waiting to be remade.

But I was not remade. None of the promised benefits of the drugs came, and I suffered still. In 1993, I went to see Donald Klein, one of the top psychopharmacologists in the country. Klein's prestige, underscored by his precipitous fees, again set me

10

off into fantasies of health. He peppered me with questions, listened thoughtfully. After an hour, he pushed his reading glasses onto his forehead and said, "Well, this is what I think you have." He opened the standard psychiatric reference text to a chapter on "disassociative disorders" and pointed to a sublisting called depersonalization disorder, "characterized by a persistent or recurrent feeling of being detached from one's mental processes or body."

I'm still not certain that this illness best describes my experience. I can't even describe myself as "clinically ill," because clinicians don't know what the hell to do with me. But Klein gave me an entirely new way of thinking about my problems, and a grim message. "Depersonalization is very difficult to treat," he said. So I was back where I started, with one exception. During our session, Klein had asked if I used marijuana. Once, I told him, but it didn't do much. After he had given me his diagnosis, he told me the reason he had asked: "A lot of people with depersonalization say they get relief from marijuana." At that time, I happened, for the first time in my life, to be surrounded by friends who liked to smoke pot. So in addition to taking drugs alone and waiting for a miracle, I looked for solace in my own small drug culture. And for a time, I got some. The basic function of antidepressants is to help people with battered inner lives participate in the world around them. This is what pot did for me. It helped me spend time with others, something I have yearned for but also feared; it sparked an eagerness to write and conjure ideas—some of which I found the morning after to be dreamy or naive, but some of which were the germ of something valuable. While high, I could enjoy life's simple pleasures in a way that I hadn't ever been able to and still find maddeningly difficult. Some might see this (and people watching me surely did) as silly and immature. But it's also a reason to keep living.

Sad to say, I quickly found pot's limitations. When my spirits are lifted, pot can help punctuate that. If I smoke while on a downward slope or while idling, I usually experience more depression or anxiety. Salvation, for me at least, is not within that smoked plant, or the granules of a pill, or any other substance. Like I said, it's a hard lesson to learn.

To the more sober-minded among us, it is a source of much consternation that drugs, alcohol, and cigarettes are so central to our collective social lives. It is hard, in fact, to think of a single social ritual that does not revolve around some consciousness-altering substance. ("Should we get together for coffee or drinks?") But drugs are much more than a social lubricant; they are also the centerpiece of many individual lives. When it comes to alcohol, or cigarettes, or any illicit substance, this is seen as a problem. With pharmaceuticals, it is usually considered healthy. Yet the dynamic is often the same.

It begins with a drug that satisfies a particular need or desire—maybe known to us, maybe not. So we have drinks, or a smoke, or swallow a few pills. And we get something from this, a whole lot or maybe just a bit. But we often don't realize that the feeling is *inside*, perhaps something that, with effort, could be experienced without the drugs or perhaps, as in the psychiatric equivalent of diabetes, something we will always need help with. Yet all too often we project upon the drug a power that resides elsewhere. Many believe this to be a failure of character. If so, it is a failure the whole culture is implicated in. A recent example came with the phrase "pure theatrical Viagra," widely used to describe a Broadway production starring Nicole Kidman. Notice what's happening: Sildenafil citrate is a substance that increases blood circulation and has the side effect of producing erections in men. As a medicine, it is intended to be used as an adjunct to sexual stimulation. As received by our culture, though, the *drug* becomes the desired effect, the "real thing" to which a naked woman onstage is compared.

Such exaltation of drugs is reinforced by the torrent of pharmaceutical ads that now stuff magazines and blanket the airwaves. Since 1994, drug-makers have increased their direct-to-consumer advertising budget sevenfold, to $1.2 billion last year. Take the ad for Meridia, a weight-loss drug. Compared with other drug ads ("We're going to change lives," says a doctor pitching acne cream. "We're going to make a lot of people happy"), it is the essence of restraint. "You do your part," it says in an allusion to exercise and diet. "We'll do ours." The specific intent here is to convince people who are overweight (or believe themselves to be) that they should ask their doctor for Meridia.[2] Like the pitch for Baby Gap that announces "INSTANT KARMA" over a child wrapped in a $44 velvet jacket, drug ads suggest—or explicitly say— that we can solve our problems through magic-bullet consumption. As the old saying goes, "Better living through chemistry."

It's the job of advertisers to try every trick to sell their products. But that's the point: drugs are a commodity designed for profit and not necessarily the best route to health and happiness. The "self help" shelves at pharmacies, the "expert only" section behind the counter, these are promised to contain remedies for all

₁₅

ills. But the wizards behind the curtain are fallible human beings, just like us. Professor Montagne says that despite obvious financial incentives, "there really is an overwhelming belief among pharmacists that the last thing you should do for many problems is take a drug. They'll recommend something when you ask, but there's a good chance that when you're walking out the door they'll be saying, 'Aw, that guy doesn't need a laxative every day. He just needs to eat right. They don't need Tagamet. They just need to cut back on the spicy food.'" It is hard to get worked up about these examples, but they point to the broader pattern of drug worship. With illegal drugs, we see the same pattern, again through that warped mirror.

Not long after his second inauguration, President Clinton signed a bill earmarking $195 million for an antidrug ad campaign—the first installment of a $1 billion pledge. The ads, which began running last summer, all end with the words "Partnership for a Drug Free America" and "Office of National Drug Control Policy." It is fitting that the two entities are officially joined. The Partnership emerged in 1986, the year basketball star Len Bias died with cocaine in his system and President Reagan signed a bill creating, among many other new penalties, mandatory federal prison terms for possession of an illegal substance. This was the birth of the drug wars' latest phase, in which any drug use at all—not abuse or addiction or "drug-related crime"— became the enemy.[3] Soon the words "drug-free America" began to show up regularly, in the name of a White House conference as well as in legislation that declared it the "policy of the United States Government to create a Drug-Free America by 1995."

Although the work of the Partnership is spread over hundreds of ad firms, the driving force behind the organization is a man named James Burke—and he is a peculiar spokesman for a "drug free" philosophy. Burke is the former CEO of Johnson & Johnson, the maker of Tylenol and other pain-relief products; Nicotrol, a nicotine-delivery device; Pepcid AC, an antacid; and various prescription medications. When he came to the Partnership, he brought with him a crucial grant of $3 million from the Robert Wood Johnson Foundation, a philanthropy tied to Johnson & Johnson stock. Having granted $24 million over the last ten years, RWJ is the Partnership's single largest funder, but the philanthropic arms of Merck, Bristol-Myers Squibb, and Hoffman-La Roche have also made sizable donations.

20   I resist the urge to use the word "hypocrisy," from the Greek *hypokrisis*, "acting of a part on the stage." I don't believe James

Burke is acting. Rather, he embodies a contradiction so common that few people even notice it—the idea that altering the body and mind is morally wrong when done with some substances and salutary when done with others.

This contradiction, on close examination, resolves into coherence. Before the Partnership, Burke was in the business of burnishing the myth of the uber-drug, doing his best—as all marketers do—to make some external object the center of existence, displacing the complications of family, community, inner lives. Now, drawing on the same admakers, he does the same in reverse. (These admakers are happy to work pro bono, having been made rich by ads for pharmaceuticals, cigarettes, and alcohol. Until a few years ago, the Partnership also took money from these latter two industries.) The Partnership formula is to present a problem—urban violence, date rape, juvenile delinquency—and lay it at the feet of drugs. "Marijuana," says a remorseful-looking kid, "cost me a lot of things. I used to be a straight-A student, you know. I was liked by all the neighbors. Never really caused any trouble. I was always a good kid growing up. Before I knew it, I was getting thrown out of my house."

This kid looks to be around seventeen. The Partnership couldn't tell me his real name or anything about him except that he was interviewed through a New York drug-treatment facility. I wanted to talk to him, because I wanted to ask: "Was it *marijuana* that cost you these things? Or was it your *behavior* while using marijuana? Was that behavior caused by, or did it merely *coincide* with, your marijuana use?"

These kinds of subtleties are crucial, but it isn't a mystery why they are usually glossed over. In Texas, federal prosecutors are seeking life sentences for dealers who supplied heroin to teenagers who subsequently died of overdose. Parents praised the authorities. "We just don't want other people to die," said one, who suggested drug tests for fourth-graders on up. Another said, "I kind of wish all this had happened a year ago so whoever was able to supply Jay that night was already in jail." The desire for justice, and to protect future generations, is certainly understandable. But it is striking to note how rarely, in a story of an overdose, the survivors ask the most important question. It is not: How do we rid illegal drugs from the earth.[4] Despite eighty years of criminal sanctions, stiffened to the point just short of summary executions, markets in this contraband flourish because supply meets demand. Had Jay's dealer been in jail that night, Jay surely would have been able to find someone else—and if not that night, then soon thereafter.

The real question—why do kids like Jay want to take heroin in the first place?—is consistently, aggressively avoided. Senator Orrin Hatch recently declared that "people who are pushing drugs on our kids . . . I think we ought to lock them up and throw away the keys." Implicit in this remark is the idea that kids only alter their consciousness because it is *pushed* upon them.

25   Blaming the alien invader—the dealer, the drug—provides some structure to chaos. Let's say you are a teenager and, in the course of establishing your own identity or quelling inner conflicts, you start smoking a lot of pot. You start running around with a "bad crowd." Your grades suffer. Friction with your parents crescendos, and they throw you out of the house. Later, you regret what you've done—and you're offered a magic button, a way to condense and displace all your misdeeds. So, naturally, you blame everything on the drug. Something maddeningly complicated now has a single name. Psychologist Bruce Alexander points out that the same tendency exists among the seriously addicted. "If your life is really fucked up, you can get into heroin, and that's kind of a way of coping," he says. "You'll have friends to share something with. You'll have an identity. You'll have an explanation for all your troubles."

What works for individuals works for a society. ("Good People Go Bad in Iowa," read a 1996 *New York Times* headline, "And a Drug Is Being Blamed.") Why is the wealthiest society in history also one of the most fearful and cynical? What root of unhappiness and discontent spurs thousands of college students to join cults, millions of Americans to seek therapists, gurus, and spiritual advisers? Why has the rate of suicide for people fifteen to twenty-four tripled since 1960? Why would an eleven- and a thirteen-year-old take three rifles and seven handguns to their school, trigger the fire alarm, and shower gunfire on their schoolmates and teachers? Stop searching for an answer. Drug Watch International, a drug "think tank" that regularly consults with drug czar Barry McCaffrey and testifies before Congress, answered the question in an April 1998 press release: "MARIJUANA USED BY JONESBORO KILLERS."[5]

II

The market must be taken seriously as an explanation of drugs' status. The reason is that the explanations usually given fall so far short. Take the idea "Bad drugs induce violence." First, violence is demonstrably not a pharmacological effect of marijuana, heroin, and the psychedelics. Of cocaine, in some cases. (Of alcohol, in many.) But if it was violence we feared, then wouldn't we punish that act with the greatest severity? Drug sellers, even people marginally involved in a "conspiracy to distribute," consistently receive longer sentences than rapists and murderers.

Nor can the explanation be the danger of illegal drugs. Marijuana, though not harmless, has never been shown to have caused a single death. Heroin, in long-term "maintenance" use, is safer than habitual heavy drinking. Of course, illegal drugs can do the body great harm. All drugs have some risk, including many legal ones. Because of Viagra's novelty, the 130 deaths it has caused (as of last November) have received a fair amount of attention. But each year, anti-inflammatory agents such as Advil, Tylenol, and aspirin cause an estimated 7,000 deaths and 70,000 hospitalizations. Legal medications are the principal cause of between 45,000 and 200,000 American deaths each year, between 1 and 5.5 million hospitalizations. It is telling that we have only estimates. As Thomas J. Moore notes in *Prescription for Disaster*, the government calculates the annual deaths due to railway accidents and falls of less than one story, among hundreds of categories. But no federal agency collects information on deaths related to legal drugs. (The $30 million spent investigating the crash of TWA Flight 800, in which 230 people died, is six times larger than the FDA's budget for monitoring the safety of approved drugs.) Psychoactive drugs can be particularly toxic. In 1992, according to Moore, nearly 100,000 persons were diagnosed with "poisoning" by psychologically active drugs, 90 percent of the cases due to benzodiazepine tranquilizers and antidepressants. It is simply a myth that legal drugs have been proven "safe." According to one government estimate, 15 percent of children are on Ritalin. But the long-term effects of Ritalin—or antidepressants, which are also commonly prescribed—on young kids isn't known. "I feel in between a rock and a hard place," says NIMH [National Institutes of Mental Health] director Hyman. "I know that untreated depression is bad and that we better not just let kids be depressed. But by the same token we don't know what the effects of antidepressants are on the developing brain. . . . We should have humility and be a bit frightened."

These risks are striking, given that protecting children is the cornerstone of the drug wars. We forbid the use of medical marijuana, worrying that it will send a bad message. What message is sent by the long row of pills laid out by the school nurse—or by "educational" visits to high schools by drugmakers? But, you might object, these are medicines—and illegal drug use is purely hedonistic. What, then, about illegal drug use that clearly falls under the category of self-medication? One physician I know who treats women heroin users tells me that each of them suffered sexual abuse as children. According to University of Texas pharmacologist Kathryn Cunningham, 40 to 70 percent of cocaine users have preexisting depressive conditions.

30   This is not to suggest that depressed people should use cocaine. The risks of dependence and compulsive use, and the roller-coaster experience of cocaine highs and lows, make for a toxic combination with intense suffering. Given these risks, not to mention the risk of arrest, why wouldn't a depressed person opt for legal treatment? The most obvious answers are economic (many cocaine users lack access to health care) and chemical. Cocaine is a formidable mood elevator and acts immediately, as opposed to the two to four weeks of most prescription antidepressants. Perhaps the most important factor, though, is cultural. Using a "pleasure drug" like cocaine does not signal weakness or vulnerability. Self-medication can be a way of avoiding the stigma of admitting to oneself and others that there is a problem to be treated.

Calling illegal drug use a disease is popular these days, and it is done, I believe, with a compassionate purpose: pushing treatment over incarceration. It also seems clear that drug abuse can be a distinct pathology. But isn't the "disease" whatever the drug users are trying to find relief from (or flee)? According to the Pharmaceutical Research and Manufacturer's Association, nineteen medications are in development for "substance use disorders." This includes six products for "smoking cessation" that contain nicotine. Are these treatments for a disease or competitors in the market for long-term nicotine maintenance?

Perhaps the most damning charge against illegal drugs is that they're addictive. Again, the real story is considerably more complicated. Many illegal drugs, like marijuana and cocaine, do not produce physical dependence. Some, like heroin, do. In any case, the most important factor in destructive use is the craving people experience—craving that leads them to continue a behavior despite serious adverse effects. Legal drugs preclude certain behaviors we associate with addiction—like stealing for dope money—but that doesn't mean people don't become addicted to them. By their own admissions, Betty Ford was addicted to Valium and William Rehnquist to the sleeping pill Placidyl, for nine years. Ritalin shares the addictive qualities of all the amphetamines. "For many people," says NIMH director Hyman, explaining why many psychiatrists will not prescribe one class of drugs, "stopping short-acting high-potency benzodiazepines, such as Xanax, is sheer hell. As they try to stop they develop rebound anxiety symptoms (or insomnia) that seem worse than the original symptoms they were treating." Even antidepressants, although they certainly don't produce the intense craving of classic addiction, can be habit forming. Lauren Slater was first made well by one pill per day, then required more to feel the same effect, then found that even three would not return her to the miraculous health that she had at first experienced. This is called tolerance. She has also been unable to stop taking the drug without "breaking up." This is called dependence. "There are plenty of addicts who lead perfectly respectable lives," Slater's boyfriend tells her. To which she replies, "An addict . . . You think so?"

III

In the late 1980s, in black communities, the Partnership for a Drug Free America placed billboards showing an outstretched hand filled with vials of crack cocaine. It read: "YO, SLAVE! The dealer is selling you something you don't want. . . . Addiction is slavery." The ad was obviously designed to resonate in the black neighborhoods most visibly affected by the wave of crack use. But its idea has a broader significance in a country for which independence of mind and spirit is a primary value.

In *Brave New World*, Aldous Huxley created the archetype of drug-as-enemy-of-freedom: soma. "A really efficient totalitarian state," he wrote in the book's foreword, is one in which the "slaves . . . do not have to be coerced, because they love their servitude." Soma—"euphoric, narcotic, pleasantly hallucinant," with "all the advantages of Christianity and alcohol; none of their defects," and a way to "take a holiday from reality whenever you like, and come back without so much as a headache or a mythology"—is one of the key agents of that voluntary slavery.

In the spring of 1953, two decades after he published this 35 book, Huxley offered himself as a guinea pig in the experiments of a British psychiatrist studying mescaline. What followed was a second masterpiece on drugs and man, *The Doors of Perception*. The title is from William Blake: "If the doors of perception were cleansed every thing would appear to man as it is, infinite—/For man has closed himself up, till he sees all things thro' narrow chinks of his cavern." Huxley found his mescaline experience to be "without question the most extraordinary and significant experience this side of the Beatific vision. . . . [I]t opens up a host of philosophical problems, throws intense light and raises all manner of questions in the field of aesthetics, religion, theory of knowledge."

Taken together, these two works frame the dual, contradictory nature of mind-altering substances: they can be agents of servitude or of freedom. Though we are deathly afraid of the first possibility, we are drawn like moths to the light of the second. "The urge to transcend self-conscious selfhood is," Huxley writes, "a principal appetite of the soul. When, for whatever reason, men and women fail to transcend themselves by means of worship, good works and spiritual exercises, they are apt to resort to religion's chemical surrogates."

One might think, as mind diseases are broadened and the substances that alter consciousness take their place beside toothpaste and breakfast cereal, that users of other "surrogates" might receive more understanding and sympathy. You might think the executive taking Xanax before a speech, or the college student on BuSpar, or any of the recipients of 65 million annual antidepressant prescriptions, would have second thoughts about punishing the depressed user of cocaine, or even the person who is not seriously depressed, just, as the Prozac ad says, "feeling blue." In trying to imagine why the opposite has happened, I think of the people I know who use psychopharmaceuticals. Because I've always been up-front about my experiences, friends often approach me when they're thinking of doing so. Every year there are more of them. And yet, in their hushed tones, I hear shame mixed with fear. I think we don't know quite what to make of our own brave new world. The more fixes that become available, the more we realize we're vulnerable. We solve some problems, but add new and perplexing ones.

In the *Odyssey*, when three of his crew are lured by the lotus-eaters and "lost all desire to send a message back, much less return," Odysseus responds decisively. "I brought them back . . . dragged them under the rowing benches, lashed them fast." "Already," writes David Lenson in *On Drugs*, "the high is unspeakable, and already the official response is arrest and restraint." The pattern is set: since people lose their freedom from drugs, we take their freedom to keep them from drugs.[6] Odysseus' frantic response, though, seems more than just a practical measure. Perhaps he fears his own desire to retire amidst the lotus-eaters. Perhaps he fears what underlies that desire. If we even feel the *lure* of drugs, we acknowledge that we are not satisfied by what is good and productive and healthy. And that is a frightening thought. "The War on Drugs has been with us," writes Lenson, "for as long as we have despised the part of ourselves that wants to get high."

As Lenson points out, "It is a peculiar feature of history, that peoples with strong historical, physical, and cultural affinities tend to detest each other with the most venom." In the American drug wars, too, animosity runs in both directions. Many users of illegal drugs—particularly kids—do so not just because they like the feeling but because it sets them apart from "straight" society, allows them (without any effort or thought) to join a culture of dissent. On the other side, "straight society" sees a hated version of itself in the drug users. This is not just the 11 percent of Americans using psychotropic medications, or the 6 million who admit to "nonmedical" use of legal drugs, but anyone who fears and desires pleasure, who fears and desires loss of control, who fears and desires chemically enhanced living.

Straight society has remarkable power: it can arrest the enemy, seize assets without judicial review, withdraw public housing or assistance. But the real power of prohibition is that it *creates* the forbidden world of danger and hedonism that the straights want to distinguish themselves from. A black market spawns violence, thievery, and illnesses—all can be blamed on the demon drugs. For a reminder, we need only go to the movies (in which drug dealers are the stock villains). Or watch *Cops*, in which, one by one, the bedraggled junkies, fearsome crack dealers, and hapless dope smokers are led away in chains. For anyone who is secretly ashamed, or confused, about the explosion in legal drug-taking, here is reassurance: the people in handcuffs are the bad ones. Anything the rest of us do is saintly by comparison.

We are like Robert Louis Stevenson's Dr. Jekyll, longing that we might be divided in two, that "the unjust might go his way . . . and the just could walk steadfastly and securely on his upward path, doing the good things in which he found his pleasure, and no longer exposed to disgrace and penitence by the hands of this extraneous evil." In his laboratory, Jekyll creates the "foul soul" of Edward Hyde, whose presence heightens the reputation of the esteemed doctor. But Jekyll's dream cannot last. Just before his suicide, he confesses to having become "a creature eaten up and emptied by fever, languidly weak both in body and mind, and solely occupied by one thought: the horror of my other self." To react to an unpleasant truth by separating from it is a fundamental human instinct. Usually, though, what is denied only grows in injurious power. We believe that lashing at the illegal drug user will purify us. We try to separate the "evil" from the "good" of

40

drugs, what we love and what we fear about them, to enforce a drug-free America with handcuffs and jail cells while legal drugs grow in popularity and variety. But we cannot separate the inseparable. We know the truth about ourselves. It is time to begin living with that horror, and that blessing.

Endnotes

1. Although I am critical of the exaltation of drugs, it must be noted that a crisis runs in the opposite direction. Only a small minority of people with schizophrenia, bipolar disorder, and major depression—for which medications can be very helpful—receive treatment of any kind.

2. Fifty-five percent of American adults, or 97 million people, are overweight or obese. It is no surprise, then, that at least forty-five companies have weight-loss drugs in development. But many of these drugs are creatures more of marketing than of pharmacology. Meridia is an SSRI, like Prozac. Similarly, Zyban, a Glaxo Wellcome product for smoking cessation, is chemically identical to the antidepressant Wellbutrin. Admakers exclude this information because they want their products to seem like targeted cures—not vaguely understood remedies like the "tonics" of yesteryear.

3. Declared Nancy Reagan, "If you're a casual drug user, you're an accomplice to murder." Los Angeles police chief Daryl Gates told the Senate that "casual drug users should be taken out and shot." And so on.

4. Many people believe that this is still possible, among them House Speaker Dennis Hastert, who last year co-authored a plan to "help create a drug-free America by the year 2002." In 1995, Hastert sponsored a bill allowing herbal remedies to bypass FDA regulations, thus helping to satisfy Americans' incessant desire for improvement and consciousness alteration.

5. The release describes Andrew Golden and Mitchell Johnson as "reputed marijuana smokers." No reference to Golden and pot could be found in the Nexis database. The *Washington Post* reports that Johnson "said he smoked marijuana. None of his classmates believed him."

6. In the 1992 campaign, Bill Clinton said, "I don't think my brother would be alive today if it wasn't for the criminal justice system." Roger served sixteen months in Arkansas State Prison for conspiracy to distribute cocaine. Had he been convicted three years later, he would have faced a five-year mandatory minimum sentence, without the possibility of parole. If he had had a prior felony or had sold the

same amount of cocaine in crack form, he would have automatically received ten years.

Discussion Questions

1. Describe the "beliefs" in American society that have made both legal and illegal drugs so popular. Then, contrast Shenk's article about drugs' effects on the body to the perspective of the mind–body connection discussed in Chapter 1.

2. Shenk claims that most of our social rituals "revolve around some consciousness-altering substance" (paragraph 14). To what extent do you believe this remark is accurate? Give examples of social rituals in which some sort of "drug" is *not* used as a "social lubricant."

3. Watch one pharmaceutical commercial on television. It is best to record the segment on a VCR so that you can review it. Make notes about what the drug-makers promise to people who try the drug offered. According to the commercial, how will it change the user's life? Analyze the strategies that the story line uses to engage the viewer in the dramatic change possible through the product.

4. Shenk claims that one appeal of illegal drugs for adolescents is "to join a culture of dissent" against "straight society" (paragraph 39) and to enter "the forbidden world of danger and hedonism" (paragraph 40). How important do you think this antisocial appeal is in an individual's choice to "get high" illegally?

Topics for Exploration and Writing

You have been reading about and discussing the impacts of contemporary medical science on the body and the ethics of choosing technological solutions for human health. To explore these ideas, analyze one realm of choice relating to medical practices, drawing on examples from your observation and experience. While most of your content should be original, brief comparisons to *at least one* of the articles in this chapter are *required* to develop your viewpoint (refer to authors by last name and to article titles). Your job as a writer is to inform your readers by presenting specific examples that you can explain in detail and then generalizing about these examples by presenting a well-informed viewpoint on a social practice. For any of these topics, if race, ethnicity, gender, sexual preference, age, body size, or disability relates to your analysis, please include these important dimensions in your essay.

1. Carefully reread *one* of the essays in Chapter 1 . Then, compare and contrast the attitude toward the body, as expressed in that essay, with the

mainstream American attitude toward the body that Shenk discusses in "America's Altered States." Be sure to consider the value our culture seems to place on drugs.

2. Henig, in "Pandora's Baby," and Hershey, in "Choosing Disability," concern themselves with "reproductive technologies." On one hand, Henig cites the real risks for "test-tube babies," which medical science has only recently discovered. On the other hand, Hershey warns of the possible discrimination of prenatal screening. In your essay, try to resolve the possible contradictions between the two authors and explain the principles they might share.

3. Hershey defines "disabiliphobia" as "a deep-seated fear of confronting the physical vulnerability that is part of being human" (paragraph 20). *If you have experienced or witnessed* this phobia, describe the experience, giving reasons for this fear among the "abled." Or, instead of focusing on the disabled, apply the quotation to experiences showing "ageism," prejudice toward the elderly.

4. Compare and contrast the dangers and potentials of medical technology as outlined by Henig and Wilmut. Do *both* authors seem to describe human needs for technology? Suppose American society accepts Wilmut's definition stating that "the embryo is a cluster of cells that does not become a sentient being until much later in development, so it is not yet a person" (paragraph 25). Does this belief, then, justify embryonic stem cell research to benefit humans who are ill or who wish to avoid genetically transmitted diseases? After discussing the viewpoints of Henig and Wilmut, define the principles that you believe should govern such research. Your purpose is to explain the controversy rationally, rather than to persuade the reader through emotional appeals.

5. Consider the metaphor of the boundary—between human bodies, between social groups or classes, and between geographical regions. Analyze the use of this metaphor in the Chapter 5 articles by Hershey—who considers the boundaries between the womb and the world, and between the disabled and the "abled"; by Wilmut—who considers the boundary between the egg cell and the genetic material of a "donor cell"; by Scheper-Hughes—who considers the boundaries between rich, white bodies and poor, brown bodies in the "slave trade" of the kidney transplant market; and by Shenk—who considers the artificial social boundary between the legal prescription drug user and the illegal drug abuser. Analyzing two or more of the articles in Chapter 5, explain the meaning of the boundary metaphor. Judge how effectively this metaphor conveys the complexities of biological and social separation.

Dance

Drid Williams has been a professional modern dancer and a teacher of ballet, Afro-Caribbean forms, and ballroom dancing, but has also worked as a professor of dance and human movement studies. In *Ten Lectures on Theories of the Dance* (Scarecrow Press, 1991), drawing from her practical and academic background, she outlines six reasons that people dance:

1. For leisure and entertainment. . .
2. Because of biological, organic, or instinctive needs . . . as a precursor to spoken language, perhaps. . .
3. To express themselves—dances as *symbolic* activities divorced from real life. . .
4. Because they feel sexy, happy or sad, or something—the dance as a prime repository of emotions. . .
5. Because a spirit has possessed them, whether good or bad—dances as hysterical, neurotic, or *quasi*-religious manifestations. . .
6. To show off or relieve their overburdened feelings—the dance as *catharsis*. . . (6)

Though Williams is careful to qualify that "all of the above answers are inadequate," her list still provides a fair starting point for discussion and evokes several metaphors for the body. In this last chapter of *Body and Culture*, her list also provides an opportunity to reassess our understandings about the body formed by previous readings in the text. It seems we might compare all these reasons to the motivations for body art in Chapter 3. Pierced and tattooed people may find some *entertainment* in rebelling against the mainstream, but also feel an *instinctive need* for "primitive" marks, which prove *symbolic* of their deeper connection to human

213

tribal history, provide *catharsis* through the pain of the procedure, and reveal the *emotions* of a newly discovered sensuality
that reaffirms their lives. On the other hand, some critics of the
"mutilated" subculture may see their motivations as *neurotic*.
Williams's reasons for dancing also apply to the athletic activities
in Chapter 2. The metaphor of the body as a "repository of emotions" may explain bodybuilding as a means to escape insecurities and attain self-confidence; it might also explain skateboarding as an activity that "reflects your mood at the time" and
expresses "the skaters' own standards for personal worth." The
catharsis theory of dance can also apply to Chapter 4 in explaining eating disorders among young women who binge and purge
to control their bodies. Likewise, *emotions* such as jubilation
over new freedoms and the *catharsis* of breaking through sexist
barriers in the workplace both explain the appeal of the sexually
liberated Maidenform bra ads to women in the 1970s.

The authors in Chapter 6 recall some of these concerns
about the body expressed in the earlier chapters. These authors
not only explore the reasons people dance, but also some of the
benefits of dancing for the mind and spirit. In the first article, "I
Am a Dancer," Martha Graham provides a personal and philosophical viewpoint from the perspective of a professional modern dancer. She explores how dance expresses "the inner landscape" through creating and performing, but she also believes
that dance draws its inspiration from a "blood memory" of instincts born of human history. Graham, like Jack Kornfield in
Chapter 1, emphasizes that there is a bodily and mental purity
required of focused human activity, whether meditation or
dance. And like Zen, for Graham dancing means "you have to be
reborn to the instant"—being alive to the moment of decision
and action.

In the second article, "The Art of Dancing," Havelock Ellis
presents a historical survey of the origins of dance in human cultures, considering its relevance in religion, courtship, art, social
custom, and education. Here, he writes in the genre of the
nineteenth-century English essay, an informal discursive style
that explores an issue from a variety of viewpoints in order to
contemplate its potential meanings and implications. As such,
the essay cites ideas from other thinkers and writers—such as
the Scottish explorer David Livingstone, the American educator
Stanley Hall, and the German philosopher Friedrich Nietzsche—
although no references are made to particular sources, as is typical of the English essay form. Still, it is a well-informed and

thoughtful examination of dance and the social meanings of an art "of which we ourselves are the stuff."

In the third article, "Disco," Peter Braunstein writes as a historian of a fairly recent social phenomenon. Since this work was published in *American Heritage* for a popular audience, there are no footnotes, but his research is evident and eclectic. Braunstein informally mentions authors throughout his writing, even though sometimes he writes like an insider to the disco scene and merely alludes to a source: the 1958 Senate Subcommittee on Juvenile Delinquency, Jane Fonda's filming of *Klute*, music journalist Carol Cooper, *Dancing Madness*—a heterosexual's guide to discos, "a reporter from *Harper's*," the biography *Simply Halston*, statistics from *Billboard*, quotations from *Interview* magazine and from Mae West. He not only records, but almost celebrates the hedonism and decadence of disco, which he argues was countercultural "in its elevation of the human body as an instrument of pleasure." Again, this metaphor for the body seems to relate to Williams's first reason for dancing—entertainment. But, oddly enough, Braunstein also alludes to the fifth reason—"*quasi*-religious manifestations"—when he writes, "personal exploration through dance, sex, or drug use was indeed a quasi-religious quest."

In the fourth article, "Ballet as a Way of Knowing," Marion Frank revisits Chapter 4's concerns about unhealthy body ideals, but also about the validation and empowerment of women. It should be noted that the original publication of this work included a bibliography of eighteen sources in social psychology or professional dance. This scholarly research has been omitted in the reprint since Frank's argument is essentially supported within her text. In the context of ballet instruction, she argues for the value of intuition, the "resources deep within. . . , the emotions and memories . . . embedded in the body." This metaphor of the body as "a prime repository of emotions" recalls Williams's fourth reason for dancing, but also her second reason, responding to "biological, organic, or instinctive needs." For Frank, as for Martha Graham, the body seems to hold "blood memory." Frank suggests such a concept of cultural and spiritual continuity in this way: "A consciousness concerning ballet's metaphors is essential [to teaching], for whatever can happen to the body can happen to the soul and psyche." Again, we seem to discover the continued significance of Williams's theory that people dance "because a spirit has possessed them." As in some previous readings, we recognize the metaphor of the body as the tabernacle of the soul.

I Am a Dancer

MARTHA GRAHAM

Born in 1894, Martha Graham was one of the most active and influential dancer/choreographers of the twentieth century, and her contributions to technique revolutionized modern dance. She became a professional dancer in 1919 with Ruth St. Denis's company and formed her own experimental dance troupe in 1926. Struggling through poverty and adversity in the early years, she was a prolific choreographer in the 1920s and 1930s, when she produced over a hundred works. She was so revolutionary in her rejection of the formal ballet tradition and so creative in her patterns of movement that she pioneered an entirely new way of communicating with the body. Graham attempted to express pure emotion, in the tradition of Native American dance, believing that "out of emotion comes form." Her pioneering technique emphasized contraction and release as the means to initiate movement, and she developed the use of falls and floorwork, pelvic tension, the flexed foot, angular positions, and percussive motions—gestures that became the new vocabulary of modern dance. At the same time, her dance was intellectually inspired by language, and she inflected her compositions with imagery and metaphor, the concept of inner space, and an exploration of the primitive. After she began including men in her company in 1936, her works explored the complexities of human relationships, Jungian psychology, and the myths of the ancient Greek and Hebrew cultures. In these productions, she invented a new genre of psychological dance-drama. Her students have included some of the luminaries of dance—Rudolf Nureyev, Mikhail Baryshnikov, Merce Cunningham, and Paul Taylor. She continued to perform until her mid-seventies, even though by then she suffered severely from arthritis. Finally, her life is a testament to the courage of the unique artist to follow her instincts and to realize her epic visions of human history in the medium of dance.

The following selection is an excerpt from the first chapter of her autobiography, Blood Memories, *published the year of her death in 1991. Before you read, write a definition of a "dancer" in several sentences. As you read, compare what you wrote to Graham's development of what she thinks makes up the dancer's experience. To what extent do your ideas converge?*

✦

I am a dancer.

I believe that we learn by practice. Whether it means to learn to dance by practicing dancing or to learn to live by practicing living, the principles are the same. In each it is the performance of a dedicated precise set of acts, physical or intellectual, from which comes shape of achievement, a sense of one's being, a satisfaction of spirit. One becomes in some area an athlete of God.

To practice means to perform, in the face of all obstacles, some act of vision, of faith, of desire. Practice is a means of inviting the perfection desired.

I think the reason dance has held such an ageless magic for the world is that it has been the symbol of the performance of living. Even as I write, time has begun to make today yesterday—the past. The most brilliant scientific discoveries will in time change and perhaps grow obsolete, as new scientific manifestations emerge. But art is eternal, for it reveals the inner landscape, which is the soul of man.

Many times I hear the phrase "the dance of life." It is an expression that touches me deeply, for the instrument through which the dance speaks is also the instrument through which life is lived—the human body. It is the instrument by which all the primaries of life are made manifest. It holds in its memory all matters of life and death and love. Dancing appears glamorous, easy, delightful. But the path to the paradise of the achievement is not easier than any other. There is fatigue so great that the body cries, even in its sleep. There are times of complete frustration, there are daily small deaths. Then I need all the comfort that practice has stored in my memory, a tenacity of faith.

It takes about ten years to make a mature dancer. The training is twofold. First comes the study and practice of the craft which is the school where you are working in order to strengthen the muscular structure of the body. The body is shaped, disciplined, honored, and in time, trusted. The movement becomes clean, precise, eloquent, truthful. Movement never lies. It is a barometer telling the state of the soul's weather to all who can read it. This might be called the law of the dancer's life—the law which governs its outer aspects.

Then comes the cultivation of the being from which whatever you have to say comes. It doesn't just come out of nowhere, it comes out of a great curiosity. The main thing, of course, always is the fact that there is only one of you in the world, just one, and if that is not fulfilled then something has been lost. Ambition is not enough; necessity is everything. It is through this that the legends of the soul's journey are retold with all their tragedy and their bitterness and sweetness of living. It is at this point that the sweep of life catches up with the mere personality of the performer, and while the individual becomes greater, the personal becomes less personal. And there is grace. I mean the grace resulting from faith . . . faith in life, in love, in people, in the act of dancing. All this is necessary to any performance in life which is magnetic, powerful, rich in meaning.

In a dancer, there is a reverence for such forgotten things as the miracle of the small beautiful bones and their delicate strength. In a thinker, there is a reverence for the beauty of the alert and directed and lucid mind. In all of us who perform there is an awareness of the smile which is part of the equipment, or gift, of the acrobat. We have all walked the high wire of circumstance at times. We recognize the gravity pull of the earth as he does. The smile is there because he is practicing living at that instant of danger. He does not choose to fall.

At times I fear walking that tightrope. I fear the venture into the unknown. But that is part of the act of creating and the act of performing. That is what a dancer does.

10   People have asked me why I chose to be a dancer. I did not choose. I was chosen to be a dancer, and with that, you live all your life. When any young student asks me, "Do you think I should be a dancer?" I always say, "If you have to ask, then the answer is no." Only if there is one way to make life vivid for yourself and for others should you embark upon such a career. . . . You will know the wonders of the human body because there is nothing more wonderful. The next time you look into the mirror, just look at the way the ears rest next to the head; look at the way the hairline grows; think of all the little bones in your wrist. It is a miracle. And the dance is a celebration of that miracle.

I feel that the essence of dance is the expression of man—the landscape of his soul. I hope that every dance I do reveals something of myself or some wonderful thing a human being can be. It is the unknown—whether it is the myths or the legends or the rituals that give us our memories. It is the eternal pulse of life, the utter desire. I know that when we have rehearsals, and we have them every day, there are some dancers, particularly men, who cannot be still. One of the men in my company is not built to be still. He has to be moving. I think at times he does not know what he is doing, but that is another matter. He's got the essence of a man's inner life that prods him to dance. He has that desire. Every dance is a kind of fever chart, a graph of the heart. Desire is a lovely thing, and that is where the dance comes from, from desire.

Each day of rehearsal for a new ballet I arrive at a little before two in the afternoon, and sit alone in my studio to have a moment of stillness before the dancers enter. I tease myself and say I am cultivating my Buddha nature; but it is really just such a comforting place for me to be—secure, clear, and with a purpose. It is that order of these elements together that led one writer to call dance "glorified human behavior." I sit with my back to our large mirrors so that I am completely within myself.

• • •

Outside my studio door, in my garden, is a tree that has always been a symbol of facing life, and in many ways it is a dancer. It began as a sapling when I first moved here and although a wire gate was in its way, it persisted and grew to the light, and now thirty years later it is a tree with a very thick trunk, with the wire embedded within. Like a dancer it went to the light and carried the scars of its journey inside. You traverse, you work, you make it right. You embody within yourself that curiosity, use that avidity for life no matter whether it is for good or for evil. The body is a sacred garment. It's your first and your last garment; it is what you enter life in and what you depart life with, and it should be treated with honor, and with joy and with fear as well. But always, though, with blessing.

• • •

And then there is inspiration. Where does it come from? Mostly from the excitement of living. I get it from the diversity of a tree or the ripple of the sea, a bit of poetry, the sighting of a dolphin breaking the still water and moving toward me . . . anything that quickens you to the instant. And whether one would call that inspiration or necessity, I really do not know. At times I receive that inspiration from people; I enjoy people very much and for the most part feel it is returned. I simply happen to love people. I do not love them all individually, but I love the idea of life pulsing through people—blood and movement.

For all of us, but particularly for a dancer with his intensification of life and his body, there is a blood memory that can speak to us. Each of us from our mother and father has received their blood through their parents and their parents' parents and backward into time. We carry thousands of years of that blood and its memory. How else to explain those instinctive gestures and thoughts that come to us, with little preparation or expectation. They come perhaps from some deep memory of a time when the world was chaotic, when, as the Bible says, the world was nothing. And then, as if some door opened slightly, there was light. It revealed certain wonderful things. It revealed terrifying things. But it was light.

William Goyen, in *The House of Breath*, wrote that "we are the carriers of lives and legends—who knows the unseen frescoes on the private walls of the skull." Very often making a dance springs from a desire to find those hidden frescoes.

In Burma, on our second Asian tour in the 1970s, I had been asked to present flowers at the tomb of the Burmese Unknown Soldier. This I did in the presence of our ambassador and the Burmese minister of culture. When I had finished, there was a tremendous stir, great sounds of conversation. The Burmese wanted to know who had coached me to present the flowers in precisely the correct manner, steps, and gestures that would be appropriate to a Burmese woman of my age and station. No one had. Just as no one had taught Ruth St. Denis to touch back generations in East Indian dance to find the true path and spirit for her solos which even the Indians at that time had lost.

But for this you must keep your vessel clean—your mind, your body; it is what the Zen masters tell their students who get too full of themselves, too wrapped up in theory and too many thoughts. They ask them, "That is all very good; but have you cleaned your dish?" For the Buddhist student lived by begging food; and how could he receive it if his bowl was not clean? He is being asked if he is ready for his next meal. A clear instruction to get back to basics. It is so easy to become cluttered.

I think that is what my father must have meant when he wrote to me when I was away from home. "Martha," he said, "you must keep an open soul."

20   It is that openness and awareness and innocence of sorts that I try to cultivate in my dancers. Although, as the Latin verb to educate, *educere*, indicates, it is not a question of putting something in but drawing it out, if it is there to begin with.

• • •

Dancers today can do anything; the technique is phenomenal. The passion and the meaning to their movement can be another thing.

At times I will tease my dancers and tell them that perhaps they are not too bright today, that all of their jumping has addled their brains. And yet they move with grace and a kind of inevitability, some more powerfully than others. This moment of rehearsal is the instant that I care about. This is the very now of my life.

The only thing we have is the now. You begin from the now, what you know, and move into the old, ancient ones that you did not know but which you find as you go along. I think you only find the past from yourself, from what you're experiencing now, what enters your life at the present moment. We don't know about the past, except as we discover it. And we discover it from the now. Looking at the past is like lolling in a rocking chair. It is so relaxing and you can rock back and forth on the porch, and never go forward. It is not for me. People sometimes ask me about retirement and I say, "Retire? Retire into what?" I don't believe in retirement because that is the time you die.

The life of a dancer is by no means simple. It is comparatively short. I am not an example of that, but I could not do certain things beyond a certain point. Old age is a pain in the neck. I didn't want to grow old because I didn't realize that I was growing old. I feel that it is a burden and a fearful thing and one I have to endure. It is not a thing to be treasured or to be loved. It is by any means a difficulty to bear.

When I stopped dancing, it was not a conscious decision. I realized that I did not have the strength or the ability to build into the interior and the soul of the artist. Before I began to dance I trained myself to do four hundred jumps in five minutes by the clock. Today, there are so many things I can't do. I get absolutely furious that I cannot do them. I didn't want to stop dancing and still do not want to. I have always wanted a simple, direct, open, clean, and wonderful life. That has been my time.

There are always ancestral footsteps behind me, pushing me, when I am creating a new dance, and gestures are flowing through me. Whether good or bad, they are ancestral. You get to the point where your body is something else and it takes on a world of cultures from the past, an idea that is very hard to express in words. I never verbalize about the dance as I create it. It is a purely physical risk that you desire to take, and that you have to take. The ballet I am doing now is a risk. That is all I can say because it isn't fulfilled yet. I let no one watch, except for the dancers I am working with. When they leave I am alone with the ancestral footsteps.

• • •

What I miss some days in a dance class is not perfection, because some of them will never achieve that moment of technical expertise. I don't demand, at the beginning, any vestige of perfection. What I long for is the eagerness to meet life, the curiosity, the wonder that you feel when you can really move—to work toward a perfect first or a perfect fifth position. There becomes an excitement, an avidity, a forgetfulness of everyone about you. You are so completely absorbed in this instrument that is vibrant to life. The great French poet St. John Perse said to me, "You have so little time to be born to the instant." This I miss in class very much. I miss the animal strength, the beauty of the heel as it is used to carry one forward into life. This, I think more than anything, is the secret of my loneliness.

I do not feel myself unique by any means, but I do know that I agree with Edgard Varèse—and I'm going to use a word that I never use regarding myself or anybody else. And that word is genius. Varèse, a wonderful French composer, who wrote some music for me, opened up new areas of musical strength in the way he used percussion that I had never experienced before. He said, "Martha, all of us are born with genius, but most people only keep it for a few seconds."

By genius he meant that curiosity that leads to the search for the secret of life. That is what tires me when I teach and I come away alone. Sometimes you will see a person on the stage who has this oneness with himself—it is so glorious it has the power to stop you. It is a common gift to all of us but most people only keep it a few moments.

30   I can never forget the evening I was staying late at the school, and the phone rang. I was the only one there and I picked it up to hear a mother ask about classes for her child. "She is a genius. Intuitive. Unique. It must be nurtured now." "Really," I answered. "And how old is she?" Her mother replied, "Two years old." I told her that we only accepted children at nine (today much earlier, thanks to vitamins and computers and home training). "Nine!" she cried. "But by nine she will have lost all of her genius." I said, "Madame, if she must lose it, it is best she lose it young."

I never thought of myself as being what they call a genius. I don't know what genius is. I think a far better expression is a retriever, a lovely strong golden retriever that brings things back from the past, or retrieves things from our common blood memory. I think that by every act you do—whether in religion, politics, or sex—you reveal yourself. This, to me, is one of the wonderful things in life. It is what I've always wanted to do—to show the laughing, the fun, the appetite, all of it through dance.

In order to work, in order to be excited, in order to simply be, you have to be reborn to the instant. You have to permit yourself to feel, you have to permit yourself to be vulnerable. You may not like what you see, that is not important. You don't always have to judge. But you must be attacked by it, excited by it, and your body must be alive. And you must know how to animate that body; for each it is individual.

• • •

When a dancer is at the peak of his power he has two lovely, fragile, and perishable things. One is the spontaneity that is arrived at over years of training. The other is simplicity, but not the usual kind. It is the state of complete simplicity costing no less than absolutely everything, of which T. S. Eliot speaks.

How many leaps did Nijinsky take before he made the one that startled the world? He took thousands and thousands and it is that legend that gives us the courage, the energy, and arrogance to go back into the studio knowing that while there is so little time to be born to the instant, you will work again among the many that you may once more be born as one. That is a dancer's world.

Discussion Questions

1. Explain what you think Graham means by "the performance of living" (paragraph 4).
2. Graham mentions another author who calls dance "glorified human behavior" (paragraph 12). Explain how another activity might also be described in this way.
3. Graham's writing seems sometimes abstract, lacking concrete examples, but she often use metaphors, such as the tree that is "a symbol of facing life" (paragraph 13). What image or metaphor did you find most striking in this selection? Explain its appeal and its meaning for you.
4. Graham calls the human body "the instrument through which life is lived" (paragraph 5). Explain in what way you think the body is an "instrument," like a tool, an implement, or a device. Does this term seem a rather inanimate metaphor for the body? What would it mean if we were to say, instead, that *the human mind* is "the instrument through which life is lived"? Which use of the term "instrument" makes more sense to you?

5. Review the "Healing through Emptiness" section of Kornfield's article on "Necessary Healing" in Chapter 1. Compare it to Graham's discussion of "blood memory" and "ancestral footsteps" (paragraphs 15–17, 26, 31).

The Art of Dancing
HAVELOCK ELLIS

Although trained as a physician, Havelock Ellis did not practice medicine, preferring a writing career as a literary critic, novelist, poet, autobiographer, translator, and essayist on such subjects as philosophy, criminality, eugenics, psychology of sex, color sense, and drug effects. In Man and Woman: A Study of Human Secondary Sex Characteristics *(1894), he attempted to distinguish biologically based differences from socially induced ones, a distinction that remains central to contemporary gender studies. His most extensive research was the seven-volume* Studies in the Psychology of Sex *(1897–1928), a frank assessment of sexual behavior based on hundreds of case studies. This work, the most influential portrait of human sexuality until the Kinsey reports of the 1950s, contributed to more tolerant British and American attitudes toward such previously taboo topics as homosexuality, masturbation, and female sexual responsiveness. Ellis was also famous for writing on the social implications of science, in such books as* A Study of British Genius *(1904),* The World of Dreams *(1911), and* The Dance of Life *(1923), the source of the following selection.*

———————— ✦ ————————

II

'What do you dance?' When a man belonging to one branch of the great Bantu division of mankind met a member of another, said Livingstone, that was the question he asked. What a man danced, that was his tribe, his social customs, his religion; for, as an anthropologist has put it, 'a savage does not preach his religion, he dances it.'

There are peoples in the world who have no secular dances, only religious dances; and some investigators believe with Gerland that every dance was of religious origin. That view may seem too extreme, even if we admit that some even of our modern dances, like the waltz, may have been originally religious. Even still (as Skene has shown among the Arabs and Swahili of Africa) so various are dances and their functions among some peoples that they cover the larger part of life. Yet we have to remember that for primitive man there is no such thing as religion apart from life, for religion covers everything. Dancing is a magical operation for the attainment of real and important ends of every kind. It was clearly of immense benefit to the individual and to society, by imparting strength and adding organised harmony. It seemed reasonable to suppose that it attained other beneficial ends, that were incalculable, for calling down blessings or warding off misfortunes. We may conclude, with Wundt, that the dance was, in the beginning, the expression of the whole man, for the whole man was religious.

Thus, among primitive peoples, religion being so large a part of life, the dance inevitably becomes of supreme religious importance. To dance was at once both to worship and to pray. Just as we still find in our Prayer Books that there are divine services for all the great fundamental acts of life—for birth, for marriage, for death—as well as for the cosmic procession of the world as marked by ecclesiastical festivals, and for the great catastrophes of nature, such as droughts, so also it has ever been among primitive peoples. For all the solemn occasions of life, for bridals and for funerals, for seedtime and for harvest, for war and for peace, for all these things there were fitting dances. To-day we find religious people who in church pray for rain or for the restoration of their friends to health. Their forefathers also desired these things, but, instead of praying for them, they danced for them the fitting dance which tradition had handed down, and which the chief or the medicine-man solemnly conducted. The gods themselves danced, as the stars dance in the sky—so at least the Mexicans, and we may be sure many other peoples, have held; and to dance is therefore to imitate the gods, to work with them, perhaps to persuade them to work in the direction of our own desires. 'Work for us!' is the song-refrain, expressed or implied, of every religious dance. In the worship of solar deities in various countries, it was customary to dance round the altar, as the stars dance round the sun. Even in Europe the popular belief that the sun dances on Easter Sunday has perhaps scarcely yet died out. To dance is to take part in the cosmic control of the world. Every sacred Dionysian dance is an imitation of the divine dance.

• • •

These religious dances, it may be observed, are sometimes ecstatic, sometimes pantomimic. It is natural that this should be so. By each road it is possible to penetrate towards the divine mystery of the world. The auto-intoxication of rapturous movement brings the devotees, for a while at least, into that self-forgetful union with the not-self which the mystic ever seeks. The ecstatic Hindu dance in honour of the pre-Aryan hill god, afterwards Siva, became in time a great symbol, 'the clearest image of the *activity* of God,' it has been called, 'which any art or religion can boast of.' Pantomimic dances, on the other hand, with their effort to heighten natural expression and to imitate natural process, bring the dancers into the divine sphere of creation and enable them to assist vicariously in the energy of the gods. The dance thus becomes the presentation of a divine drama, the vital reenactment of a sacred history, in which the worshipper is enabled to play a real part. In this way ritual arises. . . .

III

5   Dancing is not only intimately associated with religion, it has an equally intimate association with love. Here, indeed, the relationship is even more primitive, for it is far older than man. Dancing, said Lucian, is as old as love. Among insects and among birds it may be said that dancing is often an essential part of love. In courtship the male dances, sometimes in rivalry with other males, in order to charm the female; then, after a short or long interval, the female is aroused to share his ardour and join in the dance; the final climax of the dance is the union of the lovers. . . . It is the more primitive love-dance of insects and birds that seems to reappear among human savages in various parts of the world, notably in Africa, and in a conventionalised and symbolised form it is still danced in civilisation to-day. Indeed, it is in this aspect that dancing has so often aroused reprobation, from the days of early Christianity until the present, among those for whom the dance has merely been, in the words of a seventeenth-century writer, a series of 'immodest and dissolute movements by which the cupidity of the flesh is aroused.'

But in nature and among primitive peoples it has its value precisely on this account. It is a process of courtship.

• • •

In innumerable parts of the world the season of love is a time which the nubile of each sex devote to dancing in each other's presence, sometimes one sex, sometimes the other, sometimes both, in the frantic effort to display all the force and energy, the skill and endurance, the beauty and grace, which at this moment are yearning within them to be poured into the stream of the race's life. . . . When both sexes take part in such an exercise, developed into an idealised yet passionate pantomime of love, we have the complete erotic dance. . . .

IV

From the vital function of dancing in love, and its sacred function in religion, to dancing as an art, a profession, an amusement, may seem, at the first glance, a sudden leap. In reality the transition is gradual, and it began to be made at a very early period in diverse parts of the globe. All the matters that enter into courtship tend to fall under the sway of art; their esthetic pleasure is a secondary reflection of their primary vital joy. Dancing could not fail to be first in manifesting this tendency. But even religious dancing swiftly exhibited the same transformation; dancing, like priesthood, became a profession, and dancers, like priests, formed a caste. This, for instance, took place in old Hawaii. The hula dance was a religious dance; it required a special education and an arduous training; moreover, it involved the observance of important taboos and the exercise of sacred rites; by the very fact of its high specialisation it came to be carried out by paid performers, a professional caste. In India, again, the Devadasis, or sacred dancing girls, are at once both religious and professional dancers. They are married to gods, they are taught dancing by the Brahmins, they figure in religious ceremonies, and their dances represent the life of the god they are married to as well as the emotions of love they experience for him. Yet, at the same time, they also give professional performances in the houses of rich private persons who pay for them. It thus comes about that to the foreigner the Devadasis scarcely seem very unlike the Ramedjenis, the dancers of the street, who are of very different origin, and mimic in their performances the play of merely human passions. The Portuguese conquerors of India called both kinds of dancers indiscriminately Balheideras (or dancers) which we have corrupted in Bayaderes.

In our modern world professional dancing as an art has become altogether divorced from religion, and even, in any biological sense, from love; it is scarcely even possible, so far as Western civilisation is concerned, to trace back the tradition to either source. If we survey the development of dancing as an art in Europe, it seems to me that we have to recognise two streams of tradition which have sometimes merged, but yet remain in their ideals and their tendencies essentially distinct. I would call these traditions the Classical, which is much the more ancient and fundamental, and may be said to be of Egyptian origin, and the Romantic, which is of Italian origin, chiefly known to us as the ballet. The first is, in its pure form, solo dancing—though it may be danced in couples and many together—and is based on the rhythmic beauty and expressiveness of the simple human personality when its energy is concentrated in measured yet passionate movement. The second is concerted dancing, mimetic and picturesque, wherein the individual is subordinated to the wider and variegated rhythm of the group. It may be easy to devise another classification, but this is simple and instructive enough for our purpose.

• • •

10   The modern ballet, it is generally believed, had its origin in the spectacular pageants at the marriage of Galeazzo Visconti, Duke of Milan, in 1489. The fashion for such performances spread to the other Italian courts, including Florence, and Catherine de' Medici, when she became Queen of France, brought the Italian ballet to Paris. Here it speedily became fashionable. Kings and queens were its admirers and even took part in it; great statesmen were its patrons. Before long, and especially in the great age of Louis XIV, it became an established institution, still an adjunct of opera but with a vital life and growth of its own, maintained by distinguished musicians, artists, and dancers.

• • •

The Russian ballet was an offshoot from the French ballet and illustrates once more the vivifying effect of transplantation on the art of Romantic dancing. The Empress Anna introduced it in 1735 and appointed a French ballet-master and a Neapolitan composer to carry it on; it reached a high degree of technical perfection during the following hundred years, on the traditional lines, and the principal dancers were all imported from Italy. It was not until recent years that this firm discipline and these ancient traditions were vitalised into an art form of exquisite, and vivid beauty by the influence of the soil in which they had slowly taken root. . . . What we see here, in the Russian ballet as we know to-day, is a splendid and arduous technical tradition, brought at last—by the combined skill of designers, composers, and dancers—into real fusion with an environment from which during more than a century it had been held apart; Russian genius for music, Russian feeling for rhythm, Russian skill in the use of bright colour, and, not least, the Russian orgiastic temperament, the Russian spirit of tender poetic melancholy, and the general Slav passion for folk-dancing, shown in other branches of the race also, Polish, Bohemian, Bulgarian, and Servian. At almost the same time what I have termed Classic dancing was independently revived in America by Isadora Duncan, bringing back what seemed to be the free naturalism of the Greek dance, and Ruth St. Denis, seeking to discover and revitalise the secrets of the old Indian and Egyptian traditions. Whenever now we find any restored art of theatrical dancing, as in the Swedish ballet, it has been inspired more or less, by an eclectic blending of these two revived forms, the Romantic from Russia, the Classic from America. The result has been that our age sees one of the most splendid movements in the whole history of the ballet.

V

Dancing as an art, we may be sure, cannot die out, but will always be undergoing a rebirth. Not merely as an art, but also as a social custom, it perpetually emerges afresh from the soul of the people. Less than a century ago the polka thus arose, extemporised by the Bohemian servant girl Anna Slezakova out of her own head for the joy of her own heart, and only rendered a permanent form, apt for world-wide popularity, by the accident that it was observed and noted down by an artist. Dancing has for ever been in existence as a spontaneous custom, a social discipline. Thus it is, finally, that dancing meets us, not only as love, as religion, as art, but also as morals.

• • •

In the narrow sense, in individual education, the great importance of dancing came to be realised, even at an early stage of human development, and still more in the ancient civilisations. 'A good education,' Plato declared in the 'Laws,' the final work of his old age, 'consists in knowing how to sing and dance well.' And in our own day one of the keenest and most enlightened of educationists has lamented the decay of dancing; the revival of dancing, Stanley Hall declares, is imperatively needed to give poise to the nerves, schooling to the emotions, strength to the will, and to harmonise the feelings and the intellect with the body which supports them.

It can scarcely be said that these functions of dancing are yet generally realised and embodied afresh in education. For, if it is true that dancing engendered morality, it is also true that in the end, by the irony of fate, morality, grown insolent, sought to crush its own parent, and for a time succeeded only too well. Four centuries ago dancing was attacked by that spirit, in England called Puritanism, which was then spread over the greater part of Europe, just as active in Bohemia as in England, and which has, indeed, been described as a general onset of developing Urbanism against the old Ruralism. It made no distinction between good and bad, nor paused to consider what would come when dancing went. So it was that, as Remy de Gourmont remarks, the drinking-shop conquered the dance, and alcohol replaced the violin.

15   But when we look at the function of dancing in life from a higher and wider standpoint, this episode in its history ceases to occupy so large a place. The conquest over dancing has never proved in the end a matter for rejoicing, even to morality, while an art which has been so intimately mixed with all the finest and deepest springs of life has always asserted itself afresh. For dancing is the loftiest, the most moving, the most beautiful of the arts, because it is no mere translation or abstraction from life; it is life itself. It is the only art, as Rahel Varnhagen said, of which we ourselves are the stuff. Even if we are not ourselves dancers, but merely the spectators of the dance, we are still—according to that Lippsian doctrine of *Einfuhlung* or 'empathy' by Groos termed 'the play of inner imitation'—which here, at all events, we may accept as true—feeling ourselves in the dancer who is manifesting and expressing the latent impulses of our own being.

It thus comes about that, beyond its manifold practical significance, dancing has always been felt to possess also a symbolic significance. Marcus Aurelius was accustomed to regard the art of life as like the dancer's art, though that Imperial Stoic could not resist adding that in some respects it was more like the wrestler's art. 'I doubt not yet to make a figure in the great Dance of Life that shall amuse the spectators in the sky,' said, long after, Blake, in the same strenuous spirit. In our own time, Nietzsche, from first to last, showed himself possessed by the conception of the art of life as a dance, in which the dancer achieves the rhythmic freedom and harmony of his soul beneath the shadow of a hundred Damoclean swords. He said the same thing of his style, for to him the style and the man were one: 'My style,' he wrote to his intimate friend Rohde, 'is a dance.' 'Every day I count wasted,' he said again, 'in which there has been no dancing.' The dance lies at the beginning of art, and we find it also at the end. The first creators of civilisation were making the dance, and the philosopher of a later age, hovering over the dark abyss of insanity, with bleeding feet and muscles strained to the breaking point, still seems to himself to be weaving the maze of the dance.

Discussion Questions

1. Ellis points out that among primitive peoples, "the whole man was religious" (paragraph 2). Explain his meaning and contrast this religious orientation with that of *modern* peoples.
2. Ellis claims that dance, with its erotic origins, has been considered by many Christians as a "series of 'immodest and dissolute movements by which the cupidity [lust] of the flesh is aroused'" (paragraph 5). To what extent do you agree with this description? If you do *not* agree, explain why you think dance has lost its erotic nature in the modern era.
3. In Part IV of his essay, Ellis describes dancing as "art." Based on his discussion, write a definition of "art." Then, describe some other activity (such as skateboarding or snowboarding, dressing up, haircutting, cooking, auto restoration, or playing poker) and explain why you think it should be considered an "art" according to your own definition.
4. To what extent do you believe that, through dancing, you are able "to harmonize the feelings and the intellect with the body" (paragraph 13)? Explain.
5. Compare Ellis's viewpoints on dance with those of Graham. Explain the common ground that they share about the topic.

Disco

Peter Braunstein

A journalist and cultural historian based in New York City, Peter Braunstein earned an M.A. from New York University in 1992 with a thesis on the counterculture of San Francisco's Haight-Ashbury district. He publishes frequently in The Village Voice, Forbes, *the* Chronicle of Higher Education, Women's Wear Daily, *and* W *on such topics as fashion, film, celebrity culture, music, the 1960s, and technology. With Michael Doyle, Braunstein has edited the collection* Imagine Nation: The American Counterculture of the 1960s and 70s *(2001). In their opening essay, the editors criticize both the romantic and the conservative views of the period, emphasizing the need for more rigorous historical analysis. Braunstein's recent works include* Discotheque *(2004) and* Sin City: New York in the Seventies, A Cultural History *(2005). The following selection was first published in* American Heritage *in 1999.*

✦

It began in the Paris underground of World War II and evolved over thirty years into a phenomenon that so overturned cultural norms that it could not survive. Bona fide revolutions—whether political, cultural, or spiritual—occur infrequently in history, and it's possible to pass an entire lifetime without experiencing one. What, then, do transcendence seekers or would-be revolutionaries do in the meantime? One option is nightlife, one of society's few sanctioned antidotes to the monotony of the day-to-day, or what the French call *le quotidien.* The elements that prevail during times of revolution—the exhilaration of collective experience, the inversion of social roles, the supremacy of the present, the triumph of imaginative life—can all be found in the dusk-to-dawn alternative world of the nightclub. Nightlife is, in a sense, revolution during the off-season. Passions and vices that would trouble the day are exiled to the nocturnal realm of clubs, where they are transformed into virtues, encouraged, and at the same time contained and prevented from causing social upheaval.

From the juke joint to the dance hall, American clubs in the postwar era have been the center of a cultural struggle pitting the forces of hedonism, revelry, and sexual liberation against those of sociosexual stability and control. The furor generated in the 1950s by Elvis's gyrating pelvis and that era's television censorship of certain "sexually provocative" dances like the Alligator illustrated white, adult, middle-class fears of what could be called the spillover effect of dance music, the possibility that the sexualized frenzy of the dance floor might seep out onto the streets and into the suburbs of America. At an extreme the broad brushstrokes of Cold War logic painted a frightening picture of provocative dances exposing white youths to black music and culture, weakening their moral fiber, promoting juvenile delinquency, and wearing down their resistance to the perils of both miscegenation and communism. It was this chain of reasoning that led a member of the Senate Subcommittee on Juvenile Delinquency to conclude in 1958 that "the gangster of tomorrow is the Elvis Presley type of today."

No wonder that the discotheque, that salient feature of American nightlife from the 1960s to the 1980s, became an enactment zone for the cultural revolutions of the era. In the sixties discotheques served as the laboratories for new multimedia entertainment meant to complement the high provided by LSD, marijuana, and other drugs; in the seventies disco spawned a lifestyle that confronted white, heterosexual America with a composite bogeyman—a lifestyle devoted to rampant promiscuity and avid, recreational drug use, peopled by newly liberated gay men dancing to up-tempo black rhythm and blues. Disco, in short, brazenly confirmed all the old fears that under the right conditions the passions aroused in clubs might overflow their bounds and foster a broader ferment. For a short while the essential cultural tension between restraint and desire seemed to be overthrown.

From its very origins the history of disco is a story of strange bedfellows, of odd couplings and midnight encounters that take place only in clubs. Associations banished from broad daylight—between debutantes and bikers, between working-class delivery boys and high-profile fashion designers, between mobsters and newly liberated gay men—freely blossomed in the fantasy-scape of the discotheque. But for all its ephemeral one-night stands, disco itself is the product of two more lasting across-the-track love affairs: the first between Europe and America and the second between the social elite and the cultural underworld.

• • •

In the aftermath of the Stonewall Riots of 1969, gay men and   5
women won the right to dance and otherwise intermingle in their own bars and clubs without having to worry about police raids and harassment or maintaining a heterosexual facade. Since Stonewall was largely about gays' right to their own nightlife, it's not surprising that the discotheque became the main site of gay liberation. Returning to its roots established some twenty-five years earlier in wartime France, disco entered a new underground phase characterized by cloaked, celebratory club life open only to initiates. Typical of the era was Aux Puces, in New York City, one of the first gay discos, where admittance was strictly speakeasy style: Only persons known to the maitre d' were let in. The most famous—and first unabashedly gay—disco of the early 1970s was the Sanctuary, located in a former German Baptist

church on West Forty-third Street in New York. It had been started as a gathering spot for straight, moneyed celebrity types but then, under new management, inaugurated the seventies trend of mixing gays and straights together on one dance floor. Soon gay men predominated, so much so that when Jane Fonda entered the disco to film the nightclub scenes for *Klute*, she felt compelled to demand that women—at a bare minimum, gay women—be allowed into the club too.

The fact that the most legendary gay disco of the early seventies was located in a former church, its deejay booth at the altar, serves as a perfect metaphor for the quasi-religious fervor of gay disco culture. In his 1978 paean to it, *Dancer from the Dance*, Andrew Holleran remembers "the thrill of newness, and the thrill of exclusivity" in those early days, as well as the hard-core disco habitués who "lived only in the ceaseless flow of this tiny society's movements. . . . They passed one another without a word . . . hell-bent on their next look from a handsome stranger. Their next rush from a popper. The next song that turned their bones to jelly and left them all on the dance floor with heads back, eyes nearly closed, in the ecstasy of saints receiving the stigmata." The bacchanalian spirit of the Sanctuary revolved around a triumvirate of pleasures—music, sex, and drugs—that made sensual climax, in one form or another, the organizing principle of the disco era. The drugs of the psychedelic sixties, particularly LSD, were now supplanted by the "body-high" drugs of the 1970s. Predominant in the gay disco scene were poppers, amyl nitrite vials, used originally by angina sufferers, which when broken open and inhaled caused a precipitous drop in blood pressure and near-loss of consciousness. Poppers coexisted with that other quintessential 1970s club drug Quaalude, which suspended motor coordination and turned one's arms and legs to Jell-O. These two drugs were, in turn, counterbalanced by the principal upper of the era, cocaine. One journalist sardonically recalled the "Circle of Life" in disco drug culture: "The poppers gave you a 30-second rush of oblivion on the dance floor. Since you were already 'luded to the gills, this meant you stumbled around more, generally crashing into somebody who was just putting a coke spoon to his nose, making him spill the coke, causing a mass plunge to the floor by everyone in the vicinity. While you were down there, you'd usually find some old poppers, and the whole cycle would start over again."

Massive quantities of drugs ingested in discotheques by newly liberated gay men produced the next cultural phenomenon of the disco era: rampant promiscuity and public sex. While the dance floor was the central arena of seduction, actual sex usually took place in the nether regions of the disco: bathroom stalls, exit stairwells, and so on. In other cases the disco became a kind of "main course" in a hedonist's menu for a night out. Discos like 12 West were located in the marginal meat-packing district, on the extreme West Side of Manhattan, and the nearby decaying Hudson River piers became a famous after-hours "trysting spot." In the 1970s discos became the focal points of just such an eroticization of urban space, as pleasure seekers spilled out of them to colonize adjoining streets, alleys, and piers.

The last innovation in 1970s disco culture involved the music itself. While there had been discotheques in the sixties, there had been no such thing as disco music. Clubs had simply played live or recorded rock music, which wasn't ideal for dancing. Given that most rock singles of the era lasted a mere three minutes, by the time dancers "found their groove" the song was over. By the early seventies deejays and dancers were taking another approach in their search for continuous, danceable rhythms. They returned to the black R&B roots of pop music. Philadelphia had historically been a nexus for dance crazes, particularly the Twist. A decade later two producer-songwriters, Kenny Gamble and Leon Huff, reclaimed the dance-music mantle with their hit factory Philadelphia International Records, putting out what was called the "Philly Sound." Their stable of groups included the O'Jays ("Love Train"), Harold Melvin & the Blue Notes ("If You Don't Know Me by Now"), and the Three Degrees ("When Will I See You Again?"). As the music journalist Carol Cooper observed, the Philly Sound "virtually cornered the market on emotionally subtle, rhythmically kinetic pop music that was equally accessible to blacks and whites of all ages." The revival of dance music began in mid-1973, when the African singer Manu Dibango's "Soul Makossa"—generally considered the first disco song of the 1970s—hit the pop charts. A crescendo of No. 1 dance singles followed, including Barry White's "Love's Theme" and George McRae's "Rock Your Baby." Disco became a verifiable, nationally recognized phenomenon in 1975, when Van McCoy and "The Hustle" went to the top of the pop charts, set off a nationwide craze for "touch dancing," and eventually sold ten million copies. With "The Hustle," disco's underground incubation period had come to an end. The disco was now a fully actualized concept, the term comprehending both the physical venue and the new music created for it.

For the first half of the 1970s, disco was an extended conversation between black musicians and gay dancers. These were halcyon days for those in on the disco craze while it was still a glorious secret from journalists and most of the white, heterosexual world, before it became, as Andrew Holleran put it, "another possession of the middle class." But the mainstreaming of disco after 1975 was probably inevitable in a recession-plagued America. As cultural commentators ceaselessly observed at the time, paying a deejay fifty dollars a night to spin records was a lot cheaper than hiring live entertainers, and a nominal cover charge was easier on the wallet than buying a ticket to a rock concert. All told, disco promised euphoria, glamour, and decadence at a reasonable price. As the Hustle craze of 1975 elevated disco to a national phenomenon and enticed straight white people to boogie, a clash of cultures occurred. A mere half-decade after Stonewall, heterosexuals were being forced to navigate in an inverted cultural landscape whose terms were set by gay men. *Dancing Madness*, published in 1976 to capitalize on the disco craze, set down some guidelines: "The first test for the hetero male who wishes to be in tune with the basics of bisexual chic is to not feel threatened when addressed as 'baby' rather than 'sir.'" A reporter from *Harper's*, dispatched to the disco front in 1977, noted the nuanced stratagems necessary for straight entry into the world: "Now middleclass young men cruise the banquettes each weekend, but the tone of the place is sufficiently gay that a woman can protect herself by adopting a fierce gaze to indicate dykishness, or by staring fixedly at herself in a mirror, for self-absorption is respected here." The author concluded that heteros "might say they were there only as watchers, only as voyeurs, [but] they were also becoming participants, regulars in a scene which could never be theirs, outlaws in what had always been an outlaw world."

10   Indeed, disco firmly situated itself within the cultural politics of the 1970s, which ran a bizarre gamut from radical-chic terrorist groups like the Symbionese Liberation Army to orthodox feminism, from gay liberation to the environmental movement. Whereas groups like the S.L.A., representing the tail end of New Left radicalism, endowed every action—eating, sleeping, bank robbery—with political significance, disco was just the opposite. Its lifestyle contained a politics, but it was one that often remained implicit and unarticulated. What was the politics of disco? It can be found, ironically, in a statement made by a motivational-research guru named Ernest Dicter in the 1950s, who told executives: "One of the basic problems of prosperity is to demonstrate

that the hedonistic approach to life is a moral and not an immoral one." Disco, as music and as way of life, was the standard-bearer for the hedonistic fringe of liberalism that held that nothing was wrong if it felt right, that personal exploration through dance, sex, or drug use was indeed a quasi-religious quest, with a morality as valid and legitimate as the counter-morality condemning it. Disco's counter-cultural politics lay particularly in its elevation of the human body as an instrument of pleasure. It strove to rupture the tie between pleasure seeking and shame.

In fact, disco's defiance of shame was designed specifically by and for gay men, who had always found themselves on the losing end of straight society's equation of sexuality, and particularly homosexuality, with shame. Instead, disco's philosophy, fused in the rapturous gay underworld and then adopted by straight men and women, is best conveyed by the lyrics of one popular disco song: "Shame on you, if you can't dance too." The only "shame" in disco lay in the inability to get in touch with one's body through dance, drugs, and sexual exploration. However powerful it was, though, this antishame politics remained only occasionally acknowledged by its practitioners as a countermorality, and this made it highly vulnerable to attack.

The opening of Studio 54, in April 1977, expanded gay disco culture to encompass a pansexuality that united gays, straights, and the sexually undecided under the banner of disco hedonism. As Steven Gaines observed in his biography *Simply Halston*, "Studio 54 was the embodiment of the most decadent social period of any city in modern history. By 1978, Dionysus had hired a press agent and New York was headlong into an era of staggering permissiveness." Founded by gay Steve Rubell and straight Ian Schrager, Studio's immediate success also solidified, in the public mind, the connection between disco and an aristocratic sensibility. The club was further proof that in the city-state of the discotheque, the preferred government was a circumscribed democracy. Rubell was famous for the arbitrary brutality of his door policies: allowing a woman in but not her date, demanding that people strip naked before entering, telling would-be guests they would never be let in under any circumstances because they were gauche, or not well shaven, or tackily dressed. This ruthless discrimination was justified as an artistic process Rubell called "painting the picture": By preventing redundancy in the reveling crowd (too many investment bankers in suits, too many drag queens, etc.) and banning outright certain categories of people like "bagel nosh Jews" (those who looked like Rubell and came from his social background) and "Quiana from the Americana" (rich South American tourists from the nearby hotel), it ensured, according to the club owner Jim Fouratt, "that if you got in, you were in a world that was completely safe for you to do whatever you wanted"—that you were, in short, among the elect.

Disco's rising fortunes were further buoyed in December 1977 by the astounding success of the film *Saturday Night Fever*. The double-album soundtrack eventually became the biggest-selling record of all time until Michael Jackson's *Thriller*, and the film irrevocably established most of the stereotypes associated with the disco era to this day: the white three-piece suit, gold chains, precision blow-dried hair, patented dance-floor moves. *Saturday Night Fever* propelled disco fever to epidemic proportions: By 1978, 40 percent of all the music on *Billboard*'s Hot 100 was disco. Meanwhile the discofication of America proceeded: There were disco lunch boxes, disco "Snoopy" bed sheets and pillows, disco belt buckles, disco records by old-timers like Frank Sinatra and Ethel Merman, an estimated two hundred all-disco radio stations, disco dance courses, disco proms, books about the proper makeup to wear to discos—and an estimated twenty thousand discotheques nationwide.

The rise of Studio 54 and the phenomenal success of *Saturday Night Fever* made disco a ubiquitous feature of the pop-culture landscape as well as a living paradox. The media focus on celebrities like Margaret Trudeau, Andy Warhol, and Halston at Studio 54 projected an image of disco as a snob medium, an elitist music-based lifestyle adopted by name-dropping poseurs. This conceptualization surfaced, however, at the very moment when disco was gaining suburban grassroots appeal, as Americans across the nation grew accustomed to hearing the disco *Star Wars* theme piped into their malls and supermarkets. Mainstream disco was, at the same time, a de-gayed version of the original. It is no coincidence that the Bee Gees, the chief apostles of the mainstreaming, had nothing to do with the original disco constituency and didn't come from a dance-music background at all. Their songs, in fact, diverged from the hedonistic, highly sexualized genre of most early disco in favor of macho posturing ("Staying Alive") and ersatz romanticism ("How Deep Is Your Love?")—in other words, traditional pop-music themes. Kevin Kaufman, a deejay at the time at a club called Disco 2000, in Reno, Nevada, later observed, "I don't know any gay bar worth its salt in '77 or

'78 where you would ever, ever have heard them play 'Staying Alive.'"

During this heyday of mainstreaming, *Interview* magazine, which shared with Studio 54 a parasitic relationship to celebrity culture, decided to profile Olivier Coquelin, the man who had brought the discotheque to America some fifteen years earlier. Since his concept had ultimately triumphed, one might have expected an exultant Coquelin, but instead his tone was apocalyptic, sensing as he did that the entire social basis for the discotheque was slipping away. "I think the world as we know it has a few years to go," he said. "By 'as we know it,' I mean as we enjoy it—with servants, with Camembert, with fine wines. This will soon be finished. . . . What we know now—taking 'The Queen Mary' to Europe for six days and all those P. G. Wodehouse kinds of things—is gone, and it's gone forever. We have 10 years, maybe 15 or 20 years at most, to enjoy whatever is left." But even the prescient Coquelin couldn't know that, for disco, the end was still closer at hand.

No one was more alarmed by the growth of disco than were fans of rock music. They saw it as a direct and intentional challenge to rock's position at the top of pop music's ziggurat. Rock fans framed their struggle against disco as a Manichaean conflict of ideological opposites, in which disco represented all that was synthetic, aristocratic, and fake, while populist rock stood for all that was earthy and real. Rhetorical polarities notwithstanding, history told a somewhat different tale. Rock had originally lost ground to disco precisely because it demanded a relationship between performer and fans in which the latter were reduced to passive, idolatrous spectators. This dynamic was reversed by the democratic principle within disco that relegated many performers to a state of near-anonymity and made the dancers the stars. Moreover, disco stood for a new sexual order that, in the words of the writer Alice Echols, "seemed to arouse something like castration anxiety in rockers." Rock had been an ongoing celebration of uncontested straight male sexual dominance; disco bypassed hetero men in favor of black women divas, gay male dancers, and virtually any other alternative. To reaffirm their sexual primacy, rockers needed to destroy disco and the altered sexual hierarchy it stood for.

In fact, disco rejuvenated rock by serving as the kind of enemy the latter had been lacking since the generation-gap wars of the 1960s. Instrumental in the growing anti-disco movement was

Steve Dahl, a Chicago disc jockey and fervent disco hater most famous for officiating at the Disco Demolition rally in Chicago's Comiskey Park Stadium in July 1979. The idea was to detonate disco records during the intermission of a baseball doubleheader, but charged-up White Sox fans—chanting, "Disco sucks" and "Death to disco"—lost control and began tearing up the stadium. Just as the bloody Altamont concert a decade earlier had become an epitaph for the sixties counterculture, so the Comiskey riot became visual shorthand for the end of the disco era.

The year 1980 proved a fateful one for disco. In the eighteen months after Comiskey Park, the market for disco music crashed, a popular backlash against sexual license became part of a conservative wave that elected Ronald Reagan President, and a new, mysterious "gay cancer" appeared that would soon be known as AIDS. Together these developments undermined the hedonistic lifestyle that disco had sustained. This naturally came as a great relief to the rock majority, many of whom would have continued the counterrevolution until the last disco dancer had been consumed. But what emerged was a more subtle cultural tradeoff. Disco-derived music had found a lasting place in the hearts of Americans and so continued to thrive into the 1980s and beyond, taking the likes of Michael Jackson and Madonna to the very pinnacle of long-lasting celebrity and popularity. Madonna would build her persona on a watered-down version of disco-era hedonism. At the same time, the word *disco* was effectively banished from the language for the next decade—even as a term for describing a nightclub—and the lifestyle associated with it became an object of scorn, ridicule, and embarrassment.

As early as 1978 the novelist Andrew Holleran had looked back on the dawn of disco and sighed, "Any memory of those days is just a string of songs." The same may be said today, but for different reasons. Certainly the nostalgia-soaked 1990s have rehabilitated disco music and associated kitsch, but much of the original context has been erased, including the unfettered pleasure seeking that it once symbolized. Films like *54* and *The Last Days of Disco*, along with disco marathons and Studio 54 documentaries churned out by VH1, present the contours of the original disco boom while eliminating the gay content at its core. On the basis of current representations, one might conclude that disco died a natural death when the market for disco music collapsed, circa 1980, not that disco stood for an unleashed sexuality that flew in the face of mainstream mores even during the "anything goes" seventies. The ensuing AIDS crisis further called into question many of the equations set up by gay liberation and heralded by disco: that the sexual was sacred, that sexual liberation was personal liberation, that shame was the only enemy.

For this reason disco makes for bumpy nostalgia even in gay   20
circles, as everyone tries to imagine (or recall) what a consequence-free world could have looked like. And this legacy has imbued disco with a mellow aura of decadence turned innocence. It occupies an extreme place in history, a brief, dizzying, exhilarating moment when the guiding cultural principle was Mae West's axiom: "Too much of a good thing may be a great thing."

Discussion Questions

1. The author claims that night clubs allow people to express "passions and vices" that might otherwise lead to "social upheaval" (paragraph 1). First, evaluate this "pressure valve" theory of venting antisocial impulses. Then, describe other activities or places—besides nightclubs—where individuals might be encouraged to channel their potentially destructive energies.

2. Braunstein records the phenomenon of disco being an "outlaw world" invaded by heterosexuals, who then adopted it into the middle class (paragraph 9). Compare the disco scene with a more recent social practice that has moved from the edge of society to the mainstream.

3. Braunstein argues that disco music and its associated lifestyle have celebrated "the human body as an instrument of pleasure" (paragraph 10). First, summarize this interpretation. Then, consider other social activities that promote the body "as an instrument of pleasure."

4. Evaluate Braunstein's depiction of the decline of disco music as a conflict between the "straight white male sexual dominance" expressed by rock music and alternative values expressed by black female singers and gay male dancers. To what extent do you agree?

Ballet as a Way of Knowing
Marion Rudin Frank

A former ballet student and dance performer in musical theater, Marion Rudin Frank has been a clinical psychologist and medical psychotherapist for twenty years. Her specialties include gender and relationship issues, anxiety, and depression. With an M.A. in counseling from Columbia University and an Ed.D. in Adult, Group and Organizational Psychology from Temple University, Frank has also trained as a Jungian analyst through advanced seminars. Her publications include the academic articles "Chronic Illness and Self Esteem" (1996), "Feminism as a Therapy Modality" (1995), "Epilepsy Myths and Stereotypes" (1988), and "Women Crying in the Workplace" (1987). In the following selection, published in 1997, she argues for several therapeutic values of dance: it "enhances body image," it "builds confidence," and it "increases the ability to live more freely and fully." It should be noted that this reprint is an excerpt from the original work, which cited eighteen sources on psychology and dance; this information, directed mostly to other therapists, has been omitted.

Before you read, review Bordo's portrait of the emaciated fashion model in Chapter 4. Here, Frank criticizes the unnaturally thin ballerina as a "sexist ideal." As you read, compare the viewpoints of the two writers and consider what social forces reinforce the image of the masculine "Lord of the Dance."

———————— ✦ ————————

I believe that any discussion of ballet's metaphors should include the negative images which are also derived from the ballet experience. As a woman who brings feminist theory into the clinical practice of psychology, I cannot overlook the obvious sexist ideal of femininity in ballet that equates beauty and grace with excessive thinness. Relentless persistence of this often unnatural "ideal" body has caused many aspiring young women to engage in activities which result in eating disorders. Studies linking ballet dancers with anorexia and bulimia find that the majority of ballet dancers weigh significantly below national norms, are excessively preoccupied with food and weight, and engage in unhealthy methods of weight loss. For dancers immersed in the ballet world, these behaviors are socially and strongly reinforced.

In dance class, bodies are constantly on display. Often weight, more than talent, is the criterion for acceptability. The "sylph" look is a ballet tradition, and chances of getting into a ballet company (or fitting into the ballet "family") are dependent upon being thin, often excessively so.

These powerful pressures cause young women to develop an overconcern with normal development of breasts, thighs and buttocks and to believe that the road to success is starvation. It is not all that unusual for young ballerinas to diet to the point of losing menses or having erratic periods, compromising health, risking stress fractures and possible future osteoporosis. With an inner drive for perfection, a teenager with serious aspirations may practice up to eight hours a day, withdraw from friends and obsess about maintaining what is actually a prepubescent body shape. Those not genetically prone to slight bodies may encounter severe self-esteem issues or suffer other psychological consequences.

Moreover, ballet has mirrored the culture's ambiguity toward sexual expression and gender patterns. The ballerina is at once artist, idealization of virgin-like femininity, and sex object. Her body is the instrument of dance and thus the tool of the choreographer. Dance shares with other disciplines and career paths a gender-related prestige hierarchy. The well-recognized choreographers and managers are disproportionately male and the dancers are disproportionately female. In the studio or on the stage, male choreographers unintentionally may treat dancers like children; there is an expectation that they will be obedient and deferential. Ballet teachers still refer to female dancers as "girls" and male dancers as "boys."

Some contemporary writers believe that classical ballet has offered a legacy in which heterosexual, romantic, and chivalrous relationships validate male dominance. A recurring image is certainly the *pas de deux*, in which the strong male interpreted as her pedestal, dominates and supports the woman on *pointe*.   5

However, more than simply sanctioning gender-related behavior, ballet offers opportunities for fantasy. The *pas de deux* may be interpreted not only as man manipulating woman but as man enabling woman to have added freedom in movement, helping her to achieve her goals. Or it may be seen as a mutually interdependent image, with clear separation of duties.

Few attempts have been made to understand the impact of ballet on the adult development of female dancers. Susan A. Lee, in her exploration of the topic, concluded that the environment of the ballet world causes arrested development and supports dependency and immaturity. Normal developmental processes may be jeopardized if, for example, the mother plays an intrusive role in the career of her aspiring daughter, rendering the achievement of the tasks of separation and independence more difficult.[1]

Moreover, dancers deal with a unique peer group, one which is comprised of rivals. In spite of emerging sexuality, this group of adolescents may be striving not to mature physically, as would be age-appropriate. On the other hand, serious dancers are often forced to make decisions which are more characteristic of older midlife experiences. Before the age of thirty, dancers may feel forced to leave not only a job but a lifestyle and, even more importantly, a core identity.

In spite of potential hazards such as limited body image, old-fashioned gender roles, and out-of-step developmental tasks, dance has much to offer that is psychologically beneficial to women. It can promote the development of self-esteem, self-confidence, and a host of important understandings for managing life. Perhaps the primary lesson derived from the study of ballet and of particular value to women concerns the related themes of discipline and commitment. Adolescent women have less access to these and other important understandings, which men often gain from experiences in playing team sports. The ballet studio is an environment of courage. There is the dancer who dances despite realities of low wages, injury, or family hardship. A young woman sees that it is ultimately motivation which brings achievement and not simply potential. She also learns to strive for perfection as an individual, yet to adjust her individuality to the group.

10   Like any athlete, the ballet student must confront inevitable limitations—the stretch that is not perfectly turned out, the student in front whose kick is higher, the reality of her genetic structure. She learns that great effort enables her to achieve certain levels of technical competence, yet exceptional talent is inevitably born. Hopefully she learns to focus on her possibilities and potentials rather than on her limitations. Although the best ballet student is likely to be the one who lives and breathes ballet, a woman dedicated to it discovers what it means to find something that one loves to do. Its practice, like any worthwhile endeavor, is a matter of patience, endurance, pain and pleasure.

In my therapy work with women of various ages, the most prevalent and perhaps most profound of the themes which inevitably emerge concerns the concept of power. Lacking societal status and role models, women in our culture often struggle to take themselves seriously, to assert themselves, and to trust their own intuitive sense. Dance cultivates a way of learning and knowing which heightens this sense, as dance is centered in the body and the mind. As emotions and memories are embedded in the body, a heightened sense of body awareness may enhance access to them. In addition, it is obvious that a young woman can change quite dramatically through ballet training, that presence and grace can be learned, developed and mastered. Practiced movement brings with it a change in a sense of style, presence and confidence and an accompanying alteration in inner feeling. Ballet offers the opportunity to go beyond ego, to respect form and to reach for resources deep within in order to stir the audience outside. A woman learns that performing itself is at once an assertive act and an essential skill for life.

As mentors and role models, the influence of the ballet teacher cannot be overstated. The teacher of ballet has a tremendous opportunity to affect not only technique, but the values and lives of students. An awareness of psychological dynamics is essential to develop a teaching style which is validating and empowering to young women. As stereotyped conventions change, changes in the teaching of dance are also inevitable. Today, more flexible body ideals and fewer gender-specific steps convey a greater freedom and sense of empowerment for women, particularly in modern dance. In the future, even in ballet, more flexible teaching methods might emerge which incorporate psychological methods and concepts.

For example, small groups may be encouraged to work together before and after class, to focus on and help one another with specific steps or routines and to foster a true "esprit de corps." Or groups of three to five might be given responsibility for choreographing a piece, an experience to which too few dancers are exposed. These groups might also be encouraged to process their feelings about how they worked together and what they appreciated about the contributions from other members. Role reversal is a psycho-drama technique which may be used in dance class to better understand the essence of another's role and one's own impact in the performance. A temporary switch of dance roles might facilitate an understanding of the interdependency of those roles and clarify how differences in physical movements relate to different emotional responses. Male and female students might be encouraged to try each other's parts. This exercise also enables one to become more familiar with the masculine and feminine parts of one's own nature. (Teachers should expect to meet with some resistance when introducing non-traditional teaching methods, but their value will inevitably emerge.)

It is important that the dance teacher be aware of his/her unspoken message to students concerning diet and body image. Students will role-model a teacher who survives on diet soda and cigarettes. Attention to language is important as well. Students who are addressed as "men" and "women" rather than "boys" and "girls" will more likely act mature and assume adult responsibility. Most importantly, the teacher of dance teaches what it is to be an adult who loves dance. No matter what the subject, it is enthusiasm which determines the successful teacher. He/she must bring passion, not only to the work of dance, but also to the values of life which are inevitably imparted. A consciousness concerning ballet's metaphors is essential, for whatever can happen to the body can happen to the soul and psyche.

15   Ballet training may be a demanding discipline for a specified period of a woman's life, or it may be an absorbing pleasure that can last a lifetime. In an article expressing the value of dance, Armando R. Favazza, wrote, "While researchers continue their vast and complex studies of rhythms . . . which are intertwined with the experience of life, poets . . . continue their search for the perfect metaphor for life. To the latter, I would suggest that dance is as good as any."[2] As the search continues for the perfect metaphor for life, I would suggest that ballet is as good as any and that the meeting of ballet and psychology holds great promise for women.

Endnotes

1. Lee, Susan A. "Adult Development and Female Artists: Focus on the Ballet World," *Medical Problems of Performing Artists,* Vol. 4, 1 March 1989, pp. 32–37.
2. Favazza, Armando R. "Ballet de Corps," *M.D., Mirror of Medicine,* October 1976, p. 180.

Discussion Questions

1. Explain how Frank's position as a clinical psychologist shapes her viewpoint of dancers.
2. Despite the potential psychological hazards of being a dancer, Frank compares the "discipline and commitment" required of both ballet, for women, and team sports, for men. With details and examples from your own experience and/or observation, elaborate on this comparison.
3. Explain one claim that Frank makes for dance as a "way of knowing": "A woman learns that performing itself is at once an assertive act and an essential skill for life" (paragraph 11). In this learning, how does dance develop one's personal "power"?
4. Frank's largest claim seems to be that "whatever can happen to the body can happen to the soul and psyche" (paragraph 14). Paraphrase her meaning in this quotation, and then explain to what extent it seems relevant to you.
5. Compare Frank's view of the body in this quotation (Question 4) with Kornfield's view of the body in "Necessary Healing" from Chapter 1.

Topics for Exploration and Writing

You have been reading about and discussing the social and psychological relationships between the body and the activity of dance. To explore these ideas, focus on analyzing one theory about the social significance of dance,

drawing on examples from your observation and experience. While most of your content should be original, brief comparisons to *at least one* of the articles in this chapter are *required* to develop your viewpoint (refer to authors by last name and to article titles). Your job as a writer is to inform your readers by presenting specific examples that you can explain in detail and then generalizing about these examples by presenting a well-informed viewpoint on a social practice. For any of these topics, if race, ethnicity, gender, sexual preference, age, body size, or disability relates to your analysis, please include these important dimensions in your essay.

1. Reread Kornfield's "Necessary Healing" from Chapter 1. Then, compare and contrast to Ellis's "The Art of Dancing." Analyze how each author suggests connections among mind, body, and spirit. Draw examples from your own experience with "alternative healing" or with dance as a performance or social activity.

2. If you have been active as a dance participant, explain the current popularity of *one* form of social dance: folk, contra, cha-cha, salsa, swing, or tango. In your essay, incorporate ideas from *one or more* of the articles in Chapter 6.

3. If you consider yourself a dancer, analyze the "psychology of dance," synthesizing Frank's viewpoints with your own experience. If you like, include whatever is relevant in Ellis's insight: "the revival of dancing . . . is imperatively needed to give poise to the nerves, schooling to the emotions, strength to the will, and to harmonise the feelings and the intellect with the body which supports them" (paragraph 13).

4. Compare and contrast the image of the punk rockers' rebellion in Braunstein's "Disco" and in Liotard's "The Body Jigsaw" from Chapter. Evaluate the two authors' development of the descriptions and the analysis. Which author seems more precise and profound in explaining the social phenomenon? Finally, relate that author's image of punk rockers to a more contemporary group of music-makers and fans that you have witnessed or experienced.

5. Compare and contrast the authors' treatment of American drug culture in Braunstein's "Disco" and in Shenk's "America's Altered States" from Chapter 5. Consider to what extent each author attributes drug use to subculture or alternative lifestyle. Consider to what extent each author attributes drug use to mainstream American culture.

6. Compare Ewen's viewpoint on bodybuilding in Chapter 2 and Frank's viewpoint of ballet training as two forms of "discipline" over the body. Discuss to what extent this discipline is enabling and to what extent it is confining.

CREDITS